An Educator's Guide to Toddler Development

An Educator's Guide to Infant and Toddler Development is a comprehensive and approachable guide to the growth, learning and development of children from birth to age 3.

Beginning with the foundations of infant and toddler education, environments and family relationships, this essential text explores each category of development in depth. Chapters clearly explain key learning and developmental milestones, provide real-life examples and walk readers through materials and strategies for effective practice. Designed to build effective and appropriate caregiving practices, this resource is packed with reflection questions and fieldwork observations to help students continually grow their knowledge and skills.

Informative, thorough and easy to use, this is a critical guide for students, caregivers and teachers helping young children to learn and grow.

Jennifer Kaywork, EdD, is a Professor of Teacher Education and the Founder and Coordinator of the Early Childhood Certification program at Dominican College in Orangeburg, New York.

An Educator's Guide to Infant and Toddler Development
Understanding and Responding Appropriately

Jennifer Kaywork

NEW YORK AND LONDON

First published 2020
by Routledge
52 Vanderbilt Avenue, New York, NY 10017

and by Routledge
2 Park Square, Milton Park, Abingdon, Oxon, OX14 4RN

Routledge is an imprint of the Taylor & Francis Group, an informa business

© 2020 Taylor & Francis

The right of Jennifer Kaywork to be identified as author of this work has been asserted by her in accordance with sections 77 and 78 of the Copyright, Designs and Patents Act 1988.

All rights reserved. No part of this book may be reprinted or reproduced or utilised in any form or by any electronic, mechanical, or other means, now known or hereafter invented, including photocopying and recording, or in any information storage or retrieval system, without permission in writing from the publishers.

Trademark notice: Product or corporate names may be trademarks or registered trademarks, and are used only for identification and explanation without intent to infringe.

Library of Congress Cataloging-in-Publication Data
A catalog record for this book has been requested

ISBN: 978-0-367-36636-0 (hbk)
ISBN: 978-0-367-40723-0 (pbk)
ISBN: 978-0-367-80871-6 (ebk)

Typeset in Goudy
by Apex CoVantage, LLC

Printed and bound by CPI Group (UK) Ltd, Croydon, CR0 4YY

Visit the eResources: www.routledge.com/9780367407230

This book is dedicated to Hayleigh and Maximus.
I wrote this book with my memories of your infant and toddler years in my mind, and I am eternally grateful for all of the time we spent together during those very important years. It is my hope that this book will give everyone the tools to feel all of the joy and excitement that I did with you. Mommy loves you both so very much.

Contents

1 Introduction to Infant and Toddler Care   1

2 Caregiving as Infant and Toddler Education   23

3 The Infant and Toddler Environments   52

4 Partnering With Families   80

5 Perceptual Development and the Five Senses   103

6 Physical Development   129

7 Play as Learning   148

8 Attachment   173

9 Social Development and Interactions   198

10 Emotional Development   220

11 Language and Literacy Development   244

12 Cognitive Development   273

13 Early Intervention   299

Index   309

For additional material, visit: www.parentphd.org/infantandtoddlertext

1 Introduction to Infant and Toddler Care

Welcome to *An Educator's Guide to Infant and Toddler Development: Understanding and Responding Appropriately*. As a former caregiver for infants and toddlers and a parent, I have been fortunate enough to spend a great deal of time with the 0–3-year-old population. As a current practitioner of early childhood education, I strive to transfer my knowledge and experience to my students so that they will truly understand infants and toddlers. Throughout my professional work, I have realized that this important knowledge and skills should not only be meant for early childhood education students. Parents and caregivers of infants and toddlers would benefit as well. This realization became the impetus for this book. It is my hope that it will provide you with everything you need to know about infants and toddlers so that you truly understand them, can appropriately respond to them and—most importantly—enjoy them!

This book serves many purposes and populations. For undergraduate and graduate students studying early childhood education, this book is a textbook for your infant/toddler courses and will fully explain this population of children to you. For parents, this book is a manual that will tell you what is happening with your children as they move through the first three years of life. For childcare centers, this book is a handbook to follow to both come to really understand children ages 0–3 and then learn what to do as a caregiver for these children. For all of you, this book will fully explain children ages 0–3 and give you concrete ideas about what to do and say with these children to maximize their growth and development.

Throughout your reading of this book, you might come across information that you would deem not important to know based on your role in infants and toddlers' lives. For example, if you are a parent and you are reading about how a caregiver in a childcare center might work with infants and toddlers, you might think that the information isn't pertinent to your role as a parent. It is. It is important for you as a parent to know what the caregivers of your children are doing with them all day and, more importantly, what they should be doing. Your knowledge of your infant or toddler's daily experiences is important to understanding them as people. If you are a caregiver for infants or toddlers in a childcare center and you are reading about how parents could calm their children or guide them, you might think that the information isn't pertinent to you since you aren't a parent. It is. It is important for you to be aware of parenting practices because you as a caregiver of infants and toddlers must emulate the home and parents of the children you care for. Any "parenting strategy" can be modeled in a childcare center. Understanding these strategies will also allow you to understand where your infants and toddlers are coming from when they enter your classroom each day. Everything is this book is pertinent to everyone who has any extended period of contact with infants and toddlers. The more you understand them and how to care for them, the better you will be at whatever role you fulfill.

Before you begin your journey to understanding this amazing population of children, it's important for you to share your own ideas, beliefs and questions. This book will hopefully further shape these ideas and beliefs as well as answer all of your questions. It is recommended that you designate a separate journal or notebook for documenting your answers and ideas throughout the reading of this text.

Start by responding to these two questions in your journal:

1. How do you feel infants should be cared for?
2. How do you feel toddlers should be cared for?

Your feelings about caring for infants and toddlers have been shaped by how you have been cared for throughout your life as well as your own experiences with young children. These feelings will change as you learn more about the 0–3 population but will be grounded in these first ideas.

Now you need to think about questions you might have about infants and toddlers. Below is a list of the typical age groupings for children ages 0–3. These groupings are based on stages of child development. Write down any questions you have about each age group. Throughout the book, your questions will be answered, and you can write the pertinent information next to your question:

- Birth–6 weeks
- 6 weeks–3 months
- 3–6 months
- 6–9 months
- 9–12 months
- 1–2 years
- 2–3 years

Now that you have your own ideas about infant/toddler care out in the open and have documented your questions about the 0–3 population, let's get a general idea of what the care and education of infants and toddlers is comprised of. I would like to begin with the core beliefs from which this book was written. Each one is briefly described for you here and then will be expanded upon throughout the book. These beliefs hold true for educators, parents, caregivers and childcare centers who work with children ages 0–3.

The Care and Education of Infants and Toddlers

Beliefs About Infant/Toddler Care

The following seven beliefs are the framework for this book's philosophy of infant/toddler care. Why only seven and not a nice round number like ten? Because 8, 9 and 10 are to be filled in by you. The last three beliefs are your own that you will shape as you educate yourself about infants and toddlers.

1. Every experience can be a time for interaction with infants and toddlers
   - Talk to them about what you're doing, seeing and experiencing. Show them how to do it. Ask them to tell you or show you what they are experiencing.
2. Spend time observing infants and toddlers
   - Watch their actions and listen to their verbalizations. Then respond to exactly what you observe (not what you interpret).
3. Learn how each individual child communicates so you can respond appropriately
   - Always talk to infants and toddlers like they are regular people (no baby talk!) and show your emotions so they learn what they look like.
4. Provide as many sensory experiences as possible
   - Infants and toddlers learn by touching, tasting, smelling, hearing and looking at things.
5. Let infants and toddlers work on solving their own problems
   - A little stress to figure something out is OK. Talk them through it if necessary. And be there to help if it is definitely needed.
6. Be consistent and reliable so you can build a trust with the infant/toddler.
   - This trust is the backbone of the infant/toddler's entire development. Comfort with those who care for him = comfort with himself and the world.
7. Read to infants and toddlers every day and as often as possible.
   - These early literacy experiences have a profound effect on their knowledge, language and overall ability to communicate effectively.
8.
9.
10.

Think about these beliefs. What do they mean to you? Do you know what each of them looks like?

Caregivers and Caregiving

As infant/toddler educators, we call our teaching "caregiving" because we are "caring" for the children. This goes beyond "teaching" them. Therefore, throughout this book, you will see teachers referred to as "caregivers" and teaching referred to as "caregiving." But what does this caregiving look like?

In the first three years of life, relationships with responsive and reciprocal adults are essential and are considered the building blocks of healthy development. These types of relationships help infants and toddlers make sense of the world, take in all of the information that is coming at them and then assimilate and understand it better. Social competence, emotional development and academic learning are all fostered when infants and toddlers have responsive and reciprocal relationships with adults. These types of caregivers also provide predictable responses that the children come to trust; they read the children's cues and respond to their needs. Every interaction matters and has an impact on the children's lives. Infants develop their first sense of self through their observations of those who care for them.

In order for this to happen appropriately, the caregivers must not only understand the children in front of them but also how to appropriately respond to and care for them. Infants and toddlers deserve care and education that is respectful, responsive and reciprocal:

- To be *respectful* is to respect the infants and toddlers' needs, their space and their communications. Adhering to specific needs is especially important for infants, who lead the way in these interactions. Overall, infants and toddlers tell us what they need, and then it's our job to respond to it appropriately
- To be *responsive* is to respond to infants and toddlers' actions, emotions, communications and needs. This is especially true for infants because they cannot fulfill their own needs. Toddlers can begin to respond to their own needs with your guidance
- *Reciprocal* means to have "synchronous interactions." In these interactions, caregivers respond to infants and toddlers and then await their response to you. Think of it like a "dance" of back and forth interactions and communications between caregiver and child. These types of interactions give infants and toddlers a sense of security in their classroom environment, and they come to trust their caregivers and the environment. The children know that they are being cared about as much as they are being cared for, which is an important feeling for their emotional security (Gonzalez-Mena & Eyer, 2017)

Picture that you are a baby playing on the floor. Suddenly, someone grabs you from behind and, next thing you know, you are flying through air to the changing table. You are plopped down and wondering, "how did I get here?" or "what are we doing?"

> How do you think that baby feels?
> How about disrespected? Unsure?

Always remember that you don't want any "babies flying through the air." It sounds silly, but it will help you remember when you are about to grab an infant or toddler and "do" something to her without preparing her. Always tell infants and toddlers what you are about to do to them or with them. Let them know what is going on so they can be ready and trust you and your actions. This is very respectful and comforting. They should always know where they are going and what is about to happen. They also see that you understand and are responding to their needs (changing, hunger, etc.). And remember to respond to what they need, not what you think they need. This may require some troubleshooting by you as the caregiver but find out exactly what they need.

The Growth and Development of Infants and Toddlers

This book will describe the understandings and capabilities of children from ages 0–3 based on what I call a "typically developing child." It is important to remember that not every child does everything at the exact same time, so don't worry if a child you are observing isn't exactly meeting the criteria I describe. As long as he reaches it at some point around the age group, he is doing just fine. I describe the growth, development and learning of children ages 0–3 as "climbing a ladder." Everyone starts at the bottom and works their way up. The ladder is not a one-way climb. We can also take a few steps down and relearn something or reexperience something. Although the rate or speed of development varies for each child, the general order that children ages 0–3 learn skills is generally the same.

The quality of a child's life in the first three years has a profound effect on the rest of their lives. All of children's experiences in these years affect how their brain develops and how they grow as a person. This development and growth continues through the early childhood years.

The first three years of life are a time of constant emerging skills—skills that children are working on or just mastering. It is a time of figuring out the world and what it does. As caregivers of children ages 0–3, knowledge and recognition of these emerging skills is necessary. It is also important to remember that life experience has a lot to do with what skills young children acquire and when they acquire them. The concept of "nature versus nurture" is discussed often in early childhood education. Nature is the biological traits that you are born with. This comes from your biological parents and includes characteristics such as your physical stature and appearance. Nurture is your life experiences. Both influence how children grow and develop. Nurture has a larger effect on growth and development versus nature. The experiences you have in the world from the day you are born decide how you act and approach life as

6   Introduction to Infant and Toddler Care

Figure 1.1 Toddler Water Play

well as how much and what you learn. Infants and toddlers learn from every aspect of every experience.

Infants and toddlers are also strongly influenced by the environments and routines they experience each day. The physical environment, group size, daily schedules, plans and routines of their classroom environments must foster the establishment of relationships with trusted caregivers.

Infants and toddlers are also active and self-motivated learners. There should be many opportunities for them to engage in meaningful communication with their caregivers about the experiences they are having together. They must also have their communications acknowledged and encouraged.

Brain Development

Infant and toddler brains can be considered a work in progress. While the majority of the brain's cells are formed before birth, most of the connections between the cells are made during the first three years of life. The brain is primed for learning at birth but requires early experiences to wire the neural circuits of the brain to facilitate learning. These experiences involve the infants and toddlers using their five senses to explore and understand the world and continually influence the way in which the circuits, or pathways, of the brain become "wired." Sensory experiences direct brain cells to their location and reinforce the connections between brain cells.

An 8-month-old infant can have about 1,000 trillion connections, or *synapses*, and that same child will have twice as many synapses as adults by age 3. As the synapses in a child's brain are strengthened through repeated experiences, connections and pathways are formed that structure the way a child learns. If a pathway is not used, it's eliminated based on the "use it or lose it" principle. Things that a child does only once will have very little influence on brain development. When a connection is used repeatedly in the early years, it becomes permanent.

Based what we know about brain development, it is clear that the first three years of life are critical. While genetics are involved in the initial development of the brain, there is increasing evidence that early experiences can radically alter the way genes work in the developing brain. Having positive and healthy experiences will help any brain develop well. These positive and healthy experiences consist of moments where caregivers and parents interact with infants and toddlers, as well as when these children interact with the environment. Interactions involving talking, singing, playing and reading all help to build a child's brain. These moments are most critical in a child's brain development (Porter, 2007).

"Flipping the Light Switches"

So what does all of that brain information mean? Let's put it into simple terms that you can remember as a caregiver for infants and toddlers:

From birth, the brain is full of "un-flipped light switches." Positive and nurturing experiences flip those light switches up, and the child makes connections and acquires knowledge and skills. Once the switch is up, the child uses it often, and the skill ("switch") is strengthened. If a child does not have a variety of positive and nurturing experiences, the light switches are never flipped. By around age 12, any switches that aren't "flipped" die away.

Therefore, our job as caregivers of infants and toddlers is to provide the children with a variety of enriching and positive experiences. If we do, they will have a brain full of knowledge and skills. This book will give you, the caregiver, ideas about how to "flip the light switch" of the children whom you are working with. And I am not just talking about cognitive knowledge and skills. Social and emotional knowledge and skills is just as, if not more, important than learning cognitive skills. Without healthy social/emotional development, cognitive skills cannot be learned and definitely not mastered.

So how do you "flip the switches" and provide the right experiences? You must begin by becoming a careful observer of the children's needs, interests and abilities. As you do this, you will come to understand each child and then use this information to create appropriate learning experiences and explorations. Your curriculum as an infant/toddler caregiver is based on:

- Goals for the children based on where they are in their development
- What materials and experiences you will provide
- The role of the caregivers

In this type of environment, the infants and toddlers become active partners in the creating and initiating of their own curriculum. Caregivers support the children in initiating their own learning and allow each child to learn and grow at their own pace. Curriculum flows and changes with the interests and skills of the children. Infants and toddlers learn best not from adult-directed lessons but instead from having caregivers who act as facilitators of learning, taking cues from them.

Along with the environment, everyday encounters provide times for both interaction and learning. When a caregiver greets a child and tells him what is about to happen (*I am going to pick you up and change your diaper now.*), the child pays attention and anticipates what is about to happen to him. When a caregiver waits for a child to react to her communications, the child learns to respond. When a caregiver asks for cooperation or follows a child's lead (in dressing or undressing for example), a child learns to cooperate and participate and that it is an enjoyable experience. When a caregiver encourages mastery (of putting on an article of clothing, for example), the child learns to master skills and be independent. When a caregiver engages a child in a task and "plays around" with him as the task is completed (dressing, for example), the child learns the joy of completing a task together.

They key to being a good caregiver for infants and toddlers is to understand exactly what their daily lives should look like. Infant/toddler education should foster the exploratory nature of infants and toddlers. Always remember that children, and especially infants and toddlers, learn by using their senses and through firsthand interactions with people and things. As they hear, touch, taste, smell and see people and objects in their world, they learn.

Infants and toddlers want to play with materials and explore what they can do, rather than meet any specific outcome or goal. It is important to let the infants and toddlers figure out how something works or figure out the stimulation on their own. This will teach them to always approach something new with the thought of "I wonder what this does" versus looking at you and asking you to show them what it does. Overstimulation is actually worse than a lack of stimulation.

The classroom or caregiving environment is a large part of the "curriculum" for infants and toddlers. Caregivers must create a safe and interesting place for learning that responds to the individual children as well as the small group of children present. Therefore, an infant classroom and a toddler classroom should be set up in the manner that fosters this type of learning. When contemplating the layout of infant and toddler classrooms, remember that as the children get older, the open space gets smaller. In an infant room, there should be a large open space for the children to lay, crawl, scoot and roll. At this age, the infants need lots of room to work on their newly developing motor skills. Low shelves should frame out the space so that the infants can reach toys and manipulatives on their own or with a caregiver's guidance. With this layout in mind, it is important to put babies on the floor to let them play and explore. They should not be strapped into seats or swings unless it is necessary for safety or as a way to comfort them. In order for this to work, the open space must be clear of hazards and everything that is reachable by the infants must be something they can touch and explore.

In talking about putting infants on the floor, I'd like to discuss your role as a parent or caregiver while the infant is on the floor. When I am asked, "What do you DO with infants all day?" my response is always "You don't DO anything." Once this is understood, it's much easier and less stressful for caregivers. You goal is to provide them with sensory experiences to explore and learn. Infant caregivers are not there to simply stimulate the children. I tell those whom I work with that they are not the "hired entertainment for the day." You are not there to entertain the children and dangle things in front of their faces. You are not there to stimulate and occupy them.

As infants move around and explore and play, you can then respond to what they are doing through verbalizations or reciprocal actions of your own. This is very different from continuously initiating a play experience or interaction. Now, this doesn't mean that you never initiate anything with infants. What it does mean is that most of your time should be spent watching the infants move and explore and then follow their lead. Caregiving in this way teaches infants to explore and play alone, which is a very nice character trait to have as they grow up. You are always present, but you respond based on their actions and communications. This also teaches you a baby's personal communications so you can learn them.

When I wrote my doctoral dissertation, my daughter was an infant. I put her on the floor and let her explore on her own. While she did this, I wrote. This paid off because she now approaches everything with the "what does this do?" attitude and doesn't look to me or others to show her. I remember the first time she was able to grab her butterfly and squeeze it, and it played a song. The look on her face when it began to sing to her was priceless. And she did it on her own. Much better than me constantly squeezing it and showing her that it played a song. You start from infancy "training" them to play on their own.

When infants grow into toddlers, their environment should grow with them. The large open space that was once available to these children in their infant years is now gone. In a toddler room, shelves should divide spaces into small centers for exploration. Each center should have similar objects and toys and provide enough room for a few toddlers to play and explore. Toddler toys should be ones that they can manipulate extensively. Many "preschool-age" toys such as puzzles, magnetic/plastic letters and blocks are suitable for toddlers, and the earlier they are exposed to them, the quicker they will learn

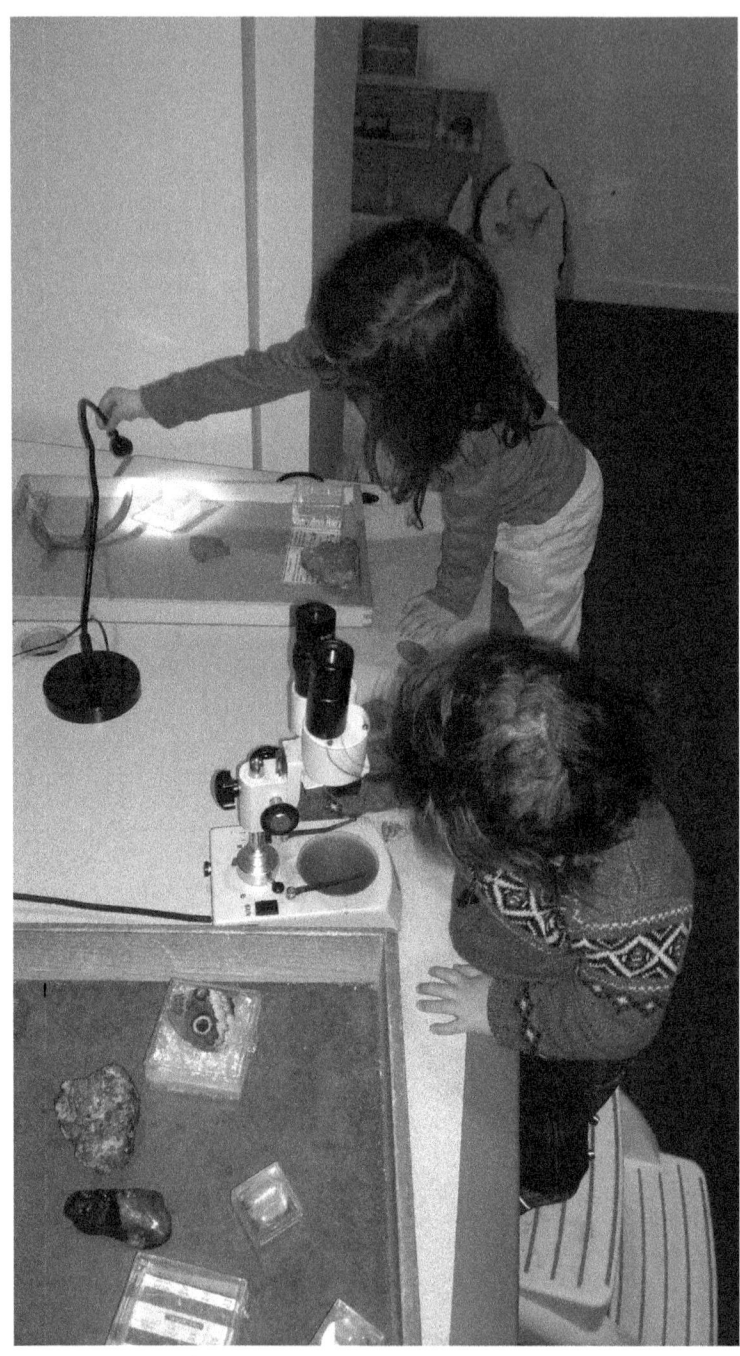

Figure 1.2 Toddlers Exploring Science Materials

from them. Many toddlers can identify their letters simply because they have been playing with them. Shelves for toddlers can be at their standing height and deeper since they are able to get things in and out of them easier.

How Infants and Toddlers Learn

Children begin learning from the moment they are born. The environment we create for them further contributes to their learning. Safe, challenging and meaningful materials and experiences are important in order to appropriately support infants and toddlers' development and learning. It is important to be aware of how infants and toddlers learn so that, as parents and caregivers, we can appropriately respond to and initiate interactions and learning experiences with these unique groups of children.

For infants, movement is exploration. Reaching for objects, grasping them, pulling them toward their bodies and eventually releasing them are how they learn about the world. As they move their bodies through rolling, scooting and rocking, they learn how their bodies feel and how they work in their environment. Infants respond to rhythm, music and calm and friendly tones of voice. Infants follow people and objects with their eyes, eventually begin to recognize familiar objects and people and then anticipate their return. They enjoy warm and comforting contact with other people and can tell by a simple tone of voice how a person is feeling.

For toddlers, we must create an environment where they feel secure enough to explore. When toddlers are engaged in meaningful activities that provide just enough challenge, they learn. Pretend play is common as they emulate the adults in their lives, and they learn how the world works by observing and interacting with the objects and materials around them. Toddlers learn from experiences and materials at their own pace.

Infants and Toddlers as Problem Solvers

A day in the life of an infant or toddler is a day of problem solving. They continually come across "problems" that they must figure out how to solve. The key is for the infants and toddlers to solve the problems on their own, although caregiver intervention is sometimes necessary.

The most common types of problems that infants and toddlers work to "solve" each day are basic physical problems like hunger and discomfort, manipulative problems like those that require them to use their fine and gross motor skills (manipulating objects and toys) and social/emotional problems such as separation from a caregiver or a need to be comforted. The key for caregivers of infants and toddlers is to recognize that these "problems" are learning opportunities and that the children should learn to solve them on their own. They need to be nearby in order to provide assistance or encouragement if necessary, but they primarily need to let the infant or toddler figure it out.

As a caregiver observes the infant or toddler working through a "problem," she must decide when, if and how to intervene. The caregiver must first *determine if the child is stressed or not*. A little stress is OK. In fact, it's a good thing. That means that the child is thinking really hard and trying really hard to figure out what is in front of her. This stress is fascinating to watch. You can almost see the wheels turning in the child's head and hypothesize about what her inner speech is as she works. Now, while a little stress is OK, you don't want a child getting so stressed that she breaks down physically and emotionally. That's why your observation skills are so important. If you see the stress level getting beyond what you think is the highest it should go, step in and intervene.

What this intervention is and how you go about it is very important. Most people would jump in and solve the problem for the infant. That's not exactly the best route to take. A slow approach is always best so as not to stress the child out even more. Then decide whether you need to *attend to the child's needs without manipulating the exploration* or *model a behavior or skill* so that the child learns how to do it correctly. Whichever you choose, verbal feedback is necessary. Here are some guidelines:

- Tell the child that you see they are having a difficult time figuring out "X."
- Describe what you see. If the child is an infant, verbalize how the child is feeling ("You can't get that shape in the hole can you? It is difficult isn't it?"). Then slowly physically intervene and help the child. If the child is a toddler, ask him if he needs help. Ask him to tell you what he needs help with ("Do you need help? You look frustrated. Tell me what you need.").

During this verbal intervention, infants are given the words, while toddlers need to give the words. You are teaching them to recognize that they are frustrated and might need help or guidance, or they may need to calm down and figure it out. Then decide how to give that help. Infants may not be able to outright tell you they need help (but will instead make noises and gestures), but toddlers can tell you, and you should work to have them tell you in the best way they can (Gonzalez-Mena & Eyer, 2017).

What Is Developmentally Appropriate Practice?

Developmentally Appropriate Practice (DAP) is a common term heard in the early childhood world. DAP is practice that adapts to the specific age, life experience, interests and abilities of the children in the group that you are caring for. Copple, Bredekamp, and Gonzalez-Mena (2011) emphasize that the cornerstone of developmentally appropriate practice is *intentionality*. By being an "intentional caregiver," you meet the infants and toddlers where they are and set up your classroom environment to allow the infants and toddlers to reach challenging and achievable goals. These caregivers are purposeful and thoughtful about the actions they take, and they base those actions on the outcomes that both the program and the children's families are helping the children reach.

Specifically, DAP does the following:

- Meets children where they are and takes the "whole child" into consideration
- Sets goals for children that are both challenging AND achievable—input from both parents and caregivers is important in the formation of these goals
- Understands that the achievement of these goals depend on child's development, knowledge, skills and life experiences

As a caregiver who practices DAP, you must take into consideration what is age appropriate, individually appropriate and socially/culturally appropriate when setting goals, creating environments and presenting experiences to infants and toddler. You must practice on what is considered typical for child development and learning, and then pay close attention to the individual children in your care in order to respond appropriately.

Copple et al. (2011) also discuss the five key aspects of a developmentally appropriate infant/toddler teacher's work. They emphasize how closely related these five aspects are and that they must be taken on equally. Throughout this book, you will learn what these aspects look like in an infant/toddler program:

- Create a caring community of learners
    - o A community is based on strong relationships. Caregivers must know all of the children both individually and how they work as a group and create a comfortable environment where the children will explore and learn. Caregivers create relationships and build trust through thoughtful and personal interactions
- Teach to enhance development and learning
    - o Infant and toddler teachers use a variety of strategies to appropriately understand and respond to infants and toddlers and then scaffold their learning. They acknowledge what the children do; encourage the children's efforts and persistence; give specific feedback; model skills and behaviors; demonstrate the correct way to do something; create or add challenge to a child's work; give cues, hints and assistance to help children accomplish things on their own; provide specific information to add to children's knowledge; and give specific instructions to guide children's play and explorations
- Plan appropriate curriculum
    - o Appropriate curriculum for infants involves following the infants' cues and routines and involves responsive interactions and explorations

between caregivers and infants. Appropriate curriculum for toddlers involves the same concepts as infants but begins to include group interactions and planned activities that incorporate a new level of problem solving and exploration

- Assess children's development and learning
    o Caregivers of infants and toddlers participate in "authentic assessment," where they observe the children and their play and use the information they gain to guide their planning and decision making. A full understanding of infant and toddler development is key to this assessment process. Assessing infants and toddlers in developmentally appropriate ways requires a caregiver to pay attention to what is age, individually and culturally appropriate for each individual child

- Develop reciprocal relationships with families
    o Making developmentally appropriate decisions about infants and toddlers requires the caregiver to know the families of the children well and interact with them often. They provide valuable information about their child that is important to consider when making decisions about the infants and toddlers while they are in your care. Caregiver-family communication also keeps the care of the infant or toddler consistent from home to school, which is comforting for the children.

Figure 1.3 Toddler Manipulative Exploration

What to Look for in Infant and Toddler Programs

The National Association for the Education of Young Children provides specific information to families about what a developmentally appropriate infant and toddler program looks like. As a parent you should analyze a potential program, and as a caregiver you should review your classroom, to ensure that it meets the criteria NAEYC emphasizes.

In infant classrooms, NAEYC emphasizes the following criteria:

- No more than eight infants and a ratio of one caregiver to three babies at the most
- Warm and supportive caregivers who make eye contact and talk to the infants about their day
- Caregivers who are alert to infants' cues and respond to them
- Caregivers appropriately participate in caregiving routines with infants
- Caregivers talk, sing and read to infants
- Infants are cared for on an individual basis—they eat when they want to, sleep when they want to and their preferences in these practices are acknowledged and adhered to
- Health and safety standards are followed (handwashing, cleaning of surfaces and toys, etc.)
- Caregivers can see and hear infants at all times
- Caregivers and families discuss infants' activities and development on a daily basis, and families are welcome in the classroom at any time

NAEYC urges families to be concerned if they do not see the above criteria being met in a potential infant classroom. Specifically, families should be concerned if they see the following:

- More than eight infants and caregivers caring for too many children at once. This will not allow them to respond to infants as individuals, which is imperative at this point in life
- Caregivers handle the infants in a "hurried" or "impersonal" manner and don't respond to infants' communications
- Infants are left in one position for long periods of time, are left in devices such as seats or cribs for long periods of time or are moved around abruptly by caregivers
- Caregivers participate in caregiving routines without warmth or attention to the infants' presence or participation
- Caregivers do not talk to infants often or appropriately and with a cold or unwelcoming tone
- Infants are expected to follow a schedule for eating and sleeping that is not determined by the individual infants
- Safety and health procedures are either not present or not followed appropriately
- Infants are left unattended at any time, especially sleeping

- Caregivers do not converse with or listen to families, and families do not feel welcome in the classroom

In toddler classrooms, NAEYC emphasizes the following criteria:

- Caregivers respond to the individual children's temperament, needs and cues
- Caregivers acknowledge toddlers for their accomplishments and help them feel confident and in control of their actions
- Caregivers respond to all types of communications because they realize toddlers cannot communicate all of their needs through language and encourage toddlers to verbally communicate their wants and needs
- Caregivers physically communicate warmth (hugs, holding on laps)
- Caregivers model kindness and respect
- Caregivers recognize that testing limits and saying "No!" are part of toddler development; establish simple rules and offer choices and alternatives when appropriate
- Caregivers frequently read, sing and do finger plays and active retells of stories to promote literacy development
- A diverse and large group of books are available for the children
- Toddlers are engaged in their everyday routines (eating, toileting, dressing) so they can learn skills and control their own behavior; independence and self-help are supported
- There are many opportunities for gross motor play both inside and outside
- Families are always welcome
- Caregivers are patient and responsive to toddlers

NAEYC urges families to be concerned if they do not see the above criteria being met in a potential toddler classroom. Specifically, families should be concerned if they see the following:

- A lack of emphasis on one-to-one relationships between the caregiver and each child
- Toddlers are criticized for their "clumsiness" as they master skills or caregivers are overprotective to the point where toddlers feel they cannot do things for themselves
- Toddlers are not allowed to touch certain things, which ignores the importance of sensory/touch experiences in their development
- Caregivers use harsh punishment to deal with children who act out or ignore aggressive or destructive behavior
- Toddlers are not allowed to assert themselves
- Toddlers are expected to sit in large group activities and watch versus participate
- There is a lack of access to books because of the fear of toddlers ripping them

- Children are dependent on caregivers for everyday tasks such as spooning food or eating with utensils
- Indoor space is too cramped
- Health and safety procedures are not followed (handwashing, cleaning)
- Caregivers leave children unattended while playing or sleeping
- Families do not feel welcome or respected by caregivers

(www.naeyc.org)

RIE and the Educaring Approach

"Educate while we care and care while we educate."

– RIE Philosophy

"Infancy is a vulnerable stage of development, therefore, it's not enough that babies receive good care, the care must be excellent."

– Magda Gerber

Infant specialist and educator Magda Gerber founded the RIE Approach in 1978 and introduced the world to the concept of an infant as "complete." Magda held a deep respect and appreciation for infants and urged us to look at them less as helpless beings. RIE's Educaring Approach:

> [E]ncourages infants and adults to trust each other, learn to problem solve, and embrace their ability for self-discovery. When allowed to unfold in their own way and in their own time, children discover and inspire the best in themselves and in others.
>
> (www.rie.org/educaring)

The approach considers young children equal members in relationships. Specifically, "RIE encourages:

- *Basic trust* in the child to be an initiator, an explorer and a self-learner
- An *environment* for the child that is physically safe, cognitively challenging and emotionally nurturing
- Time for *uninterrupted play*
- *Freedom to explore and interact* with other infants
- *Involvement of the child in all care activities* to allow the child to become an active participant rather than a passive recipient
- *Sensitive observation* of the child in order to understand his or her needs
- *Consistency*, clearly defined limits and expectations to develop discipline (www.rie.org/educaring)

Major Areas of Development

Here are some brief definitions of each of the areas of development so that you understand what you are reading about. An entire chapter is devoted to each one:

Perceptual Development—learning through the senses
Physical Development—fine and gross motor skills
Attachment—connections and relationships with caregivers
Social Development—communication and social skills
Emotional Development—understanding and expressing emotions
Cognitive Development—learning knowledge and skills
Language Development—listening to and responding with actions and verbalizations

Each of these distinct developmental stages is very different from each other. The type of care and experiences given to the children should change when the stage changes and should also recognize transitions between stages.

Observation and Documentation

As a caregiver of infants and toddlers, you must be an excellent observer. Observing the children can help you determine their needs and interests as well as totally come to understand what they are actually doing (not what you think they are doing or should be doing).

Anecdotal and Running Records are common observation forms that caregivers use when observing infants and toddlers. They allow caregivers to write down exactly what they see and hear and then interpret that information LATER—not at the same time. As humans, we are always trying to figure out what something means, usually before we've finished observing or fully understanding it. The goal for infant/toddler caregivers is to interpret later and spend the observation time writing down exactly what is going on in front of them.

The hardest thing for caregivers to do is not interpret what is happening in front of them right away. This is because that is what we are trained to do as teachers and caregivers—figure out what is happening in front of us so we can respond appropriately. Caregivers of infants and toddlers must work to do the interpreting later.

Example: Anecdotal/Running Record

    Child's Name _____
    Location of Observation _____
    Time Frame of Observation _____
    What I Saw (Exactly what the child(ren) did during the observation time):
    What I Heard (Exactly what the child(ren) said during the observation time – use *specific dialogue*):
    Interpretation/Inferences:

Daily or weekly logs and journals are also common ways to document what caregivers observe and find important to highlight about the infants and toddlers in their classrooms. These logs/journals can be by:

Individual child
Each day
Specific areas of child development
Materials/learning areas in the classroom

Example: Daily Journal/Log

    Child's Name _____
    Center/Activity Child Participated in: _____
    Anecdotal Notes (Actions/Dialogue):
    Development:
    Social/Emotional:
    Cognitive:
    Physical:
    Language:

For additional material, visit:
www.parentphd.org/infantandtoddlertext/ch1/

Reflection Questions

How do you feel infants should be cared for?
How do you feel toddlers should be cared for?
What are the similarities and differences in these two sets of beliefs?

Document your questions about the following age groups and then hypothesize what information you will need to locate in this text to answer your questions:

Age Group and Questions	Information to Find
Birth–6 weeks	
6 weeks–3 months	
3–6 months	
6–9 months	
9–12 months	
1–2 years	
2–3 years	

> Bove, C. (2001). Inserimento: A strategy for delicately beginning relationships and communications. In L. Gandini & C. Edwards (Eds.), *Bambini: The Italian approach to infant/toddler care*. New York, NY: Teachers College Press.

"Inserimento" is a term used in Italian early childhood education to describe the period of time when relationships and communications begin between adults and children entering childcare. The adults are the child's primary caregiver and his/her teachers. This chapter explains what Inserimento looks like through descriptive steps and examples. It is a wonderful way to view young children and their transition into a childcare community.

Questions to answer after reading:

Questions	Your Response
Briefly describe in your own words what Inserimento looks like in Italian infant/toddler classrooms. What is expected of parents? What is expected of caregivers? How do you think the infant/toddler feels after participating in this type of transition into care? What stands out to you about infant/toddler care in Italy? How is infant/toddler care in Italy different from what you know about infant/toddler care in the United States? The same? What specific aspects of the Italian approach to infant/toddler care can you emulate in an American childcare setting?	

Bibliography

Bove, C. (2001). Inserimento: A strategy for delicately beginning relationships and communications. In L. Gandini & C. Edwards (Eds.), *Bambini: The Italian approach to infant/toddler care*. New York, NY: Teachers College Press.

Copple, C., Bredekamp, S., & Gonzalez-Mena, J. (2011). *Basics of developmentally appropriate practice: An introduction for teachers of infants & toddlers*. Washington, DC: NAEYC.

Educaring approach. (2013). Retrieved from www.rie.org/educaring

Edwards, C. P., & Raikes, H. (2002). Extending the dance: Relationship-based approaches to infant/toddler care and education. Faculty Publications, Department of Child, Youth, and Family Studies. Paper 16. Comments published in Young Children, 57(4), 10–17.

Elicker, J., & McMullen, M. B. (2013, July). Appropriate and meaningful assessment in family-centered programs. *Young Children*, 22–27.

Gonzalez-Mena, J., & Eyer, D. (2017). *Infants, toddlers, and caregivers: A curriculum of respectful, responsive, relationship-based care and education* (11th ed.). New York, NY: McGraw Hill.

Lally, J. R. (1998). Brain research, infant learning, and child care curriculum. *Childcare Information Exchange*, 5, 46–48.

Lally, J. R. (2008). *Caring for infants and toddlers in groups: Developmentally appropriate practice*. Washington, DC: Zero to Three.

Miller, K. (2001). *Ages and stages: Developmental descriptions and activities, birth through eight years*. West Palm Beach, FL: Telshare.

National Association for the Education of Young Children. (2013). What to look for in a program. Retrieved from http://families.naeyc.org/what-to-look-for-in-a-program

Porter, P. (2007). Early brain development: What parents and caregivers need to know! Retrieved from www.educarer.com/brain.htm

Shonkoff, J., & Phillips, D. (Eds.). (2000). *From neurons to neighborhoods: The science of early childhood development.* Washington, DC: National Academy Press.

Shore, R. (1997). What have we learned? In *Rethinking the brain* (pp. 15–27). New York, NY: Families and Work Institute.

2 Caregiving as Infant and Toddler Education

This chapter will focus on what the "education" of infants and toddlers looks like. How we "educate" children ages 0–3 is very different from older children, even those only 1 month beyond the age of 3. Having the specific knowledge, skills and understandings necessary to care for infants and toddlers is essential if you are planning to work with this population of children.

Caregiving routines, self-help skills and meeting the needs of infants and toddlers make up the knowledge and understandings necessary for an infant/toddler parent or caregiver. You may not realize it, but you already have opinions about each of these concepts. Use your opinions and current understandings as a starting point as you now read about what is developmentally appropriate practice for infant/toddler caregivers in each of these areas.

Let's begin by having you answer some self-awareness questions. You have to know what you think about infant/toddler education (how you think infants and toddlers should be cared for) before learning about it. Often, I ask both parents and caregivers of infants and toddlers to contemplate their own experiences and opinions about a topic before delving deep into it. Those experiences helped to shape the opinions that will eventually translate into practice. Briefly answer the following questions:

- What do you remember about your caregiving routines when you were ages 0–3?
- Is self-help encouraged in your family/culture?
- How are children's needs met in your family culture?
- How does your family/culture believe infants (ages birth–1 year old) should be cared for?
- How does your family/culture believe toddlers (ages 1–3) should be cared for?

Now that you have documented your own experiences and opinions, think about how they influence how you work with young children. This chapter will provide developmentally appropriate information that will strengthen and further shape this work.

24 *Caregiving as Infant and Toddler Education*

Throughout this book, I will refer to infant and toddler education as "caregiving" because the education that you the caregiver provides links education and care. Infant/Toddler curriculum includes everyday caregiving experiences and constant exploration. It is a wonderful way to think about how to create an appropriate environment for infants and toddlers. Caregivers follow specific caregiving routines, and these routines become the "curriculum" that is followed in the classrooms. As caregivers meet the children's needs in following the routines, they also develop the children's interests. For *infants*, the routines are individualized. For *toddlers*, they are done as a group, although each child's needs are still individually met when necessary. Caregiving as a curriculum helps infants and toddlers learn:

- How to *cooperate* with another person by actively engaging in a routine with a caregiver
- *Self-help skills* as their caregivers slowly transfer routines and skills over to them after continual practice together
- That their lives are *predictable* because each caregiving practice is familiar to them
- What it means to have an *attachment* to those who care for them
- How to *communicate* their needs, ideas and excitement through constant interactions with their caregivers

(Gonzalez-Mena & Eyer, 2017)

Figure 2.1 Infant Connecting With Caregiver

It is also important to be consistent in the caregiving curriculum. Infants and toddlers come to depend on "what is coming next." They remember the order of events for the day, and they anticipate them. This is why it is important to not change the routines for the children unless you absolutely have to. And if you do, you must prepare the children and prepare yourself to work with those who are having a hard time working with the change.

The Primary Caregiving System

The concept of a "Primary Caregiving System" is an often-used practice in infant/toddler classrooms. The premise behind this type of system is that a caregiver is "assigned" to each kid. This person is the primary caregiver for that child and is the main caregiver who helps with the transition into the classroom as well as in meeting the needs of the child. It's almost as if the caregiver is the other "parent" in the child's life when he is at school. This type of system is also helpful if there is a large number of infants who all have different routines and ways they have their needs met. A primary caregiver can really remember three to four children's routines instead of everyone trying to remember the whole class's information.

The Primary Caregiver System gives the infant a caring one-on-one relationship while in childcare and helps him to develop a trust in that person, and then eventually the world. The primary caregiver learns that particular child's needs, interests and ways of communicating. She can then respond appropriately, giving the infant a sense of calm and familiarity. The primary caregiver also develops a bond with the infant's family, which deepens the infant's security with the caregiver. The security and trust that infants feel because of their participation in these close and strong relationships gives them the confidence to explore their environment and have a positive experience in childcare (Bernhardt, 2000).

Some schools even have the teachers "loop" with the children into the next school year and the next classroom so that an infant's teacher will also be her toddler teacher. This ensures that the toddler will be well known by the caregiver in a new school year and in a new classroom. If this cannot happen, have the old teacher participate in the transition to the new classroom and teacher with the child. Perhaps the old teacher can meet the child on the first day of the new school year and bring him to his new classroom and hand him over to the new teacher.

I have used the Primary Caregiver System in my own practice and added my own twist to it. I used it with preservice teachers. When I was a toddler teacher, I worked at a lab school at a university, and I had early childhood education students in my classroom as assistants for the school year. I had one student who was very hesitant to work with toddlers. Erin wasn't sure what to do with them or what they could do. Therefore, she didn't seem very happy or comfortable in the classroom. I decided to make her the primary caregiver for one of the toddlers who also had some difficulty transitioning into the toddler classroom. Anna always needed some "coaxing" to join the class. Once I explained the system to my preservice teachers, I asked them to participate in the transition of the child into the classroom and be available to their particular child to meet her needs or provide comfort. I know Erin was a bit skeptical of the whole process, but she participated from day one. As the days passed, I watched both Erin and Anna blossom into happy people who were excited to come to school each day. Erin recognized that Anna like art, so she suggested that we have art explorations available for her when she came to the door in the morning so that she could immediately get comfortable. Anna found comfort in Erin's presence and wanted to enter the room to play with her or show her what she could do. It was a success, and since that time I have added my own "twist" to the Primary Caregiver System to also recognize a caregiver's needs.

Knowledge and Skills of Infant/Toddler Caregivers

In order to provide the appropriate caregiving to infants and toddlers, it is important for caregivers to have a complete understanding of 0–3 children's development. This will ensure that they are participating in the caregiving routines appropriately and that they can anticipate and interpret a child's actions. Beginning in chapter five of this book, each area of child development as it pertains to infants and toddlers will be discussed in a way that will help you to not only understand what it means and what it looks like but also how to appropriately respond to the child based on your knowledge of his development. But before exploring each specific area of development, you must understand your role as an infant/toddler caregiver.

Caregiving Routines

Caregiving routines are the cornerstone of infant/toddler "education." Each routine is an opportunity for interaction and learning. This next section will discuss each of the key caregiving routines for children ages 0–3. It will give you a complete understanding of what the routine involves, the knowledge and skills that infants and toddlers can learn from participating in the routine and clarify any misconceptions or dispel any myths that you may have read about. The information in this section comes from my own experiences as a parent and caregiver to infants and toddlers, as well as recommendations from trusted sources such as the American Academy of Pediatrics and the National Association for the Education of Young Children (NAEYC). Gonzalez-Mena and Eyer (2017) also provide information for caregivers about caregiving routines that mirror much of my own work.

It is important to remember to always involve infants and toddlers in their caregiving routines. Do not give them a toy to hold or something to distract them. Talk to them about what you are doing, ask them to hold things that you need for the routine (diapers, a spoon) and ask them to help you out if they can. The caregiving routines are routines that concern infants and toddlers and are important to them, and they should never feel like they are being "done to" them. Caregivers should consider participation in a routine with an infant or toddler quality time spent with the child. While each caregiving routine is different and requires different knowledge and skills, they all make up the daily learning experiences for infants and toddlers (Sussman, 2012).

Before reading about each caregiving routine in this chapter, you should document your questions about the caregiving routine in your journal. Then, as you read, you should document the answers to your questions and the opinions your form as you learn about the routine. Your questions and uncertainties are a great place to start when coming to truly understand each important and valuable caregiving routine.

Eating/Feeding

Caregivers must make sure that they are feeding infants and toddlers food that is appropriate for their age, physical condition and cultural or religious traditions. The eating habits that children develop in the first three years of their lives can influence them for the rest of their lives. The eating environment and interactions with caregivers during the eating and feeding process should be comfortable and reinforce both good eating habits and a positive attitude about food.

Infants—Breastmilk or Formula

Infants drink either breast milk or formula. If it is possible, breastfeeding should be encouraged. The American Academy of Pediatrics (AAP) promotes breastfeeding because of the many benefits it has for infants. Breastfeeding boosts an infant's immune system at a time when it is weak and early forming, it lowers the risk of allergies and it naturally has the right amount of fat and protein that an infant needs. Breastfeeding also teaches the infant to know when she is full and should stop eating. Breastfed babies stop eating when they are full—versus bottle-fed babies, who are typically expected to finish the specified number of ounces in a bottle.

If you cannot or do not want to breastfeed, bottle feeding is fine and is in no way detrimental to infants. In fact, while I encourage breastfeeding with mothers that I work with, I also remind them that breastfeeding is a commitment of time, energy and emotion. Nursing mothers must be willing to fully commit to the process. If you force it, your baby will pick up on your unhappiness with the process, and it will get in the way of your bonding and attachment.

Regardless of a mother's choice to breast or bottle feed, milk is given to infants in bottles while they are in childcare and the mother is away from her baby. Therefore, infant caregivers must be fully aware of how to appropriately participate in a feeding caregiving routine with an infant. Caregivers must also be aware of how to store and use breast milk if mothers bring it in for their children.

For both breast milk and formula, do not heat bottles in the microwave because it can cause hot spots that will burn infants' mouths. Use warm tap water or place in a container of warm water for a few minutes. Be careful not to let milk sit for long periods of time at room temperature, because it can become contaminated. Make sure that breastmilk is stored in the refrigerator or freezer and that each container is labeled with the name of the child, date of collection and number of ounces. Refrigerated breast milk should be discarded after 48 hours, and you should not refreeze the milk after it has been defrosted. Formula should be prepared when the infant is ready to eat.

As with many caregiving routines, feeding is a "dance" between caregiver and child. Feeding an infant should be a time of calm and bonding. This important time should also be as free of distractions as much as possible so that you both can concentrate on the process of feeding. ALWAYS hold infants in your arms when you are feeding them. The close contact between the two of you is comforting to the infant and will show him that the eating time is an important and valued time. Bottles should NOT be propped up for an infant to drink on their own while they are sitting alone in a seat or swing. This is a very disconnected and impersonal interaction between caregiver and child.

When infants can completely hold their own bottles, then it is more appropriate to allow them to sit and eat without a caregiver's assistance. Giving infants this opportunity adds to their independence as an eater, but I still encourage holding the infant in your lap or sitting nearby as she eats so that the feeding/eating time is still an important time together. Typically, infants should be burped about halfway through the feeding until they are able to burp on their own (at about 6 months old and on). Burping helps them to slow down and swallow less air, which can upset their stomachs.

Infants—Introducing Solid Foods

Breast milk or formula is an infant's only source of nourishment for at least the first four months. Solid food can be introduced between 4–6 months, in which time the infant gets his nourishment from both the milk and the food. When infants are still hungry after a full feeding of breast milk or formula for a few feedings, they are sending you the sign that they are ready for some food. When introducing solid foods to infants, I ask parents and caregivers to remember the "who, what and where of babies and solid foods."

Who

The American Academy of Pediatrics (AAP) provided specific guidelines about infant readiness for solid foods in their book *Nutrition: What Every Parent Needs to Know*, and these guidelines can help parents and caregivers decide if an infant is ready for solid food. Again, infants tend to let you know when they are ready for more than just milk through their hunger after a typical bottle/breast feeding. Beyond this sure sign, consider the following:

- The infant should be able to sit in a highchair, feeding seat, or infant seat with *good head control*.
- The infant *opens his mouth* when food comes his way, watches you eating, reaches for your food and seems eager to be fed.
- The infant can *move food from a spoon into his throat*. Since he's never had anything thicker than breast milk or formula before, try diluting it the first few times and then gradually thicken the texture. I recommend making the food thicker and thicker as your infant is ready for it.
- The infant has *doubled his birth weight* (usually at about 4 months) and/or weighs about 13 pounds or more.

When introducing solid food, do it before nursing or bottle feeding so that the infant is hungry. Infants tend to be more willing to try food if they are hungry versus being full from a liquid feeding. As you learn the balance of liquid and solid food with the infant, you can decide if you would rather give the liquid before or after.

Figure 2.2 Infant Grasping Her Food

What

According to AAP, for most babies it does not matter what the first solid foods are. The only big "NO" for infants is to never give a child under the age of 1 honey or corn syrup. Both may contain a certain kind of spore that causes food poisoning that only infants are susceptible to. If you have food allergies in your family, you should be a bit more cognizant of what your baby is eating since she may have similar intolerances. This should be discussed with the child's pediatrician so that you can come up with a plan for these foods.

Commonly infants start on infant cereal (rice, oatmeal or whole wheat are common choices), and then you add pureed fruits and vegetables. However, there is no medical evidence that introducing solid foods in any particular order has an advantage for a baby. You can begin with baby cereals or go right to pureed fruits and vegetables. When introducing foods to infants, it is best to try a new food every few days. If the infant rejects it, wait a week or so and try again. As you introduce new foods, wait a few days in between each introduction and watch for a reaction such as diarrhea, rash or vomiting. You are looking for a *major* reaction to the food as a sign of intolerance. A bit of gas or other small change in the baby is just his body getting used to the new food and should not be a cause for alarm. If the infant has some type of reaction to the food, wait a few weeks and then try it again. Many infants have an *intolerance* to a food in the beginning, but it eventually goes away. Allergies are not typical and would produce an obvious repeated reaction that you should then discuss with the infant's pediatrician.

While there is a large variety of baby food for purchase, it is easy to make your own baby food using regular food. I recommend boiling both fresh and frozen fruits and vegetables and then pureeing it for infants. All you need is a pot, water and a food processor to "make" baby food. A hand blender is an even quicker and easier appliance to use. The food processor/hand blender will allow you to puree the food to whatever consistency is appropriate for the child you are feeding. You then increase the consistency of the puree to make it thicker and thicker as the infant learns to eat food and can handle thicker portions. Eventually, you will get to the point where you can mash the food with a fork and put away the appliances. After pureeing the food, portion it into small plastic containers and freeze. Take one out as needed and defrost. It's that easy!

While it isn't necessary to buy baby food, it is a fine and convenient alternative for babies to eat. When purchasing baby food, look for ingredient lists that list the food and very little additions. Your goal should be for the infants to taste as much real food as possible as early as possible. They will be more apt to try food if they are always eating regular food and tend to be less picky eaters.

If your child is eating store-bought baby food, after about six months you can start to puree or mash the table food that you are eating and give it to the infant for her meals. Infants who are breastfed have tasted the food their mother eats since birth, so they will be more tolerant of spice and adult food flavors quicker. Every feeding for breastfed babies tastes a little different based on what the mother ate. Formula fed babies are not too far behind though, so don't worry. They will just have to get used to the different flavors of food they eat.

Infants can have dairy products at 6 months. Try whole milk yogurt and cheese at 6 months and then small samples of whole milk at 9 months. The old story that children can't have any dairy until they are a year old is just untrue. When you start to integrate whole milk at 9 months, put a small amount in a sippy cup at meals. This will get the infant used to using a cup and the taste of the milk. This milk should NOT replace regular breast milk/formula feedings. It is simply an addition to infants' diet and a way to introduce them to something they will have on a regular basis at a year old. Most often, the infant will play with the cup, gnaw on it and maybe drink a few sips. As he becomes used to the cup at meals, he will drink more, although you should not expect more than a few sips or gulps at each meal.

As you introduce solid food, the infant will begin to "drop" breast/bottle feedings. This should be gradual as the infant learns to balance the liquid/solid food menu in his life. Infants will eat small meals of food and eventually by a year you can have them on the typical breakfast, lunch and dinner menu with small snacks in the morning and afternoon if necessary.

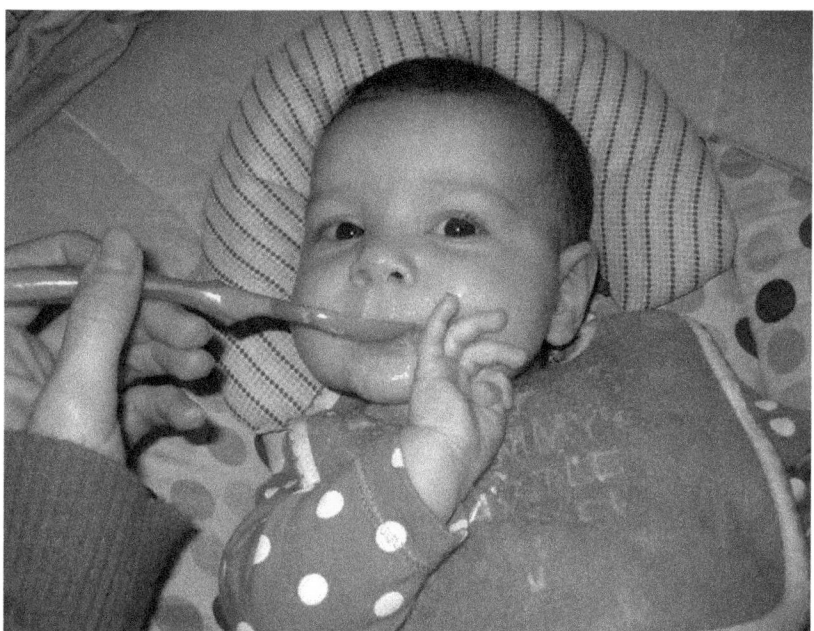

Figure 2.3 Spoon Feeding an Infant

32 *Caregiving as Infant and Toddler Education*

Where

Infants should first be placed in a bouncy seat to eat and then eventually a highchair or eating/sitting seats. The eating/sitting seat should NOT be used before an infant has some strength to sit up on her own. Infants do not have to be completely independent sitters, but they should be close. Wedging a too-small infant into a seat or highchair is not appropriate and frankly quite uncomfortable for her. A good way to know is to put her in the seat and if she doesn't slump over, she is ready to sit in it.

Once infants are in some type of "eating seat" and are able to bring their hands or other objects to their mouths, you can start to give them "finger foods" to pick up and eat on their own. This will start the learning process of feeding themselves. Infants do not need to be proficient at grabbing objects and reaching their mouths—just showing the motions to do so. To avoid choking, make sure that the food is soft, easy to swallow and cut into small pieces. Cheerios and Puffs are great starter finger foods. They are small and dissolve in their mouths quickly. Once they master their "pincer grasp" (using thumb and forefinger to pick up objects—see the Chapter 6 for a more detailed explanation of this motor skill), they will be able to pick up the food easily. They then work on their hand-eye coordination so they can get the food into their mouths. Lots of concentration is needed to eat! Infants chew with their gums,

Figure 2.4 Infant Focused on Picking Up His Food

so you don't have to wait for teeth for them to eat anything solid. Infant gums are strong and can work hard at food. Some examples of finger foods suggested by the AAP include:

- Small pieces of banana
- Wafer-type cookies or crackers
- Scrambled eggs
- Well-cooked pasta
- Well-cooked chicken finely chopped
- Well-cooked and cut-up yellow squash, peas and potatoes

Toddlers

When children reach the toddler years at a year old, you can start to give them more independence in their eating. Let me warn you—this is messy. But is also necessary. Toddlers want to practice their newly developing motor skills as well as fulfill their desire for independence. By allowing them to take more responsibility in the eating/feeding experience, you are teaching them skills and participating in a positive interaction with them.

When giving a toddler food, always start with a small amount of food and then give the toddler more if he asks for it. It is better for toddlers to ask for more than to overload their plate with food. You also do not want to force them to "clean their plates." Toddlers need to learn to recognize that they are full and no longer hungry. They will be able to do this if you give them an appropriate amount of food and respond to their signals that they are finished.

As a caregiver, you can now co-participate with the toddler in the eating experience. Take turns putting food into the toddler's mouth and give them an opportunity to feed themselves. At about 18 months, you can introduce silverware, although it is rare that toddlers will use them right away or use them well. Often times, they hold the silverware in one hand and use their other hand to feed themselves. You can model the use of the silverware by using it to feed them. Toddlers will slowly begin to use silverware, and by about 2 ½ years old, they should be skillfully using a spoon and fork to eat their food.

When introducing cups, start with the cup that has two handles, then no handles, then those with a straw and finally a regular plastic cup with no top or handles. The cup with no top should come at about 18–24 months and when the child is steady enough to not spill it every time they pick it up. Start with a small amount of liquid so he can find some success. Add more and more liquid as the toddler becomes more proficient at holding the cup and getting it to his mouth with as little mess or struggle as possible.

Toddlers can scoop, pour and serve their own food as soon as they are able to hold onto utensils and pitchers and aim it in the appropriate place. Encourage toddlers to serve themselves. This will build confidence and independence, as well as hand-eye coordination and motor skills. If they spill (which

Figure 2.5 Infant Drinking From Her First Sippy Cup

they will!), have them help clean it up and then try to serve themselves again. Practice makes perfect in this instance!

Some things to remember:

- The key to eating/feeding is to relax and follow the signs of the children. They will let you know when they are hungry, when they are full, when they like something and when they don't
- Remember that not all cultures view independence, self-feeding and big messes in the same way. While you may not agree with a family that asks you to spoon feed their child when you feel the child is at an age where she can feed herself, you must follow the wishes of the family
- Be careful about giving hot dog pieces, marshmallows, popcorn, whole grapes or any other food that might lodge in toddlers' throats. Cut them up into small pieces
- With all food, start with small amounts and small pieces. Gradually get larger as the child can handle chewing and swallowing the food.

Something to think about:

At my children's school, families are asked to NOT bring their own food for the toddlers and older unless it is for health, medical or religious reasons. They follow the philosophy that if all of the children have the same food, they will all be more willing to try it. If there is a child with something different, they all want that, and there can be issues getting the children to eat what the school is serving. They have found success in this strategy. What do you think?

Diapering

Infants and Toddlers

Diapering should be a time of interaction between caregiver and child. A caregiver can judge when an infant needs a diaper change based on smell or appearance of their bottom. A caregiver should then approach the infant face to face, let him know that he needs his diaper changed, and then pick the infant up and bring him to the changing table. Caregivers should then talk the infant through the process and/or simply respond to his verbalizations. Don't give children something to "distract" them from the changing process. If giving an infant something to hold while you are changing him is helpful, give him the materials you are using to change him (lotion bottle, diaper). This will keep him engaged in the process. This becomes especially helpful when children reach the toddler years and have a hard time lying still during changing time.

For sanitary purposes, it is important to make sure the changing area is separate from any other area of the classroom. Nothing else should happen on the changing table except the changing of diapers, and it should be sanitized after each use. It is also recommended that caregivers wear plastic gloves while changing children in order to prevent the spread of germs.

Below is a simple diapering procedure to follow. Each step ensures both appropriate and sanitary diapering experience:

1. Have the following with you at the changing table:
    a. Non-absorbent changing table paper (if used)
    b. Diaper
    c. Wipes
    d. Plastic bag for soiled clothes
    e. Gloves
2. Lay the child on the table
3. Put on gloves
4. Remove soiled diaper and place in a hands-free trash container
5. Use wipes to clean the child's diaper area from front to back
6. Use additional wipes to clean soil from adult and/or child's hands
7. Put on new diaper
8. Remove gloves
9. Re-dress the child
10. Return child to play area

11. Clean and sanitize the diaper area using bleach/water or soap/water solution and paper towels
12. Clean and sanitize adult's hands
13. Record the diaper change in the child's daily log

Potty Training

Toddlers

The move from diapering to toilet training should be a natural transition. Toilet training/learning is a developmental process and is something that cannot be done until a toddler is ready. It should never be a power struggle or something that a child is forced to do.

The ability to potty train is as much a cognitive process as it is a physical process. Toddlers need to have the cognitive ability to:

- Feel that they have to go
- Tell themselves that they have to go
- Hold it in
- Get to the potty
- Pull down their pants
- Sit on the potty and go

That's a long list of steps! This complicated cognitive process is paired with the physical ability to hold it in while they get themselves to a potty. It takes time to get both in sync, but when the child does, it usually syncs for good. When a toddler is potty training and even when she has trained, it is important to dress a toddler in clothing that is easy to get up and down so that going to the potty is easier for her. You want her to be independent in the process, and getting off her clothes is a big part of the independence.

Potty training can begin any time after a child is a year old. Before 12 months of age, children cannot control their bladder or bowel movements. Even those who show signs that they are ready cannot control their eliminations. Potty training tends to happen somewhere after 18 months; look for signs of independence and an understanding of what it means to go to the bathroom like a grown-up.

Typically, girls train earlier than boys. It is all about consistency; when you decide to do it, you need to fully commit. Get rid of the diapers with the child, and don't go back. Boys can start sitting and then stand or stand from the beginning. Give them something to aim at (Cheerios or Fruit Loops) in the toilet and have lots of wet towels for cleanup.

There are different physical, behavioral and cognitive signs that indicate that a child is ready for potty training. Not every child will show every sign, but showing a few of each category indicates that he is ready to move out of diapers and into independent toileting.

Physical signs

- Coordinated enough to walk steadily
- Urinates and has regular bowel movements at relatively predictable times
- Has "dry" periods of at least two hours *or* during naps

Behavioral signs

- Pulls pants up and down with some independence
- Shows signs of going to the bathroom and might tell you when he has gone
- Expresses dislike of a wet or dirty diaper and asks to be changed
- Shows interest in others' bathroom habits
- Demonstrates desire for independence
- Takes pride in accomplishments

Cognitive signs

- Understands the physical signals that mean he has to go to the bathroom and:
    o Tells you before it happens
    o Can hold it until he has time to get to the potty
- Can follow simple instructions, such as "sit down on the chair"
- Understands the value of putting things where they belong
- Has words for urine and stool

Pull-Ups

These are often a point of debate between parents and caregivers. They were created so that toddlers could "pull up" their own diaper/absorbent underpants, but if they had an accident it would absorb the waste. It feels like a diaper because it is. While there are varied opinions about the use of pull-ups, I will offer my viewpoint based on child development knowledge and personal experiences.

I suggest that pull-ups are only used for sleep when you are potty training and that you should get rid of them as soon as you can. Call them "night pants," not diapers, and explain to the toddler that she wears them when she sleeps because she needs to stay dry during that time. Immediately remove them when she wakes up for good; do not put them on until right before getting into bed.

Staying dry during sleep is hard and is typically mastered after normal potty training. Staying dry during naps comes first and then all night. Put the toddler on the potty before naptime and when they get up, and they will eventually stay dry while they sleep for those few hours. Nighttime is much longer and will take more time, so you want to follow the same potty practices but avoid giving toddlers a lot to drink close to bedtime. They should also be taught to get up during the night if they have to go to the bathroom, and you may want to put a portable potty in their rooms overnight in the beginning so it is close by. Toddlers will get used to the pull-ups and will go in them as long as they have them, so as quickly as you can do the night training, the easier it will be. Most children have mastered staying dry at night by age 5.

Based on my own experience potty training my children, here are my "Top Tips" for potty training a child:

BEFORE you are even considering potty training:

1. Bring infants and toddlers into the bathroom with you so they can see what happens in there. Tell them what you are doing
2. Buy toddlers a potty as soon as they can walk. Have them sit on it when you are in there in order to get used to it

WHEN you think a child is ready for potty training:

1. Get rid of the diapers and changing table completely from the start. Do it with your child
2. Start naked. The act of pulling the pants down can throw off the act of holding it in all the way to the potty
3. Put a pile of books next to the potty and read to them while they sit
4. Be patient and get REALLY EXCITED when they use the potty successfully
5. Wear "night pants" (Pull-Ups) at night at first. Training at night is a completely different skill that can come after day training is successful and consistent.

My favorite potty book

"A Potty for Me!: A Lift-the-Flap Instruction Manual" by Karen Katz: *Katz wrote two versions—one for a girl and one for a boy. The story is easy to understand, it rhymes, the pictures make sense and the children can open the flaps to reveal each "step" in the story/potty training experience.*

Bathing and Dressing

The acts of getting and keeping themselves clean and dressed are exciting tasks for infants and toddlers. The feeling of the water on their hands and the pride in putting on (or pulling off!) a sock is a big deal in the first three years of life. Involve infants and toddlers in these routines and make each one an enjoyable experience, regardless of whether or not you have 5 minutes or 50.

Bathing

Infants

Ever run water over an infant's hands and watch his reaction? It tends to be one of amazement and curiosity. Capitalize on this interest by involving infants in their bathing time. It is a period of bonding and communication, as well as a time to settle down from the day. Massage and rub infants gently while you talk to them or sing to them. You goal is to make it a calm and comforting experience.

As infants enter the second half of their first year of life, they become more mobile. This desire for mobility and physical activity will translate to the bathtub, too! Infants will want to continue their exploration of water and bathing by splashing and swimming around. This physical activity should be encouraged but monitored closely. Infants can easily fall over and hurt themselves or drown in very little water. Roll up your sleeves, hold on to them as much as you need to and let them play in the water. When infants are sitting up strongly on their own in the tub and can maneuver around with some stability (usually around 8 months), you can sit back and only reach out to hold them when they need you to. Be ready to react quickly if an infant is about to fall hard and really hurt himself. A lighter roll or fall, on the other hand, requires you to react slower and calmer, giving the infant time to react on his own and right himself.

Toddlers

As children turn 1 year old and enter the toddler years, they can take on more and more responsibility for bathing themselves. If you have talked through their bathing in the first year, they already know the words and actions of this routine. You can now give them their own washcloth to wash themselves while you do it. Eventually, you will be able to step back and let them wash themselves, providing verbal guidance when necessary.

Toddlers also love to wash their hands. The feeling of the water on their hands is still intriguing to them, and their active participation in the routine teaches them independence and self-help skills. Have a stool ready for toddlers to reach the sink and allow them to wash their own hands with as much independence as is necessary for them to get clean.

Because water and handwashing is so fun, you may find that you can't get toddlers away from the sink. If this is the case, it is time to bring out the water table. This can be something as simple as a plastic bin filled with water. Put it somewhere that can get wet underneath (they will never keep all the water in the bin—what fun is that?!). Giving toddlers the opportunity to participate in water play will help with the need to continually play in the water, as well as provide a fun and sensory experience. And . . . if you put soap in the water,

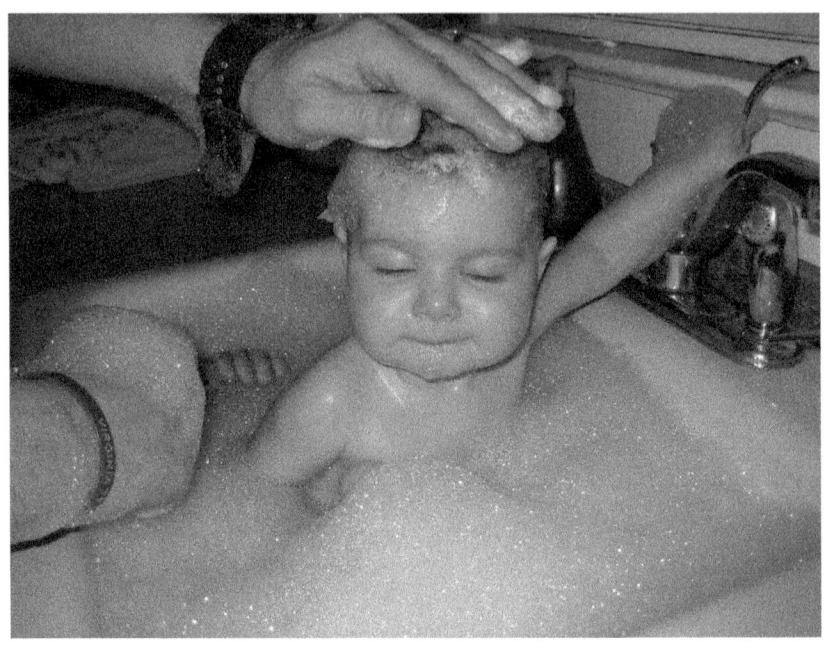

Figure 2.6 Caregiver Bathing an Infant

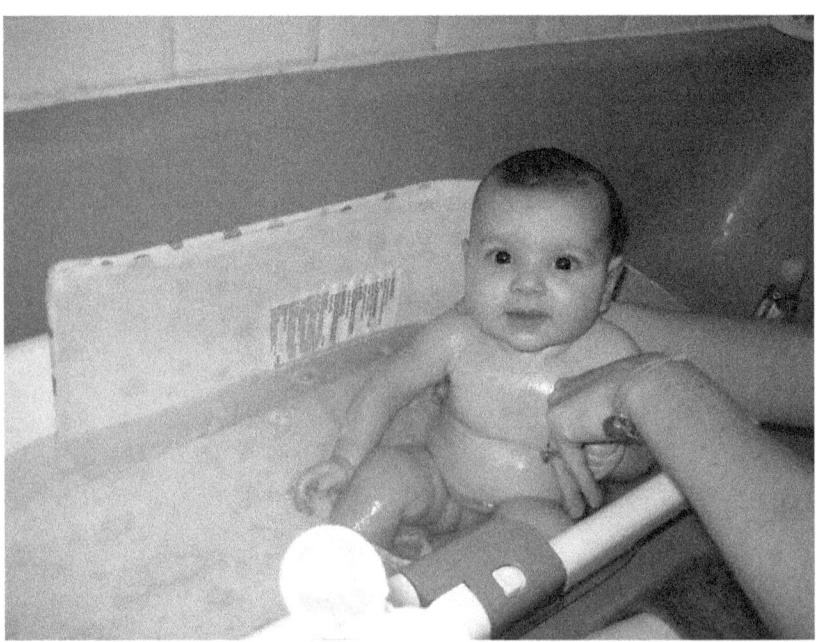

Figure 2.7 Infant Bathing in Her Own Tub

you are keeping their hands clean and altering the sensory experience at the same time.

Dressing

Infants

Dressing infants is a prime time for interaction. You are face to face throughout the whole process and have the opportunity for direct eye contact for the entire routine. Always talk infants through the dressing process, telling them what body parts you are covering and what piece of clothing you are putting on. Infants will listen to you and learn about their bodies. When they talk back to you by making verbal noises, they are participating in the caregiving process with you. As infants become more mobile, they can start to participate in the dressing routine with you. They may hold their arms up for you to put a shirt on or help take their socks off. Take the time to dress an infant; it will be both enjoyable and easy for both of you.

Toddlers

As children move into the toddler years, they will want to get more involved in their dressing routine. This directly corresponds with their desire for more independence and involvement in the daily routines of their lives. This desire for independence and control is normal and developmental, and it is important for parents and caregivers to respond positively to it.

When you see toddlers working to remove articles of clothing, take that as a cue that they want to help. If you respond to this independent behavior positively versus working to get them to "sit still" while you dress them, dressing becomes an interactive learning experience.

Socks and shoes are typically the articles of clothing that toddlers work to take off on their own first. If you see them beginning to do so, respond positively and encourage them to continue. Ask them to do it the next time you dress them. Toddlers may also want to choose their own clothing at some point. This is a way to exert their independence and have control over a specific aspect of their lives. In order to respond appropriately and still get them dressed in reasonable attire, choose two or three pieces of clothing or shoes that you would want them to wear and tell them they can choose. This will fulfill their need for independence and you still have them wearing something you would want. I call it giving them "selective choices." Dressing themselves helps work on hand-eye coordination as well, as they work to get clothes and shoes on and eventually button and zipper them.

Sleeping

Sleeping helps both infants and toddlers relax. Each child has a different sleeping routine and comfort items, so it is important for caregivers to be aware of them so they can use them in school and emulate the home experience as closely as possible. Infants should have exactly the same routine as at home. Toddlers can have some of the similarities (comfort items) but will need to move with the schedule and routine of the group. It is easy to get toddlers on this "school schedule" after a few days, so just explain it to them and incorporate some of their familiar things from home.

Always ask the parents how the child slept the night before so that you are ready for his mood and energy for the day. As the school day progresses, look for signals that an infant or toddler is tired and respond to that by putting him down to sleep. An infant can quickly get overtired and then have difficulty falling asleep. Toddlers can rest quiet in a quiet area of the classroom until it is rest time if they are showing signs that they are tired.

Infants

Infants should sleep on their back at all times. Even when they are able to roll over and do so when you put them to sleep, you should still always put them to down on their backs. It is the safest sleeping position. Most childcare centers legally must put all infants on their backs to sleep. Putting infants on their stomachs to sleep increases the risk of SIDS (Sudden Infant Death Syndrome). SIDS is discussed at the end of this section. Young infants are not strong enough to lift their heads up to breathe, so their faces stay in the mattress and they can suffocate. As they get stronger, they can begin to lift their heads, but it isn't guaranteed that they will do it well enough to breathe appropriately. Infants should sleep in their own cribs and should sleep on whatever schedule their parents use at home or ask you to implement while they are in care.

The goal for parents and caregivers of infants should be to teach infants to fall asleep on their own and not have to rely on anyone or anything to fall asleep. These abilities aren't something that they are innately born with, but they can be shown through modeling. Infants who can fall asleep on their own are in tune with their bodies and their sleep cycles and will be able to get themselves back to sleep if they wake during the night. This ability leads to infants sleeping through the night, which is something that all parents want. Contrary to what you may have heard, the goal is not to get infants to "sleep through the night." It is more of an eventual outcome to teaching infants to fall asleep on their own without anything aiding in the process.

To get an infant to fall asleep on his own, you must guide him through the learning process. This takes time but will work if you approach it positively and don't look for it to happen overnight. Start off by rocking the infant completely to sleep. This could take up to a half an hour—infants might look like they are asleep within a few minutes of rocking, but the second you put them down they jar awake. Infants need time to fully fall asleep. Look for signs like a deep sigh and muscles loosening. Throughout the first six months, gradually put them to sleep more awake and more awake. This takes some time, but your eventual goal is to put them down completely awake, and they then drift off to sleep on their own. If you find that they still wake up when you put them down, hold them right next to their crib, rock them for a minute or two and then put them down again. A small amount of "fussing" is sometimes necessary for an infant to settle himself down to sleep. If an infant cries lightly or yells for a minute or two when he is put down fully awake, he may need to get out his last bits of energy or communications before drifting off. This type of crying/yelling is much different from a cry of distress. I also recommend that you do not use mobiles or anything that is mean to catch the attention of infants while they are in the crib. The crib is a place for sleeping, not playing. Mobiles, mirrors and sound devices will distract an infant from the act of sleeping and will not help them to fall asleep.

My two children had very different behaviors when being put down to sleep for the night. They taught me that all infants are different and have different needs when going to sleep. We went through the process described above for both of them. When my daughter was put down for the night fully awake, she would almost immediately fall asleep. She might talk to herself for a minute or so, but it was rare. My son was very different. When we put him down for the night fully awake, he would almost always "fuss" for one to two minutes. This "fussing" was sometimes light cries or just yelling/talking. After a minute or so, he became silent and fell asleep. The first few times he did this, I went into his room and held him because I thought that was what he wanted. He would struggle to get out of my arms and fuss even more. One night I didn't go in, and he fell asleep after two minutes. I repeated this behavior the next night and got the same response. I realized that he needed that couple of minutes to get out his last bits of energy, and then he could sleep. I responded to his needs and his communications for "him time" at the end of the night, and he was much happier.

Toddlers

It is important for toddlers to have a routine for bedtime, although I recommend that you are "flexible" with it. Being flexible means that you still have a series of steps or tasks to complete before getting into bed, but there isn't a strict order or time period. When you are flexible, toddlers can cope with a change in routine, a removal of a step for one evening or a change in materials or location.

A typical toddler routine is simple and could involve the following:

1. Put on pajamas
2. Brush teeth
3. Go to the bathroom
4. Read a book
5. Go to bed

Toddlers like to anticipate the order of events and will usually be the ones to guide all of you through the nighttime routine. Nighttime routines should be meaningful times for everyone and should move at a reasonable pace. If a toddler finds it hard to settle down after reading a book, you can offer him 10–15 minutes of "reading time" where he can look at a book in his bed. When that time is up, lights off and time for bed. I found that one of my children needed this time after the book, and it calmed her down enough to quickly fall asleep after we turned off the light. Do what works best for each individual child.

An abbreviated version of this routine can work just as well for naps and while in care. Nap/childcare routine can involve the following:

1. Go to the bathroom
2. Get out cot/blankets/comfort items
3. Read a book
4. Go to bed

It is also appropriate to offer toddlers a quiet activity like looking at a book as an alternative to napping. They must stay on their cots and be quiet but not be "forced" to sleep. Often times, toddlers fall asleep doing this quiet activity because the room is set up for sleep. Dim the lights and play soft music in order to get the group ready for sleep and to actually sleep.

While in care, toddlers sleep all at the same time, usually after lunch. Playing outside for a short period of time before naptime also helps to get a group of toddlers to sleep. The fresh air and physical activity helps to naturally tire them out, and their sleep tends to be productive and restful when they come inside.

Some Helpful Tips for Sleeping

Swaddling helps infants to sleep on their backs. We called it "burrito time" in our house because the infant looks like a burrito when they are tightly swaddled in a blanket. It looks tight and uncomfortable to you, but it feels like the womb to infants and is very comfortable. They have what is called the "moro reflex" (see Chapter 6's section on reflexes). Basically, this is the reflex where their arms come up and hit them in the face. Infants cannot control this, so that is why they are constantly awakened when they are sleeping on their backs. Swaddling stifles the moro reflex (Karp, 2015).

Some infants hate the swaddle at first, but eventually most of them either love it or learn to deal with their moro reflex. After three months, you can start to test the fading of the moro reflex by taking one arm out of the swaddle at a time. Some infants will work their way out of the swaddle on their own, which is telling you that they are probably ready to not have it so tight or at all to sleep. As the reflex fades, infants can be put down unswaddled and in a sleep sack. Blankets should not be used with infants because of the risk of it covering their faces during sleep and making it difficult to breathe. Companies like Halo and Kiddopotamus make comfortable sleep sacks in many different sizes. They are safest for the first year.

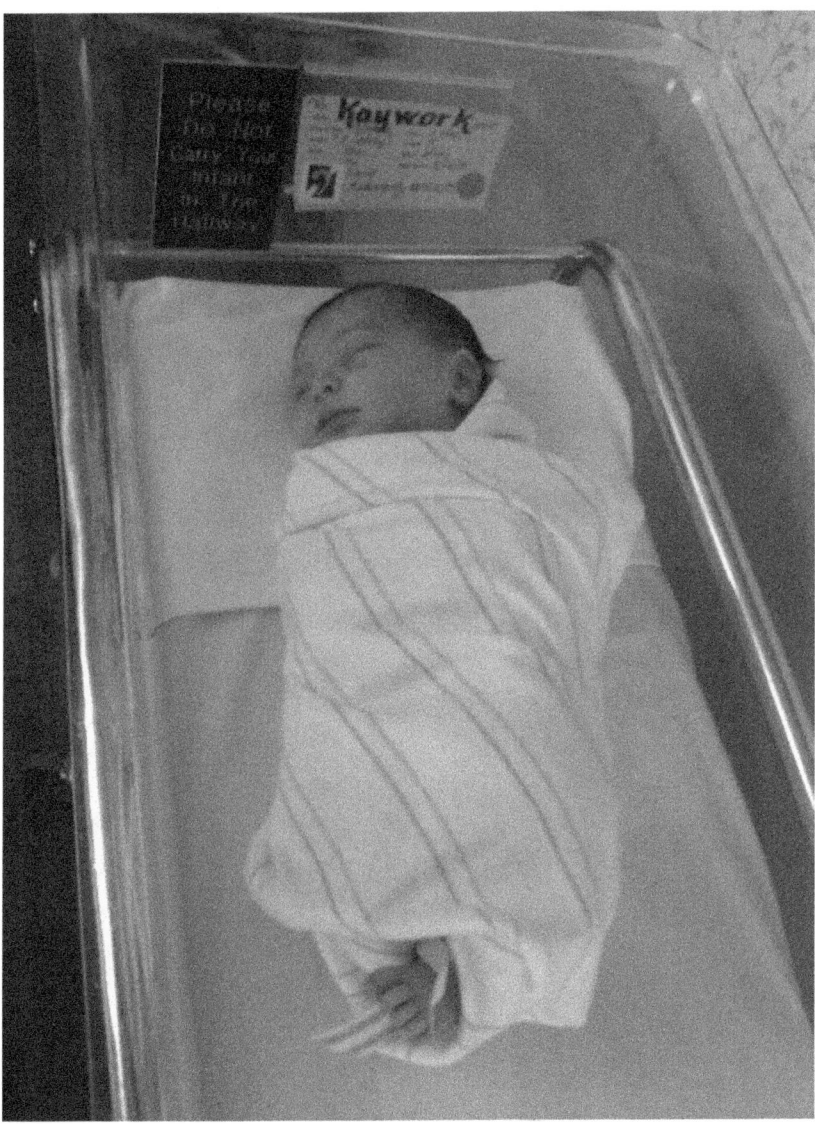

Figure 2.8 Swaddled Infant

It is also helpful to *not associate feeding with sleeping*. Nursing or giving a bottle and then immediately putting infants or toddlers to bed for the night gets them accustomed to always having a feeding or bottle in order to fall asleep. Have their last feeding at least an hour or so before bedtime and do not associate it with your bedtime routine. You should do the same for naptime.

46   *Caregiving as Infant and Toddler Education*

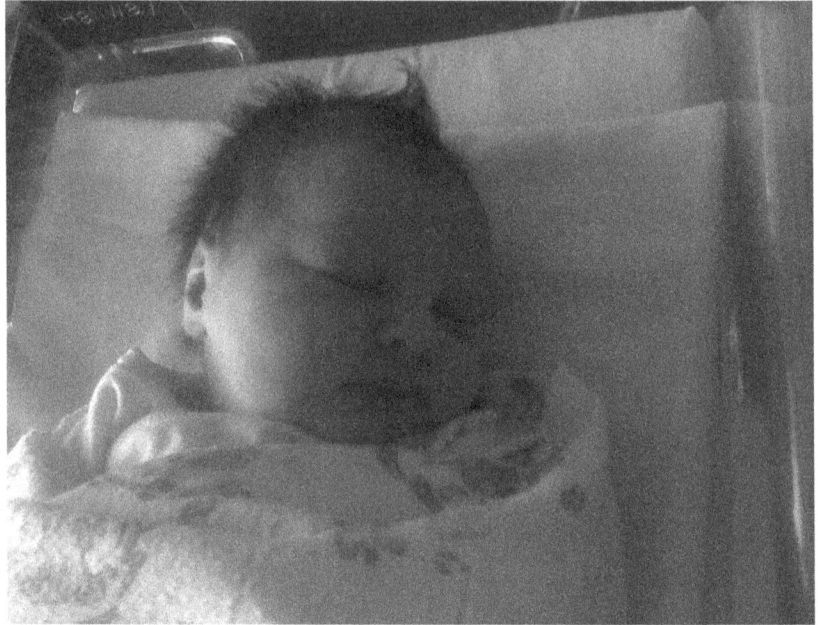

Figure 2.9 Infant Sleeping

This doesn't mean that if an infant is hungry before bed you shouldn't feed her. Always feed infants when they are hungry. The goal is to not make it a regular behavior, and the infant will not make the association. Always feed infants out of the crib and do not put them to sleep with a bottle in hand. This, too, can become a habit that is very hard to break. Toddlers should be on the family's eating schedule so a bottle or milk before bed would not be a normal request.

"The Happiest Baby on the Block"

By Dr. Harvey Karp

When it comes to calming crying infants, a caregiver's goal should be to initiate the infant's "calming reflex." This reflex will stop the crying and basically calm the infant down. The best way to calm an infant is to emulate the womb. The womb was a tight and comfortable place where infants heard a constant sound similar to a low vacuum cleaner running. Dr. Harvey Karp, author of the book *The Happiest Baby on the Block*, provides key strategies for calming an infant. And they work. His "ingredients of calm" are known as the "5 S's":

1. Swaddling—tight wrapping
2. Side/Stomach—laying a baby on her side or stomach

3. Shushing—loud white noise
4. Swinging—rhythmic, jiggly motion
5. Sucking—sucking on anything (nipple, finger, pacifier)

These techniques must be performed correctly and usually all together, and they will calm a crying/upset infant. Using the techniques individually can calm a mildly fussy baby.

The first three months of an infant's life is still very fetal. If you care for infants in the first three months by imitating the uterus, you will have a calmer and happier baby. Dr. Karp describes the differences between newborn babies and babies in their fourth month, when they have left the fetal stage:

Table 2.1 Newborn vs. Four-Month-Old-Babies

Newborns	Four-Month-Old Babies
Sensory Abilities	
Can focus on objects 8–12 inches away	Can easily focus on large objects across the room
Enjoys light/dark contrasts and designs	Can turn their head to find where a sound comes from
Social Abilities	
Prefers the human voice over music	Will wait for you to stop talking before talking with coos, grunts and giggles
Can recognize mother's voice from the womb	Enamored with parents' faces and will smile and coo to make parents smile; may become upset if ignored
Motor Abilities	
Can get cross-eyed	No longer cross-eyed
Can follow only slow-moving objects	Can now follow objects swiftly and smoothly as they move about the room
Can have jerky eye movements	More able to reach out and touch objects
	Can get their fingers in their mouth and keep them there for an extended period of time
Physiological Characteristics	
Hands and feet are blue much of the time	No longer gets blue hands and feet unless cold
Bodies can get jolted by hiccups, jittery tremors or irregular breathing	Rarely hiccups or tremors; breathing is smooth and regular
Has little ability to control body movements	Much better at controlling body movements
	Can roll over, spin around and lift head high off the mattress

Source: (Karp, 2015).

Sudden Infant Death Syndrome (SIDS)

Sudden infant death syndrome (SIDS) is the unexpected and sudden death of a child under age 1 in which an autopsy does not show an explainable cause of death. Almost all SIDS deaths occur without any warning or symptoms when the infant is thought to be sleeping. Doctors and researchers have determined that there are several different factors that can contribute to an infant dying from SIDS, such as problems with the baby's ability to wake up and an inability for an infant's body to detect a build-up of carbon dioxide in the blood. They have also determined that the following are linked to an infant's increased risk of SIDS:

- Sleep on stomach
- Exposure to cigarette smoke in the womb and after birth
- Having a mother who smokes or does illegal drugs
- Co-sleeping with parents
- Too soft bedding in the crib
- Multiple births
- Premature birth
- Having a sibling who died from SIDS
- Being born to a teen mother
- Short time between pregnancies
- Late or no prenatal care
- Living in poverty

In 1992, the "Back to Sleep" (later renamed "Safe to Sleep") campaign began and urged parents to put their infants to sleep on their back to reduce the risk of SIDS. SIDS rates have dropped dramatically since then, but it still remains a significant cause of death in infants under one year old. SIDS is most likely to occur between 2 and 4 months of age, although it can occur in older infants. SIDS occurs more often in the winter and is more likely with boys than girls (https://safetosleep.nichd.nih.gov/; www.sids.org).

Reducing the Risk of SIDS

There are many things that caregivers can do to help reduce the risk of SIDS. Whether you are a parent at home with your own infant or a caregiver caring for infants in a childcare setting, it is important to follow these guidelines:

- Place infants to sleep on their backs
- Use a firm mattress and put nothing else in the crib but the infant (no blankets, bumper pads, positioning devices or toys/stuffed animals)
- Have the infant sleep in the same room with the mother for the first few months, possibly until 6 months old. Studies clearly show that infants are safest when their beds are close to their mothers
- Do not let infants sleep in bed with adults or with adults on a couch or chair
- Use a sleep sack instead of a blanket and do not over-clothe infants

- Keep the room at a temperature that you find comfortable—infants do not need to be warmer, and overheating an infant might increase the risk of SIDS
- Do not expose infants to tobacco smoke or have them in a house or car with someone who is smoking. Exposure to tobacco smoke increases the risk of SIDS
- Breastfeed infants. Breastmilk decreases the occurrence of respiratory and gastrointestinal infections, and breastfed babies have a lower risk of SIDS compared to formula-fed babies
- Avoid exposing infants to people with respiratory infections and ask people to wash their hands before touching infants. Clean anything that comes in contact with infants and clean their hands if you feel they may have touched something with germs on it. This should be common practice for caregivers, not something that you are constantly worried about or overly cautious about. Just take care in who and what infants come into contact with
- Give infants a pacifier to suck on for the first few months. The act of sucking keeps infants breathing and their mouths occupied
- If your baby has periods of not breathing, going limp or turning blue, tell your pediatrician at once
- If an infant stops breathing or gags excessively after spitting up, discuss this with a pediatrician to rule out health risks that might contribute to SIDS.

(www.sids.org)

Baby Sign Language

Infants communicate from birth. They make eye contact, they make noises to talk and they cry when they need something. An important part of your role as a caregiver for infants and toddlers is to continually communicate with the children. Your verbalizations and actions teach the children about the world around them and what communications elicit different responses. Caregivers must also continually respond to an infant's communications. This shows the infant that what he says is recognized and responded to. Respond with your own words and emulate the infant's sounds. As infants grow up and eventually become toddlers at age 1, they are always communicating. They understand what they are trying to say to you and expect you to do the same. It is also important for caregivers to teach the infants and toddlers how to communicate. When infants and toddlers have a way to communicate their wants and needs, they are understood. When they are understood, they are less frustrated.

An easy way to teach your infant to communicate before she can clearly talk is to use baby sign language. By using a few simple signs to correspond with your words, you are teaching the child how to communicate back to you. By teaching infants a few basic signs to communicate their wants and needs, you eliminate the frustration of them verbalizing and you not understanding what they are saying. Infants who sign are not only less frustrated because their caregivers understand what they are communicating, but they also talk earlier because they already know the words and phrases they need to say to communicate. The goal is for an infant to eventually drop the sign and say the word. They will begin by signing, then signing and saying the word or phrase and finally only saying the word or phrase.

The basic signs I recommend are milk, eat, drink, sleep, more, all done, please and thank you. Any others that caregivers feel is necessary for the child's communication are fine as well. And you do not have to do the sign in the exact manner it is shown. Many families have their own variations to signs or have made up their own signs all together. Using sign language not only strengthens infants' language development but also strengthens their social/emotional development because they can effectively communicate with others.

"Teaching" infants sign language is easy. Start at birth, and usually by 9–12 months an infant will start to sign back at you. That first nine months, they are taking in your communications and learning them, so do not think your hard work is going to waste. Start with milk and move to include the other signs as they become relevant in the child's life. It is never too early to sign for "please" and "thank you." As infants gain more control of their motor skills in the first year of life, they will begin to sign back. When they do, be sure to acknowledge their communications and reciprocate them with words and signs. This will tell the infants that their communications were heard and understood, and they will continue to do it.

When teaching infants sign language, say the word/phrase and do the sign. Consistently respond to the infant's communications. If he is crying and you know he is hungry, do the sign for eat or drink and say, "You want to eat/drink?" Eventually, the infant will sign his communications. Once that first sign is shown, the rest will follow rather quickly. The key is to always say the word/phrase while both of you sign so that the infant learns the verbal communication that coincides with the sign. As they begin to talk after one year, they will know the word/phrase and then eventually say it instead of signing.

For additional material, visit:
www.parentphd.org/infantandtoddlertext/ch2/

Reflection Questions

- Cite one example for each:
    o   respectful caregiving
    o   responsive caregiving
    o   reciprocal caregiving
- In your classroom/fieldwork setting, look for examples of the "kinds of problems" that infants and toddlers encounter. Write a description of one of these experiences and then describe the child's approach to solving the problem (include specific behaviors and verbalizations).

Bibliography

American Academy of Pediatrics. (2013). Breastfeeding articles. Retrieved from www.healthychildren.org/English/ages-stages/baby/breastfeeding/Pages/default.aspx

American SIDS Institute. (2009a). Reducing the risk of SIDS. Retrieved from www.sids.org/nprevent.htm

American SIDS Institute. (2009b). What is SIDS? Retrieved from www.sids.org/ndefinition.htm

BabyCenter Medical Advisory Board. (2011, August). Potty training readiness checklist. Retrieved from www.babycenter.com/0_potty-training-readiness-checklist_4384.bc

Bernhardt, J. (2000, March). The Primary caregiving system for infants and toddlers: Best for everyone involved. *Young Children*, 74–80.

Dietze, W. H., & Stern, L. (2011). *Nutrition: What every parent needs to know* (2nd ed.). Elk Grove Village, IL: American Academy of Pediatrics.

Gonzalez-Mena, J., & Eyer, D. (2017). *Infants, toddlers, and caregivers: A curriculum of respectful, responsive, relationship-based care and education* (11th ed.). New York, NY: McGraw Hill.

Kaneshiro, N., & Zieve, D. (2011, August 2). Sudden infant death syndrome. Retrieved from www.ncbi.nlm.nih.gov/pubmedhealth/PMH0002533/

Karp, H. (2015). *The happiest baby on the block*. New York, NY: Bantam.

Katz, K. (2004). *A potty for me! A lift-the-flap instruction manual*. New York, NY: Little Simon.

Sears, W. (2013). 8 infant sleep facts every parent should know. Retrieved from www.askdrsears.com/topics/sleep-problems/8-infant-sleep-facts-every-parent-should-know

Sears, W., Sears, M., Sears, R., & Sears, J. (2013). *The baby book: Everything you need to know about your baby from birth to age two* (Revised ed.). New York, NY: Little, Brown and Company.

Sussman, F. (2012). The power of using everyday routines to promote young children's language and social skills. Retrieved from www.hanen.org/Helpful-Info/Articles/Power-of-Using-Everyday-Routines.aspx

3 The Infant and Toddler Environments

Close your eyes and imagine a room for children. Picture natural light coming through the many windows and many shapes and sizes of furniture to climb on and around and to explore. Materials are spread around that encourage sensory exploration and play. All of your senses are alive and stimulated when you are in this room.

Were you able to easily visualize this kind of room? Would you feel comfortable in it? It isn't a difficult environment to create! This next chapter will guide you toward a full understanding of what a developmentally appropriate infant/toddler environment looks like. Infant and toddler environments are complex and need to be created with care.

Infants and toddlers need safe indoor and outdoor spaces for quiet and active play, spaces for sleeping and spaces to interact one-on one with their caregivers. Within the environment, they need toys and activities selected primarily for their individual interests and abilities rather than one-size-fits-all group play.

Infant and toddler environments are comprised of three key components:

1. **The physical/learning environment**
    - Includes the classroom set-up, spaces and materials
    - Sets the stage for children's explorations and learning and influences their behavior

2. **The social/emotional environment**
    - Comprised of the relationships between the children *and* the children and the caregivers
    - Classrooms that function as a community and have close and caring relationships between caregivers and children help children relate positively to others and are comfortable places for exploration and learning

3. **The routines and transitions of the classroom**
    - These important and predictable events bring order to the day and give the children a sense of comfort

Caregivers must pay careful attention to each of these three components. They are of equal importance and deserve equal attention.

When these three aspects of infant and toddler environments are developed appropriately and with care, children feel like they "belong." Infants and toddlers feel a *sense of security* because the environment is safe and their caregivers understand and accept them. They feel a *sense of engagement* with their caregivers and their surroundings. They feel a *desire to explore and learn*, using all of their senses to discover everything in as many ways as they can. It is also important to remember that infants and toddlers are most comfortable in a classroom environment that has similar sights and sounds as their homes. When the classroom is warm and friendly for the children, it is also warm and friendly for their families. When families feel similar comfort feelings as their children, they are more willing to share ideas and contribute to the classroom (Gonzalez-Mena & Eyer, 2017).

The Physical/Learning Environment

The first aspect of infant and toddler environments is the one that comes to mind immediately when the term "environment" of a classroom is mentioned—the physical set-up of the classroom. The first things to consider in the physical environment are adult-child ratios and safety. The National Association for the Education of Young Children (NAEYC) has established the following guidelines for adult-child ratios in infant and toddler classrooms:

Table 3.1 Teacher-Child Ratios by Group Size

Age of Children	Group Size	Teacher:Child Ratio
Infant (0–15 months)	8 (maximum group size)	1:4
Infant (0-15 months)	6	1:3
Toddler 1 (12–28 months)	12 (maximum group size)	1:4
Toddler 2 (21–36 months)	12 (maximum group size)	1:6

Source: (www.naeyc.org).

These ratios are set to ensure the safety and adequate care of the children in the classroom. NAEYC states that ratios are to be lower when one or more children in the group need additional adult assistance to fully participate in the program due to ability, language fluency, developmental age or stage. Teachers can be lead teachers, assistant teachers, teacher aids, program administrators or substitute teachers. When infants and toddlers are in mixed age groups, the ratio for the youngest child applies. When two or more adults must be present during naptime, at least one of the adults present must be a teacher or assistant teacher/teacher aide. For example, a group of five to eight infants would require at least two people, one of which is a teacher or assistant teacher/teacher aide, to be present to meet the ratio. Additional adults may be staff members or other adults who function in a different role.

After appropriate ratios have been established, an environment must also be deemed safe and healthy. When ensuring that an infant/toddler environment is safe and healthy, there are many aspects of the classroom that must be analyzed. The following is a checklist that can be used to check your classroom to see if it is meeting adequate safety standards for caregivers and children:

54 The Infant and Toddler Environments

Physical Environment Safety Checklist
Table 3.2

Aspect of Environment	Checked—SAFE	Checked—UNSAFE
All electrical outlets covered		
All heaters covered/out of children's reach		
Drapery cords tied up or removed		
Windows have safety latches		
Plan for a fire is posted		
First aid kit is available and fully stocked		
All staff knows first aid and CPR		
Emergency numbers are posted		
No poisonous plants		
No broken or unstable furniture		
No broken toys or small parts loose		
Cribs meet the current consumer protection safety standards		
All medicines and cleaning materials are stored high and away from children's reach		

A healthy environment is as important as a safe one. Sanitation is key to keeping the environment safe and the caregivers and children healthy.

(www.naeyc.org)

Figure 3.1 Infant Exploring Blocks and the Rug

Physical Environment Healthy and Sanitary Checklist

Table 3.3

Aspect of the Environment	My Environment Meets This Criteria
Wash hands often	
Wash children's hands often	
Do not allow children to share personal items	
Clean toys that have been in a child's mouth immediately	
Wear socks or slippers in infant rooms—no shoes	
Vacuum rugs/mop floors daily	
Each child should have his/her own crib/bed/cot and corresponding linens	
Diapering area should be clean and away from all other activity; clean and sanitize after each use	
Store food appropriately and wash dishes/utensils in very hot water	
Make sure all children are up to date on immunizations	
Learn to recognize signs of common illnesses	
Have clear policies about when a child should and should not be in school during an illness	
Have a permission slip for parents to sign before administering medication	

(www.naeyc.org)

Children's behavior is directly influenced by the classroom environment. When the physical/learning environment meets children's developmental needs to belong and feel safe and comfortable, children become more independent and confident learners. In this section, we will discuss the layout, developmental appropriateness and how to assess the quality of your infant and toddler classrooms. First, let's begin with a general checklist that pertains to the physical layout of the classroom. Use this checklist to ensure that your classroom is the appropriate layout for the children. Read the first column and fill in the second column. The third column will be addressed later.

Classroom Layout Checklist

Table 3.4

Layout	How My Classroom Meets This Criteria	DAP
Designated area for arrivals and departures with cubbies for individual children's belongings		
Sleeping area apart from the play area		
There should be a crib or cot for each child		

(Continued)

Table 3.4 (Continued)

Layout	How My Classroom Meets This Criteria	DAP
Diaper area should be a separate area that is close to a bathroom and/or sink		
All diapering materials should be accessible to the caregiver during the changing process		
Toilets should be child-sized and have access to sinks, soap and paper towels that the children can reach on their own		
While the eating tables may be used for other purposes during non-eating times, during eating times there is only eating occurring in those areas—no play materials		
Small tables and chairs that the children can get in and out of are ideal. Bouncy seats or a caregiver's arms are available for infants who cannot sit up in these types of tables and chairs yet.		
Indoor play area should be inviting to exploration and all materials should be accessible to the children		
Outdoor play area should be inviting to exploration and all materials should be accessible to the children		

Once you have completed the second column of the previous checklist, it is time to look back at your classroom and analyze its developmental appropriateness. Having a developmentally appropriate environment is extremely important; infants thrive in an environment set-up for infants, and toddlers thrive in a totally different environment made for their age. Developmentally appropriate also means that caregivers have to be flexible; the children grow up quickly, so the environment must respond to the children as they grow and develop over time. Here are some basic criteria for developmental appropriateness for infants and toddlers. After reading through these two lists, go back to the previous checklist and fill in column three with information about how each criterion is or is not developmentally appropriate.

When planning a physical space for infants and toddlers, be sure to arrange the room so all of the children can be seen at all times. The room should be efficiently organized so that there are clear spaces for specific routines and experiences and different floor coverings, furniture and space for each one. The next few sections focus on what developmentally appropriate environments look like for infants and toddlers and offers suggestions for what materials and experiences should be in these environments. The information in these sections come from my personal experience as an infant and toddler caregiver and parent who created an environment in my home. Many concepts and tips from Dodge, Rudick, and Berke (2015); Greenman (1982, 1993); Gonzalez-Mena and Eyer (2017) and NAEYC mirror my ideas and have been naturally incorporated throughout these sections.

A Developmentally Appropriate Physical Environment for Infants

- A confined area (small mat or bouncy seat) for very young infants
- Large and open floor space for movement and exploration
- Support for "cruising"—bookcases, shelves and other furniture to hang on while standing and beginning to walk
- Cribs are only used for sleeping; infants sleep better if the only thing they do in their crib is sleep. Hanging toys, mobiles and music boxes in cribs sends a mixed message about what the crib is used for
- A comfortable eating/feeding environment. Children should be in chairs that they can fit in comfortably

A Developmentally Appropriate Physical Environment for Toddlers

- An environment that encourages independence:
  - Stools for sinks and changing tables
  - Pitchers to pour their own drinks and utensils to scoop their own food
  - Cloths to clean up their own spills
  - A place to put their dirty items after eating
- More space to accommodate new gross motor skills
- Places for manipulative play (tables, rugs) to accommodate new fine motor skills
- "Center-like areas" where a certain type of play or material has a designated place to take out, play with and then be put away
- Contains a variety of age-appropriate toys and equipment that develop active, creative and manipulative skills

A Developmentally Appropriate Physical Environment for Infants and Toddlers in the Home

Whether your home is used for childcare or just a place where you and your children spend their time, there are ways to set up the environment to be

58 The Infant and Toddler Environments

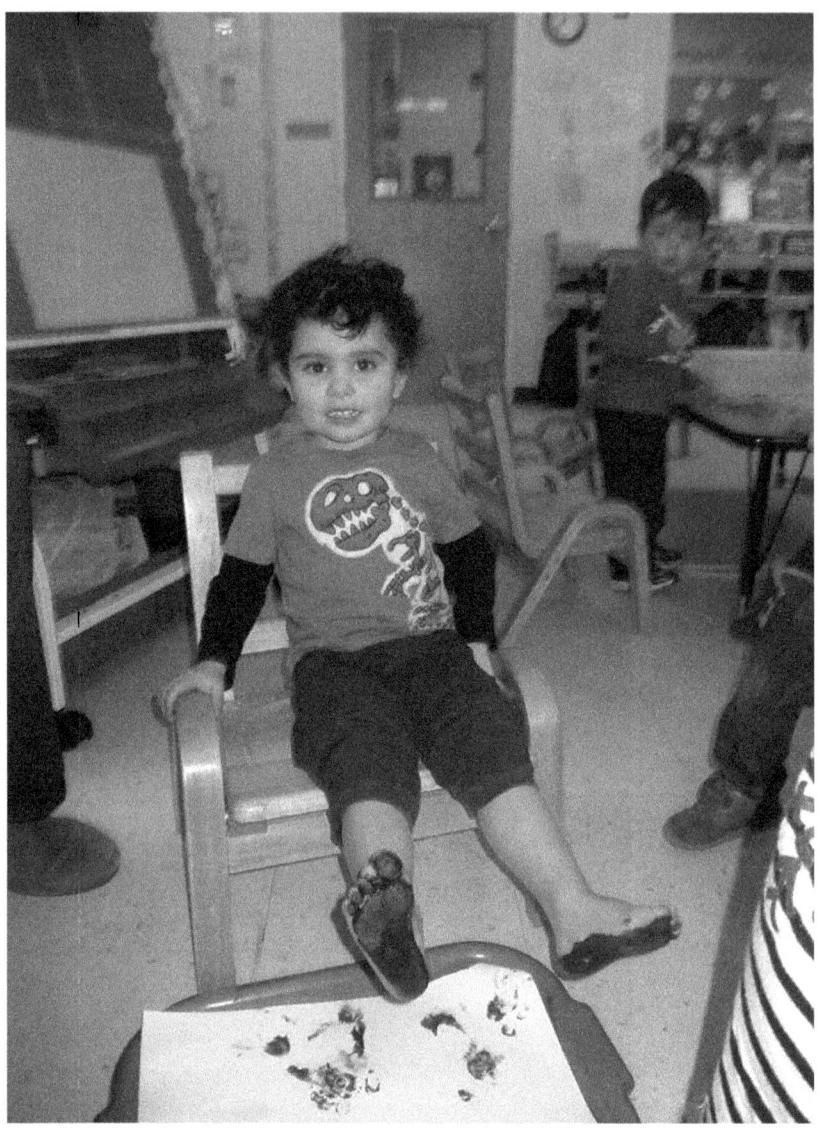

Figure 3.2 Toddler Painting With His Feet

conducive to one or more children in the infant and toddler years. Here are some tips:

- Use area rugs to define play spaces
- Store toys/materials in cube organizers so that the children can access them easily as well as use them for "cruising" and standing

Figure 3.3 An Infant and a Toddler Playing Outdoors

- Designate one cabinet in the kitchen for the children; fill it with Tupperware, plastic spoons and any other kitchen items that are safe and fun to play with
- Have furniture around the play area that the children can sit on with you (infants) and eventually climb on themselves to sit (toddlers)

Safety gates can be used at the tops and bottoms of stairs to protect the children from unsafe climbing. I recommend portable gates so that they are used only when necessary. Gates should not be placed in every entryway or doorway in order to "cage in" children into one area. They should be free to roam around under the watchful eye of a caregiver or parent. If you are concerned about something being unsafe at an infant or toddler's level, move it to a safer place or redirect children away from it to safer and more appropriate items.

Designing Spaces for Infants and Toddlers

The Creative Curriculum program describes specific characteristics of spaces for young infants, mobile infants and toddlers. They urge caregivers to design spaces that accommodate each child's developmental needs, abilities and interests. It is important to change the environment as the children get older in order to keep them safe, offer new challenges and stimulate new interests (Dodge et al., 2015).

The following is Tables 3.5, 3.6 and 3.7 provide a summary of their suggestions for the physical environments of children ages 0–3:

Young infants need soft and comfortable spaces, good lighting, many views from the floor and soft toys.

60 The Infant and Toddler Environments

Table 3.5 Young Infant Physical Environment

What Young Infants Can Do	Ways to Arrange the Environment	How This Supports Development
Look at what is around them	Place pictures at their eye level on walls, shelves and ends of cribs	Encourages focus and attention to objects
Differentiate between familiar and unfamiliar sights and sounds	Have familiar items such as clothing, music and voices	Provides comfort of home
Reach for, swat at, grasp objects	Place toys within reach	Encourages use of fine motor skills to and exploration objects
Put toys in their mouth to explore them	Have a bin for mouthed toys so they can be cleaned at the end of the day	Supports their most used avenue of exploration (the mouth) and keeps materials sanitary
Respond to being held or rocked	Have comfortable places to hold the children	Helps build trusting and secure relationships
Eventually gain the ability to roll, sit and crawl	Provide soft surfaces so infants can move safely	Promotes their gross motor skills

Table 3.6 Mobile Infant Physical Environment

What Mobile Infants Can Do	Ways to Arrange the Environment	How This Supports Development
Pull themselves up into a standing position	Have sturdy furniture that they can pull themselves up on	Free and safe exploration and gaining of balance
Repeat an action or movement to master it	Provide space and time for undisturbed play	Development of attention and motor skills
Push, pull, fill and dump objects	Have a variety of toys and containers	Development of motor skills, hand-eye coordination and understanding of cause and effect
Comforted with familiar things from home	Display family pictures	Helps to become comfortable in care because of connection to home
Use caregivers as a "home base" for exploration	Low dividers so adults and children can see each other	Promotes feelings of safety and security

Mobile infants are now moving around. The environment needs to support this desire for movement, whether it be crawling, furniture surfing or walking. Play spaces should also become more defined and designated for different experiences.

Table 3.7 Toddler Physical Environment

What Toddlers Can Do	Ways to Arrange the Environment	How This Supports Development
Jump, climb, walk and run	Provide enough space for this type of movement	Encourage free and independent exploration
Make their own choices and have favorite things to play with	All materials should be on low shelves and be labeled	Supports their independence in choosing and playing with materials
Eat in a group	Have low tables and chairs	Shows them how to be a member of a group and encourages them to converse with each other
Sleep at a scheduled time with their classmates	Provide cots or mats with their own sheets and comfort items	Provides a clear naptime and space so they can get the rest they need
May want to do more than they are able to do	Have materials and experiences that match what the children can do and also provide some challenge	Challenges the children and at the same time minimizes frustration
Play near and with other children	Have duplicates of materials and toys and enough room for more than one child to play in an area	Promotes social play

Source: The Creative Curriculum for Infants, Toddlers and Twos: The Foundation.

Toddlers are active learners whose needs and desires change often. They need space to play alone and space to gather in a group. It is time to add more materials, props and spaces for gross motor play. As these children turn 2, you can designate different play centers and communal gathering areas (eating, group time) in the classroom.

What to Give Infants and Toddlers to "Play" With

Simple play materials, individualized attention and a safe environment that promotes interaction are essential components to infant and toddler play. Such conditions help children develop long attention spans, concentration and other manipulative and physical skills. When providing materials for the children to explore and play with, age appropriateness is key. As children grow through the infant and toddler years, they gain more knowledge, skills and curiosities. The play materials must change with the children. I suggest materials that are as simple as possible. You want the children to explore it and figure out "what it does" on their own. Almost anything that is safe and interesting can be a learning tool for infants and toddlers. The chart below is

Table 3.8 Matching Infant and Toddler Skills and Abilities to Their Environment

Age	Large Muscles	Small Muscles	What to "Play" With
0–3 months	Most arm and leg movements are reflexes Can lift head briefly	Cannot control hands—often clenched Will grasp what is put into hand as a reflex Faces are the most interesting thing to look at	Mat, rug or blanket to lie on and look around Faces to look at
3–6 months	Less reflexes and more voluntary control of arms, legs and head	Will reach for objects but hands will still be in a fist Will attempt to grab objects but often miss	Mat, rug or blanket to lie on and play Washable and mouthable objects to grab for (soft toys/books, rubber and plastic blocks)
6–9 months	Full head control Can roll from back to stomach and stomach to back May creep or roll around	Can grab objects, hold onto them and manipulate them Thumb and forefinger grasp beginning to develop	Mat, rug or blanket to lie on and play Hard floor to vary what is under their body Materials with a variety of textures Introduce a "light table" and put a few colored and see-through manipulative objects on it. Use the light table throughout the infant/toddler years, continually adding more objects for the children to explore on it.
9–12 months	Can crawl around, sometimes holding objects Can pull themselves up on furniture and eventually stand without holding on "Cruises" around on furniture Can get into a seated position on their own	Can pick up small objects using thumb and forefingers Hand-eye coordination is growing stronger	More room and more objects to explore – plastic or wooden blocks, puzzles, cars/trucks, letters, nesting/shape sorting objects, balls Different levels of pillows, platforms or furniture to safely explore/climb on
12–18 months	Stands without holding on Crawling turns into walking Can climb up and down stairs	Can use both hands at the same time for different things Uses thumb well Begins to show preference for a hand	These suggestions are for a children ages 12–24 months: Enjoy taking walks and exploring the environment Sensory tub for water, sand and other sensory experiences Vehicles with and without peddles Swings Plastic and wooden blocks of different sizes

Age	Development	Materials
		Puzzles with pegs and without
Playdough
Stringing beads
Shape sorters
Instruments
Objects to sort (beads, shape pieces)
Dolls to dress and undress
Puppets
Flannel board and pieces
Dramatic play materials (prop boxes work well)
Kitchen materials and a child-sized kitchen
All types of books (big, small, board, paper)
All types of art supplies (finger paint, markers, crayons, dot paint, paper, bubble wrap)
18–24 months	Walks and eventually runs
Can walk up stairs, first holding a hand and eventually on their own
Can use crayons to draw and paintbrushes to paint
Gains more and more control of utensils and cups when eating, though will still spill
Turns the pages of a book – moving from thicker board books to paper pages	See above
24–36 months	Walk, run, climb and throw with control
Jump in place
Balance on one foot
May pedal a tricycle
Can put clothing and shoes on but still working on buttons, snaps and tying shoes
Feeds self
Scribbles and paints with control
Will use manipulatives more dramatically	Everything listed for 12–14-month-olds, but you can add larger and more challenging versions; can also start to use some preschool toys

a breakdown of children from ages 0–3 in terms of their skills and abilities and the materials you can provide for them. How many do you have in your home or childcare environment?

Now that you have set up your infant or toddler environment and have chosen your play materials, here is a final checklist to ensure that you have created the best possible environment for the children. These nine criterions are extremely relevant and are used by many infant/toddler practitioners to assess the quality of their environments.

Published by Teachers College Press, The Infant/Toddler Environment Rating Scale (ITERS) is widely used to assess the quality of infant and toddler programs. The scale consists of 39 items organized into the 7 subscales of space and furnishings, personal care routines, listening and talking, activities, interaction, program structure and parents and staff. I recommend referring to the

Table 3.9 Criteria of Quality Infant and Toddler Environments

Criteria of Quality	How My I/T Environment Promotes It
There is a balance of both soft materials (cozy furniture, pillows, blankets, stuffed animals) and hard materials (hard floors to learn to walk on)	
Low windows to allow intrusion of the outdoor environment and places for children to go when they want to be secluded and alone	
Environment must encourage the children to be mobile and active safely	
Toys should be visible and open for children to grab and explore; toys should be both open-ended (no one way to do it or many ways to do it) and close-ended (one way to do it). The younger the children, the more open-ended objects should be available.	
Both simple and complex materials should exist in the classroom, and the possibility of making a simple toy (an empty water bottle) more complex (adding sand) should also exist.	
All furniture should be to scale with the size of the children (Rule of thumb—if things are about at hip height and below for an adult, it is appropriate for infants and toddlers).	
The room should be visually appealing—use natural light whenever possible and neutral colors.	
Pay attention to the noise in the room and be aware of background noises. Too much noise can be over stimulating for infants and toddlers.	
The room should have a sense of order and everything should have a place. This provides comfort and stability for the children and the caregivers.	

Figure 3.4 An Example of an Organized and Accessible Environment

ITERS when planning an infant or toddler program, and particularly when creating the classroom spaces.

Kaplan Early Learning Company has created the "Kaplan FloorPlanner Tool," which provides sample, interactive floorplans designed to support the ITERS and NAEYC accreditation standards. When you access this website: www.kaplanco.com/resources/floorPlannerSamples.asp, you can choose to "look inside" a classroom and view a typical layout, as well as create your own custom floorplan using Kaplan's designs as starting points.

The Social/Emotional Environment

The second aspect of infant and toddler environments is the social/emotional environment. The social/emotional environment of infant and toddler classrooms focuses on the relationships between the children, the children and their caregivers and the overall comfort of the classroom. This aspect of the environment is not as easy to "see" as the physical environment, but it is incredibly important. Without a healthy social/emotional environment, the children will not grow and learn appropriately. The infants and toddlers learn a great deal about themselves and the world from the behavior of their caregivers. Therefore, regardless of what type of caregiving situation you are in with infants and toddlers, you must know how to create a positive and healthy social/emotional environment. The following section will give you an understanding of what this type of environment looks like and how to establish it in your caregiving environment.

Infants and Toddlers Forming Their "Sense of Self"

Infants and toddlers are continually in the process of forming their own identity, or sense of self. They are slowly coming to understand their likes and dislikes and who they are in the world. The way that they establish these aspects of their identity is to watch and listen to their caregivers and see how these caregivers perceive them. They also observe how their caregivers react to situations and express their emotions.

Infants and toddlers can learn many lessons from their caregivers who help them form their sense of self. They can learn what to fear, which behaviors are appropriate, how messages are received and acted upon, how successful they are at getting their needs met, what emotions they can display and at what intensity and how interesting they are. Infants and toddlers then take this information and use it to decide how they and others should be treated and how to express their emotions. Every interaction leaves an impression on the children. Therefore, if you spend any significant amount of time with an infant or toddler, you directly influence the person he turns out to be. You have helped to create each little person. Think about that for a minute!

Infants and toddlers' sense of self is comprised of many facets, and it is important to understand what each one means. *Self-concept* is a child's feelings about himself. The way that an infant or toddler is treated by caregivers affects self-concept and his *self-esteem*. Self-esteem is an infant or toddler's confidence and satisfaction with himself. Infants and toddlers must have healthy and strong attachments to caregivers in order to have a healthy and strong self-concept and self-esteem. We will discuss attachment in a forthcoming chapter but know that is a relationship with a caregiver that tells the child that he is important and cared for. Healthy attachments obviously start at home with primary caregivers but quickly extend to childcare situations when a child spends a significant amount of time in the care of other people.

Self-image, body awareness and *cultural identity* also make up a child's self-concept. Self-image is a child's perception of herself in relation to body image and awareness. Body awareness is learning and knowing the capabilities of her body. Cultural identity is the culture or cultures the children come from and how those cultures influence their thoughts and actions. It is important for caregivers to listen to the families of the infants and toddlers they care for and to emulate their cultural practices as much as they can. You should carry on the cultural caregiving from the home into your classroom each day that the child spends with you. We will discuss this more in the next chapter on communicating and working with families. The culture of the classroom is another key part of each child's cultural identity, and you as caregivers establish this and act upon it on a daily basis.

A final part of self-concept is *gender identity*. While children are aware early in their lives whether they are a boy or girl, what it means to be a boy or girl is shaped by their interactions and experiences. As a society, we influence children's ideas about how they should behave as a boy or girl. Think about this:

If you were asked to purchase a present for an expectant mother, what color clothing would you purchase for a girl? A boy? I'm pretty sure you said pink for a girl and blue for a boy. If you purchased a pink outfit for a boy, how would other people react if he wore it? Would they think he was a girl? Probably. This is just a quick example of how gender roles are established very early on in life. As a caregiver, you must be aware of your own ideas about sex role stereotyping and work hard to not have different expectations for boys and girls. These expectations influence the children's self-concept. They notice what is expected of each gender by hearing simple remarks, the clothes they are asked to wear and the toys they are given to play with. Gonzalez-Mena and Eyer (2017) suggest four strategies for caregivers to help them expand children's ideas about gender roles in your classroom:

1. Be careful not to treat boys and girls differently. Do you expect boys to "tough it out" when hurt whereas you provide support and sympathy to girls in the same situation? Do you suggest that the girls play with dolls and the boys play with blocks?
2. Model gender roles yourself. Show the children that women can fix things and men can cook a meal
3. Avoid exposing children to media messages that show stereotyped gender roles. Since infants and toddlers should NOT be watching any television,

Figure 3.5 Infant Playing With Mirror

this more refers to you finding books and pictures of men and women in a variety of occupational and caregiving roles
4. Watch your language. Make sure you do not link occupations to gender. Say "police officer" instead of "policeman".

Why You Never "Sneak Out"

An important part of infants and toddlers' sense of self is their comfort with and awareness of who they are with and where they are. Leaving an infant or toddler in the care of some else requires you to prepare and inform the child of the separation that is about to occur. You then must follow through with the separation. It is important to never "sneak out" when you are leaving an infant or toddler with a caregiver. Always say goodbye. And then leave. And don't come back. Reappearing after telling a child you are leaving is even more stressful and confusing than the initial separation. Telling infants and toddlers goodbye may make them sad because you are leaving, but it also tells them that you are leaving them and that you are coming back. If you sneak out, they don't know where you went, when you left and if you are coming back. Imagine how stressful that must be.

Guidance and Discipline

You might find it interesting that guidance and discipline is discussed in the part of this book that discusses the environment. The way that you guide and control the behavior of the infants and toddlers in your care directly affects their ideas and feelings about themselves. Your strategies and solutions help to develop the social and emotional environment of home or classroom where infants and toddlers spend their time. The following discussion about guidance and discipline will provide information and strategies for both caregivers and parents.

The Physical Environment Sets Limits

The physical environment that children are in sets specific limits. In an infant or toddler classroom, this means that everything that is accessible to the children is something they can touch, open or play with. You shouldn't have to tell children not to touch something that they can easily reach. Move it or put it in a locked cabinet if it is only for adults. Baby gates can also block off areas such as diapering/handwashing areas so that the children can only go in there with an adult. They can also be used in the doorway of the classroom so that the children can look out and interact with people that walk by but cannot leave the classroom unaccompanied.

In the child's home, the physical environment and the limit it sets is different. I actually suggest that you don't lock your house up like an institution and put away anything breakable until your child goes to college. It's not necessary, and, quite frankly, it isn't respectful to the child. It is her home, too. You just need to teach her about what she can and cannot touch and watch her to ensure that she is paying attention to those guidelines. She can be taught to touch only certain things and look at other things with her eyes or with the assistance of an adult. Back in the section of the chapter on the physical environment, you read about the use of baby gates. Your home should not be a giant maze of baby gates. Infants and toddlers should be able to roam freely through the rooms of a house under the watchful eye of an adult caregiver. Gates at the top or bottom of the stairs are essential for safety until a child is old enough to walk up and down them safely. I suggest buying portable gates that you can take down when not needed or move from stairwell to stairwell depending on where you are with your child in the house. This will also not cause adults to have to go through gates to use the stairs of your house when your children are not around.

Redirection and Guidance

In terms of actually guiding infants and toddlers' behavior, caregivers and parents should think of it more as *redirection* and less like discipline. When you redirect children, you guide them away from what they are not supposed to be doing to something they can do. An example is if a child throws a toy, give him a ball to throw safely instead. Redirection is not distraction. Distraction is manipulative and attempts to keep the child from any action altogether. Redirection channels the energy to a more appropriate activity. While this might not always work and a child may have to be removed from a situation, persistence is key. Stay the course, and children will learn their limits. Before any type of redirection or guidance, it is important for the parent or caregiver to clearly define the unacceptable behavior. Tell the child exactly what she did and that it was not ok. Then move on to redirection and guidance.

Newborns and young infants don't need any type of discipline. They are simply innocently exploring the world and are not testing limits or "acting out" for any attention. Caregivers must guide infants toward an understanding of appropriate behaviors and expressions. When we guide infants, we show them how it's done. If we want to show them "gentle," we say "gentle" and then model it with our own hands. The key is the showing or "modeling" of the skill. The term "modeling" is used often in early childhood education because as caregivers we are constantly showing the children how things are done or appropriate behaviors. As children grow to be older infants and then toddlers, guidance strategies change.

With toddlers, the modeling doesn't go away, but a simple verbal reminder tends to work because they have some experience with the guidance and appropriate action. Toddlers test limits all day every day. This is how they learn about the world. As toddlers test a limit, they wait for a reaction (positive or negative) from a caregiver. This reaction lets them know what the limit is and how far they can go. Through the constant cycle of limit testing and limit enforcement, toddlers learn about the world, and they learn how to behave appropriately. A caregiver and parent's goal is to teach toddlers what they can and cannot do and how to behave appropriately in the world. This can be done with strict limits, strict reinforcement of the limits and explanations of the limits when necessary.

It is also important to be honest about your feelings when toddlers act out. Remember that you must express them appropriately because you are teaching them not only what the different emotions look like but also the acceptable way to express them. If you are upset by their behavior, say that you are upset and show it on your face. This will teach toddlers what being upset looks like, that it is OK to be upset when expressed appropriately and that their behavior caused you to have this emotion. The same goes for happy emotions. Tell toddlers how you feel and why you feel that way.

When my daughter was a toddler, I would tell her when I was not happy with her behavior if she acted out in a way that was inappropriate and required me to let her know it was unacceptable. She got to a point where she would ask me, "Mommy are you happy?" after she did something that she probably knew was inappropriate and even if she behaved appropriately and knew that she had. I made sure to tell her the truth every time. She soon learned what behaviors triggered happy emotions and what ones triggered unhappiness because I had to redirect her. Her recognition of these emotions was a big step in her social/emotional development. She learned that it was OK for her to express any emotion and say she felt a certain way as long as she did it appropriately.

It also may be necessary to remove a toddler from a situation to cool down. I call this taking some "time to think." In a classroom, this time can be taken away from the situation that caused the misbehavior or conflict. At home, a stair is a good place to move away for a minute, calm down and think. If you don't have stairs, try a doorway. The key is that the toddler takes a moment to cool down and pull himself together before returning to play. When integrating the "time to think" moments, tell the child that he need some "time to think" after defining the unacceptable behavior. Walk with him to whatever area (stair, doorway) you have decided. Make sure it is close by so the toddler doesn't forget what he did on the way over! Sit the toddler down and tell him to take a deep breath in and out. Do it with him. Then explain that the inappropriate behavior was unacceptable and that you are both going to sit and think/calm down for a minute. Sit with the toddler when you first begin to implement this guidance strategy. You may find that as you implement the strategy more, the toddler can sit by himself or even announce that he is taking a "time to think" without your direction. After a minute or less, talk to the child about why he is there, redefine the acceptable behavior and return to play. You may have to do this numerous times at first, but it does help the child calm down and learn to pull himself together. The concept of regulating their own behavior is a skill that all children need to learn, and this guidance practice helps this process along.

Guidance and redirection are behaviors that you "do" to and with a child. There are also some behaviors that come directly from you and help children

The Infant and Toddler Environments 71

Figure 3.6 Open-Ended Toddler Nature Art

to learn how to behave appropriately. *First*, caregivers and parents should always model socially acceptable behavior. If you want children to say please and thank you, you need to always say it. If you want children to ask politely for a toy instead of grabbing it, you need to always ask politely for things. Trust me, it works! *Second*, use positive reinforcement to acknowledge socially acceptable behavior. If a child uses manners, point it out. The other children will hear it and want to garner recognition as well, so they will work to exhibit the good behaviors. *Third*, reorganize a situation and prevent harmful behavior from happening. Keep an eye on children who might act out with certain behaviors and intervene before it happens. If there is a conflict between children, work with them to work it out and/or make sure that there are enough materials or room for both children to play together. *Finally*, as I stated earlier, sometimes you need to redirect the energy. If your toddlers are really active and keep running around the room, take them outside or to an indoor space where they can run and get the energy out. Overall, caregivers and parents need to recognize what the children need and address it quickly and appropriately. This is your job as the person guiding and teaching the children. Try different strategies and don't give up. Always be reliable and consistent. One day it will all click, and the children will be working with you to regulate their behavior instead of against you (Gonzalez-Mena & Eyer, 2017).

Bargains Versus Bribes

The key to toddler guidance is that you work to have them see the logic in complying with your request or behaving appropriately because it will then allow them to do something that *they* want to do. When guiding and disciplining toddlers, I suggest taking a "Bargain versus Bribes" viewpoint. A *bargain* is allowing a toddler to do something she enjoys in return for following directions, completing a task you ask her to do, or to calm down and behave properly. Example: "If you clean up your blocks now, we have enough time to read a story before dinnertime." A *bribe* is different. Example: "If you clean up your blocks now, you can have a piece of candy." See the difference? Bargains are more logical and will work over a long period of time. They teach children cause and effect—if I complete a task, I will have time for something I look forward to or enjoy. Bribes might work right away, but you are basically training the toddler to behave for a treat, and it will get harder and harder to fulfill her idea of a "treat" as she gets older. And believe me—if the toddler doesn't comply with your request and you "don't have time" for the task that she enjoys, it makes much more of an impact versus "ok, no candy for you."

Routines and Transitions

The third and final aspect of infant and toddler environments is the routines and transitions of the classrooms. This final aspect of the environment focuses on consistency and security for the children. The daily routines and transitions in the classroom should be consistent and familiar to the children. This gives the children a sense of safety and security as they go through their day. When children know what is coming next and how it will happen, they feel as if they have some control of their daily life in the classroom. Then they, in turn, will be more independent and self-directed in their explorations and play. The more they play and explore openly, the more they learn. These consistent and familiar routines look very different for an infant classroom and a toddler classroom (Sussman, 2012).

Infant Classrooms

Routines and transitions occur on an *individual basis* in an infant room. Each infant's needs and expectations for care are different, and caregivers must be consistent and familiar to infants on an individual basis.

As discussed in chapter two, the caregiving routines that occur each day with the infants comprise the majority of their daily schedule. The rest of the time should be spent exploring materials on a large open space on the floor or venturing outside in a stroller to explore the outdoor environment. Each infant's routines and transitions are different, and the children are cared for individually rather than as a group. It is important for caregivers to be consistent with how they perform the caregiving routines with the infants so that it is a familiar and pleasurable experience for the children. Caregivers should know how each infant likes to be held when going to sleep, when eating and how to interact with them during diaper changing or bathing. Caregivers should then be consistent in this care each time it happens.

When transitioning infants from one caregiving or exploratory experience to another, caregivers must be consistent by alerting the infant to what is about to happen, looking the infant in the eye while talking and manipulating them and then carefully and calmly carrying the infant to the next experience.

Here are examples of typical infant classroom experiences that occur throughout the day:

- Caregiving routines
- Sensory play
- Floor/Manipulative play
- Outdoor play/walks
- Story time
- Music and movement
- Breakfast
- Lunch
- Snack

Since the children are cared for on an individual basis, when these experiences occur must be flexible yet "ready to go" at any moment. This "list" of routines and events is important to share with the families of the children so that they know what is happening during their children's day. As infants get closer to age 1, they also begin to follow typical eating and sleeping times, and the classroom must devote time to this transition.

Toddler Classrooms

Routines and transitions occur *as a group* in a toddler room. The children are at an age where they can move as a "class" through the daily schedule. Some toddlers, especially younger toddlers (ages 1–2), may still have individual needs that need to be met, and caregivers should do so with the same consistency and familiarity that they did for the toddlers when they were infants.

As discussed in chapter two, toddlers experience the same caregiving routines as infants but now at a more advanced level. Their skills and their desire for independence allow them to participate more with the caregiver and sometimes perform a caregiving routine on their own. Different from infants, though, these caregiving routines are only a part of a toddler's day. A toddler room's daily schedule is comprised of much more than these caregiving routines, and the children move through the schedule as a group.

While a toddler's daily schedule is a mix of caregiving and play, it is important to have consistent routines. Daily events that occur at the same time each day and in the same manner each day help to keep your classroom managed and the children feeling safe and secure. Toddlers feel as though they have more control of their lives if they know what activity or routine is coming next, and this knowledge gives them the opportunity to be independent and self-directed in their play. Every event in a toddler's day can be used as an opportunity to promote some aspect of their development and learning. Some events that take place every day in a toddler classroom are:

- Large-group meetings (morning meeting/circle time)
- Small-group time (work on a planned experience with a few children)
- Choice time (centers/interest areas)
- Mealtimes
- Rest times
- Transitions

Each of these events can be learning opportunities for children if they are well thought out and planned based on what you know about how children develop and learn. It is important to display the events of the day at the children's eye level and use both pictures and words.

So what are the characteristics of an appropriate daily schedule for toddler classrooms? The schedule should be well balanced and flexible, with orderly events scheduled throughout the day help the day go more smoothly. Remember—when children know what to expect, they feel safe. There should be a balance of different types of activities and should include both active and quiet times and outdoor and indoor play times. Toddler schedules should also have a balance of the following:

- Large-group activities
- Small-group activities
- Time to play alone
- Time to play with others
- Child-initiated activities
- Teacher-directed activities

Consistency does not mean you cannot be flexible or make changes. Just remember that when making any major changes, it is important to prepare children ahead of time. Illustrating a schedule and using it to guide children as they move from one activity to the next promotes both literacy and an understanding of sequence.

A toddler classroom starts to resemble a preschool classroom in the way that each "experience" or "exploration" has a designated space for it to occur. Toddlers can then start to make choices about what they want to play with and retrieve the materials themselves from designated shelves and centers. Here are examples of typical "centers" in a toddler classroom:

- Books
- Blocks
- Manipulatives
- Home/kitchen
- Art

It is clear that infant and toddler environments are complex and great care must be taken to develop each part appropriately. In his article "Places for Babies: Infants and Toddlers in Groups," Jim Greenman provides this evaluation form from the perspective of an infant or toddler. It is wonderful way to evaluate the appropriateness of your infant or toddler classroom and encompasses all three aspects of infant toddler environments: the physical environment, the social/emotional environment and the routines and transitions.

Quick Evaluation of an Infant or Toddler Learning/Caring Environment

If infants or toddlers could choose their own setting, they might ask:
How many places are there where I can:

climb up? _____
climb in? _____
climb over? _____
climb on? _____
go through? _____
go under? _____
go in and out? _____
pull myself up? _____
reach? _____
kick? _____
jump? _____
How many semi-enclosed places are there?
How many different places to be are there for me, places that feel different because of light, texture, sound, smell, enclosure and sight lines?
When you put me in an infant swing or bounce chair, am I only there for a short time and I get out when I want to get out?
How often do I get out of the room?
How often do I go for stroller or cart rides?
How often do I get to get out of the stroller/cart and walk/crawl around?
How often do I get to play with messy things—water, sand, dough, paint?
What is there to transport? push/pull? collect/dump? throw?
Do I get to feed myself as soon as I can hold a spoon, bottle, or cup?
Do I have to wait to be changed or use the toilet?
When I talk my talk, will someone listen and respond?
When you talk to me, will you look at me and use words I am learning to understand?
Will someone read to me?

(Greenman, 1993)

For additional material, visit:
www.parentphd.org/infantandtoddlertext/ch3/

Reflection Questions

In either your fieldwork or life experience, when have you seen an example of each of the four steps of Guidance and Redirection? Provide at least one descriptive example for each of the four steps.

First, caregivers and parents should always model socially acceptable behavior.

EXAMPLE:

Second, use positive reinforcement to acknowledge socially acceptable behavior.

EXAMPLE:

Third, reorganize a situation and prevent harmful behavior from happening.

EXAMPLE:

Finally, sometimes you need to redirect the energy.

EXAMPLE:

Complete these two evaluations of your classroom/fieldwork's infant/toddler setting:

Quick Evaluation of an Infant or Toddler Learning/Caring Environment

If infants or toddlers could choose their own setting, they might ask:
How many places are there where I can:

climb up? _____
climb in? _____
climb over? _____
climb on? _____
go through? _____
go under? _____
go in and out? _____
pull myself up? _____
reach? _____
kick? _____
jump? _____

How many semi-enclosed places are there?
How many different places to be are there for me, places that feel different because of light, texture, sound, smell, enclosure and sight lines?
When you put me in an infant swing or bounce chair, am I only there for a short time and I get out when I want to get out?
How often do I get out of the room?
How often do I go for stroller or cart rides?
How often do I get to get out of the stroller/cart and walk/crawl around?
How often do I get to play with messy things—water, sand, dough, paint?
What is there to transport? push/pull? collect/dump? throw?
Do I get to feed myself as soon as I can hold a spoon, bottle, or cup?
Do I have to wait to be changed or use the toilet?
When I talk my talk, will someone listen and respond?
When you talk to me, will you look at me and use words I am learning to understand?
Will someone read to me?

(Greenman, 1993)

Quality Criteria Chart

Criteria of Quality	How My I/T Environment Promotes It
There is a balance of both soft materials (cozy furniture, pillows, blankets, stuffed animals) and hard materials (hard floors to learn to walk on).	
Low windows allow intrusion of the outdoor environment and places for children to go when they want to be secluded and alone.	
Environment must encourage the children to be mobile and active safely.	
Toys should be visible and open for children to grab and explore; toys should be both open-ended (no one way to do it or many ways to do it) and close-ended (one way to do it). The younger the children, the more open-ended objects should be available.	
Both simple and complex materials should exist in the classroom, and the possibility of making a simple toy (an empty water bottle) more complex (adding sand) should also exist.	
All furniture should be to scale with the size of the children (Rule of thumb—if things are about at hip height and below for an adult, it is appropriate for infants and toddlers).	
The room should be visually appealing; use natural light whenever possible and neutral colors.	
Pay attention to the noise in the room and be aware of background noises. Too much noise can be over stimulating for infants and toddlers.	
The room should have a sense of order and everything should have a place. This provides comfort and stability for the children and the caregivers.	

Source: (Gonzalez-Mena & Eyer, 2017).

Bibliography

Copple, C., & Bredekamp, S. (2009). *Developmentally appropriate practice in early childhood programs serving children from birth through age 8* (3rd ed.). Washington, DC: National Association for the Education of Young Children.

Dodge, D., Rudick, S., & Berke, K. (2015). *The creative curriculum for infants, toddlers and twos: The foundation* (3rd ed.). Washington, DC: Teaching Strategies.

Gonzalez-Mena, J., & Eyer, D. (2017). *Infants, toddlers, and caregivers: A curriculum of respectful, responsive, relationship-based care and education* (11th ed.). New York, NY: McGraw Hill.

Greenman, J. (1982). Designing infant/toddler environments. In R. Lurie & R. Neugebauer (Eds.), *Caring for infants and toddlers: What works and what doesn't* (Vol. 2). Redmond, WA: Childcare Information Exchange.

Greenman, J. (1993). Places for babies: Infants and toddlers in groups. *Childcare Information Exchange, 7*, 46–49.

Harms, T., Cryer, D., & Clifford, R. (2007). *Infant toddler environment rating scale* (Revised ed.). New York, NY: Teachers College Press.

Jones, E., & Prescott, E. (1978). *Dimensions of teaching-learning environments 2: Focus on daycare*. Pasadena, CA: Pacific Oaks.

Kaplan Early Learning Company. (2013). Sample floorplans. Retrieved from www.kaplanco.com/resources/floorPlannerSamples.asp

Lally, J. R. (1998). Brain research, infant learning, and child care curriculum. *Childcare Information Exchange, 5*, 46–48.

Lally, J. R. (2008). *Caring for infants and toddlers in groups: Developmentally appropriate practice*. Washington, DC: Zero to Three.

National Association for the Education of Young Children. (2008). Teacher-child ratios within group size. Retrieved from https://dphhs.mt.gov/Portals/85/hcsd/documents/ChildCare/STARS/Kits/3to4centerteachertochildratiochart.pdf

Sussman, F. (2012). The power of using everyday routines to promote young children's language and social skills. Retrieved from www.hanen.org/Helpful-Info/Articles/Power-of-Using-Everyday-Routines.aspx

4 Partnering With Families

The following chapter will focus on the caregiver/family relationship. It will cover the expectations of both groups of people, communications between them and ways to foster a strong home-school connection. When the relationship between caregivers and families is strong, both parties, and especially the children involved, benefit. A good childcare program for infants and toddlers emphasizes a partnership between families and caregivers. Each offers the other support and insight, has strong listening skills and respects each other's perspectives about childrearing and childcare.

Caregivers and family members must act as partners in the caring and education of the children. This means having an open and communicative relationship based on respect and mutual understanding. As a caregiver, it is important that you look to families for insight about their children and guidance about how to care for them. As family members, it is important that you share your parenting practices with caregivers so that they can emulate them at school and communicate your happiness and your concerns with them openly. A good relationship between families and caregivers allows for better communication between everyone and allows both parties to effectively provide for the child's changing needs.

There are many benefits to partnering with families for both the school and caregivers. Think about these benefits and what they mean to you:

- Children come into childcare rooted in the context of their family and community
- When a childcare program focuses on families and their importance, children's learning and development are heightened
- Early childhood caregivers have different kinds of knowledge and skills than family members do—sharing this information with each other is very beneficial for all involved
- The goal of child rearing is to produce a child that fits into their family/community/culture—families and caregivers must work together to do this
- Caregivers and families might have different outcomes that they expect for the children

- Preserving diversity is important for caregivers, parents and children
(Edwards & Raikes, 2002; Gonzalez-Mena & Eyer, 2017).

How can you recognize and foster these benefits in your classroom or with your infant/toddler's caregiver?

Making Families Feel Comfortable

Families who put their children in care as infants and toddlers might have mixed feelings about sharing the care of their child with someone else, and caregivers should be prepared to help with this transition. Caregivers should be prepared to deal with concerns and hopes from the families such as if their children will be safe, feel comfortable and happy and will receive enough attention. Families want to ensure that their children have caregivers who are warm, loving, responsive and, most importantly, understand the age group they are working with. More specifically, family members may have the following feelings and desires for their children:

- Miss them and their home and still love them the most even with the introduction of new caregivers
- Have lots of opportunities to explore and play and have interesting experiences
- Learn to get along with other children and be social
- Hear lots of language and be given the opportunity to communicate often both verbally and non-verbally
- Have caregivers who will respect their family and their cultural practices
(Edwards & Raikes, 2002; Gonzalez-Mena & Eyer, 2017)

Caregivers should remember that the parents (or whoever the primary caregivers are) are the most important people to the child and know the child best. This relationship can never be replaced or reciprocated by a caregiver. However, family members may look to caregivers for advice, guidance or simply an ear to listen to. Even if family members are not outwardly forward with the desire for this companionship, caregivers can listen and figure out how to offer guidance or reassurance.

In order to make your families as comfortable as possible, both the school and each classroom should create a welcoming environment. From the moment someone walks into the door of your classroom, he or she should receive the message that he or she is always welcome and that you are a partner in the care of his or her child. Some environmental things to consider:

- Each child should have a cubby where she can keep her belongings and where caregivers can put messages and daily sheets for the family members to pick up. The cubby should have the child's first name and picture clearly displayed on it

82 Partnering With Families

- Hang a bulletin board at the entrance to the classroom. This board can have daily/weekly activities posted, as well as messages and important information for families to see and read
- Pictures of the children and their families should be posted where everyone can see them
- The room should be "decorated" with the children's work and pictures of the children exploring and playing at school. If you can decorate the hallway to the classroom with these displays as well, it will welcome the families before they even enter the classroom. It is a wonderful feeling to be surrounded by your children and their work when you enter the classroom
- Have a place for families to sit with their children before leaving. Some children might need time to transition in, and a rocking chair provides the opportunity for the family member to participate in this experience comfortably. In an infant room, this rocking chair can be used for breastfeeding mothers as well. They should always have a place to nurse their babies that is comfortable and can be made semi-private if necessary.

Each infant and toddler reacts differently to a transition into a childcare setting. Some children cry, while others withdraw until they feel comfortable. Skilled caregivers help the children *and* the families work through this important transition and adjustment. The goal for everyone is for the children and

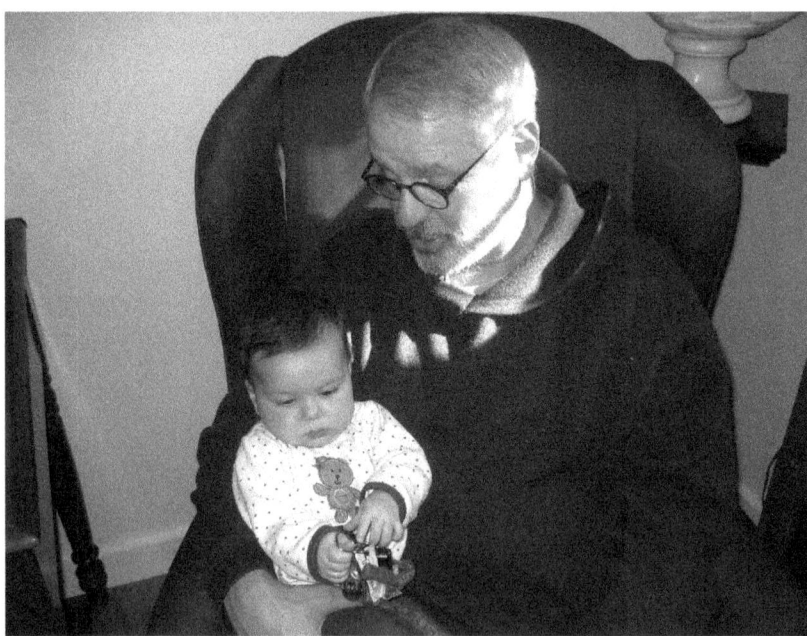

Figure 4.1 Infant Bonding With Family Member

their families to feel comfortable, secure and confident in the childcare setting. It is important for each classroom to have a process for handling transitions that is shared with everyone. Refer back to the "Inserimento" reading from chapter one. What transition procedures are followed in Italy?

In chapter three, we briefly discussed the concept of *cultural identity* in our infants and toddlers. Children bring their cultural identity with them into your classroom; you bring your own cultural identity with you. Together, you create a cultural identity as a classroom community. Because each child in your care comes from a different culture, it is important to practice multicultural and multilingual education in your infant or toddler classroom. In doing this, you help the children appreciate their culture as well as cultural differences. But what is multicultural/multilingual education in infant/toddler curriculum?

Multicultural/Multilingual Infant-Toddler Curriculum

Having a multicultural and multilingual curriculum in your infant or toddler classroom is not difficult and will contribute to a comfortable environment for you, the children and their families. This type of curriculum begins with a family questionnaire – this questionnaire should ask a variety of questions of the families about their family structure, practices, culture and traditions. An example is provided at the end of this chapter. Reading through the families' answers and understanding how they care for their children (and want you to care for their children) is the first step in acknowledging and respecting their culture. If you have questions about their responses or requests, be sure to openly discuss them and find a way to make it all work.

Family pictures should also be displayed in the classroom. You can take them of the families when they come for orientation or the first day of school or ask the families to send some in with their children. Displaying family photographs brings comfort to children. I have witnessed infants and toddlers touching or sitting near the pictures of their family at times when they needed comfort. In order for this to be possible, be sure to display the pictures at the children's level. That way they can see them easily and interact with them when they want to.

While questionnaires and pictures are small things that can be done to recognize the cultures of the children, they are not the only strategies. In fact, if this is all you do, you are missing a large portion of the family connection that you should be making with those involved in your classroom. The purpose of a multicultural and multilingual curriculum is to keep children connected to their families and their culture and give them opportunities to recognize the cultures of others in their class.

If there are dual language learners in your class, then they have a different home language than English and will most likely use your childcare environment to learn English. Infant/toddler caregivers must engage the children in this learning process while still supporting the children's home language.

Bilingual children benefit from knowing more than one language and tend to have more developed linguistic skills because of it. A caregiver's goal should be to continue to help children develop their home language while at the same time learning English. This also means that if the families use sign language at home with their infant or toddler to help them communicate, you need to do the same in your classroom.

Caregivers must also discuss caregiving practices with families to ensure that they are emulating what is happening in the home. This is especially important for infants, who must have consistency in their caregiving from home to school. How an infant is fed, changed or generally cared for should be understood and modeled by a caregiver in a childcare environment. This consistency brings comfort to the infant and respects the family's cultural practices. For toddlers, specific caregiving practices that the families want carried over into the school environment should be discussed and adhered to as much as is possible in a toddler classroom environment. Toddlers move through the day more as a group and less as an individual as they get older, so specific cultural caregiving practices that are a necessity at school must be addressed and understood (Edwards & Raikes, 2002).

Working Together Through Conflicts

As a caregiver for infants and toddlers, your goal is to act as a partner with the family in the life of the child. You share in the care and caregiving of the child. Caregivers act as supplements and supports to the parents rather than substitutes for the parents. Whether you spend a few hours a day or 40 hours per week with an infant or toddler, your role as a caregiver should emulate but not take the place of the parents or other primary caregivers in the child's life. When you take on the role of partner in the infant or toddler's care, you are able to form a mutual relationship with the family that provides opportunities for open communication

You may find that you have a conflict of beliefs with the families. Perhaps they don't value independence like you do or want their children to be cared for in a way that you do not feel is necessary for the age of the child. In any case, invite parent input and then figure out how to do in your classroom. You may be able to comply with a request after a discussion with the family members, while other times you might require more clarification and discussion where you both share your beliefs and why you have them. Either way, you must continue to work toward resolving the conflict.

Understanding the family's point of view as parents and giving the family an opportunity to understand your point of view as a caregiver might open up both of your perspectives about the topic. This work can also help you both expand your cultural awareness. You and the family might come to an agreement where the child is cared for differently in home and school, or perhaps you will find some middle ground.

Partnering With Families 85

Figure 4.2 Infant Playing With Family Member

Here are some simple steps to follow when working through a conflict or disagreement with a family member.

1. Remain calm and help the family member remain calm
2. Clarify the problem
3. Agree on the goals to solve the problem
4. Generate solutions together
5. Check back in

(Gonzalez-Mena & Eyer, 2017).

Let's look at an example that I experienced as a toddler teacher:

Nate is a 20-month old child in a toddler classroom. One day during pick up time, his mother approaches the caregiver and seems very upset.

MOTHER: Yesterday when we got home, I took Nate out of the car, and he had a large BM. This happens almost every school day, and it is a mess! I want you to bring him in early from outside play time (outside play occurred right before pick-up) and change him so he is clean when I arrive to pick him up.

CAREGIVER: OK, you seem really upset. You are upset because Nate is sitting in a BM on the car ride home? That is definitely not a comfortable thing for him.

MOTHER: Yes. He must be doing it while he is playing outside at the end of the day. I can't get here earlier than pick-up time, and we have to leave right away to get home. He needs to be changed before pick-up time.

CAREGIVER: Yes, we don't want him sitting in a BM the whole ride home, and I want him ready for you to pick him up and not make you late.

MOTHER: Exactly. I want you to bring him in early from outside time and change him so he's ready to go when I get here.

CAREGIVER: OK. The goal is to not have him get in the car with a BM and for you to leave on time, right?

MOTHER: Yes. He needs to be changed at the end of the day.

CAREGIVER: OK, I understand. State licensing rules prevent me from leaving my assistants on the playground with the children. I have to always be out there. I could send Nate in with an assistant early to be changed, but I worry that it might upset him or confuse him to leave the playground early and without his friends. We always line up and leave together, and it is a routine that he knows. It is very comforting for him. So let's think of how to solve this...

MOTHER: I don't want him to be upset leaving his friends. And I'd rather you take care of his diaper changes.

CAREGIVER: I agree. You know, we always do a diaper change before we go outside to play. Perhaps we can shift that change time to after outside play. We can go out ten minutes earlier and come in ten minutes earlier, and then he is changed and ready at pick-up time. What do you think?

MOTHER: Will that mess up the other kids and your schedule? I don't want to do that. What if a child needs to be changed before going outside?

CAREGIVER: It will have to be something we gradually change. We could do it over a few days so it isn't a big shock to all of the children. We also do frequent individual checks of the children's diapers throughout the day so they are changed when they need it, so we would still do that and plan accordingly. But we want Nate to be comfortable and work with you, so this might be the best solution. What do you think?

MOTHER: Great. Let's try it. Thanks so much for helping me to figure this out. I feel better.

CAREGIVER: No problem at all. I'm glad you shared your concern with me. I'll start the shift in our routine tomorrow and check back in with you over the next few days to see Nate's condition when you get home. Keep me posted, OK?

MOTHER: Will do. Thanks again.

CAREGIVER: No problem at all!

Now let's analyze this interaction using the steps to work through a conflict/disagreement. Using information and/or specific dialogue from the interaction, develop a step-by-step plan for resolving this conflict.

1. Remain calm and help the family member remain calm
2. Clarify the problem
3. Agree on goals to solve the problem

Partnering With Families 87

4. Generate solutions together
5. Check back in

Documenting a Child's Day

Families appreciate hearing about what their children do in care during the day. Communicating this information helps them feel connected to their child while they are away and gives them a good understanding of what their children are learning and exploring. Keeping a notebook handy with a page for each child where you can jot down notes or quick anecdotes will give you information to share with the family either in person when they pick up the child or on their daily sheet that goes home with the child.

When I taught toddlers, I found that post-its were a great resource for this type of quick note-taking. I hung a thick poster board over the main greeting/ sign-in area with a picture of each child's face glued to it. Each face had room under it for me to place post-its with notes on them throughout the day. If a child did something that I wanted to share with the families, I would jot it down on a post-it and place it under that child's face. When the families came for pick up, they had something to read about their child. These post-it anecdotes sometimes sparked a conversation between us where I gave more information, or they were simply little notes that families could take home and share.

Another aspect of documenting a child's day is to make sure that you check often for injuries. This should definitely happen when the children come in from playing outside (my children's school calls it a "Boo Check"), and after any other period of active play. Any injury—even a small scratch—should be

Figure 4.3 Toddler Free Drawing

documented on an accident report that both you and a family member must read and sign. In childcare, nothing is too small to not document. Accident reports should document the state of the injury, how it happened and what the caregiver did about it (ice pack, band-aid, etc.). After both parties sign a copy, it should be sent home and another copy should be put in the child's file at school. This heavy documentation is a way for the childcare center to cover their bases when it comes to acknowledging and dealing with injuries to the children and should be taken very seriously. An example Incident Report is included at the end of this chapter.

Ongoing and Open Communication With Families

Here are a few tips for caregivers to help foster open communication with families:

- Develop your listening skills
- Develop a problem-solving attitude
- Try to talk to each parent each day
- Regard communication as a two-way process

It is important to talk with each child's family on a daily basis, both when they drop their child off and when they pick them up. Be sure to greet each family individually and personally—a quick "hello" and "how are you today?" is all that is necessary. The child should also be greeted individually, with perhaps a more extensive interaction to help with the transition process. The drop-off conversation is usually quick and should involve transitioning the child and making sure any information from the parent is received and understood. The pick-up conversation should be longer and should involve sharing some information about what the child accomplished that day, played with or explored.

Active Listening

Active listening is a skill that all caregivers must practice. When you actively listen, you actually *listen* to what the other person is saying and then respond to their words. This is opposed just letting the other person talk, all the while thinking of what you want to say, and waiting for the person to stop talking so you can share your idea. These are two very different behaviors. If you actually listen to what the family member is saying to you and respond to their actual words, the family will feel as if they are heard and their input is recognized and important.

Remember that this family member is the first caregiver for the child and knows the child best. They have a perspective very different from yours about the child and his or her care. Active listening opens up a conversation where both parties listen to each other and respond to each other openly and honestly. It does wonders for your communication and relationships with the families of the children in your care. If you are a parent, you should also actively listen to the caregivers of your children. They have the perspective of a highly trained and educated caregiver of infants and toddlers and have a great deal of information and perspective to share with you. This reciprocity between both caregiver and family member is a way to establish an open and communicative relationship where two people work together to raise a child in a healthy and comfortable way.

When communicating with families, it is important to notice how you are feeling, look at the interaction from the child's point of view and partner together (caregivers and families) to develop a plan for the child. Begin by tuning in to your feelings so you are aware of them and can share them appropriately. Then tune into the child's experience and look at the experience from his/her perspective. This will allow you to reframe the issue in a way that doesn't make the parent feel bad and that also helps him or her understand the complexity of the child's behavior. Then develop a plan together with parents on how to handle the situation. This helps you move forward as partners, instead of competitors. Use "I" statements, ask for the parent's perspective and look for how you can compromise. It is important to clarify the parent's feelings and beliefs on the issue. Ask questions to learn, not to pass judgment. Ask the parent if he or she has ideas for next steps. What can the two of you agree on? What can you both work on? Then make sure you check in with parents to see how things are going, how your agreed-upon plan is working and where you might need to make some adjustments. This communication is the key to making any partnership work and will help your relationship to grow in a positive direction.

Parent Conferences

Parent conferences should be a time for caregivers and families to sit down and discuss what the child is doing at school and his developmental progression. Caregivers should have examples of the children's explorations to share with families, including actual artifacts and photographs. Portfolios are an excellent way to organize this information. Portfolios can be elaborate or simple. In general, a portfolio should document each area of development and provide examples of how the child exhibited growth or activity in each area of development. As caregivers talk with the families, they can move through the portfolio and use the examples inside as a way to describe the child's growth and development. As an infant/toddler caregiver, you should be documenting the children's experiences anyway in order to track and document their developmental growth, so the portfolio process should not be a difficult one. It allows you to put all of the information you've collected together in one aesthetically appealing place for you and families to share. An example Portfolio Page is included at the end of this chapter.

When conducting a parent conference, find a comfortable place for you, the family members and the child. The child should be included in the conference (even babies). You are talking about him, after all. If you are using artifacts and photographs, the child will have an opportunity to revisit experiences in the classroom and possibly participate in the conversation.

In general, families come to conferences wanting to know how their child gets along in a group and with peers, and what experiences they are having in the classroom on a daily basis. Again, portfolios are a great way to communicate this information. Here are some tips for parent conferences and an example of a portfolio page:

Before the Conference:

- Organize all photographs and artifacts in a way that will allow you to effectively communicate the information to the families. This can be by areas of development or by specific experiences in the classroom
- Prepare short summaries about the child's progress in each area of development
- Prepare a written statement about any problems or concerns that you have. These statements should include your specific observations over time and then your concern about the child
- Prepare any questions you have or clarifications you need to make with the families in written list form so that you do not forget to ask them.

Conducting the Conference:

- Always remember to talk in normal language—avoid professional jargon that only people studying child development would understand. Also be sure to explain what each area of development means so that the parents have a small framework for the information you are going to share
- Begin by discussing how the child has adjusted to the classroom, citing specific examples of their transitions into the classroom and their interactions with caregivers and other children
- Review the child's developmental growth based on each area of development. Cite examples and show photographs and artifacts
- Invite families to share their observations and concerns for their child
- Discuss any problems or concerns that you might have for the child. This discussion should be partnered with *specific* examples of the child's behavior
- Discuss specific goals for the child based on child development and learning, as well as what the family members wish for their child.

Throughout the conference, be sure to *participate in active listening* and *ask open-ended questions*. Pay attention to the family members' body language so that you can respond appropriately. If you feel as though the family members are responding negatively to what you are sharing, stop and ask them to share how they feel about what you are saying. Be sure to respect culturally based

Figure 4.4 Infant Exploring Book

communication practices and respond to any and all concerns. When advice is sought, offer it partnered with specific suggestions for caregiving and practice.

Reporting Child Abuse

As a childcare provider, you are required by law to report any signs of child abuse that you see in your classroom. Everything should be documented in writing. If a pattern of injuries forms, it is important that you inform the director of your center. You can then take the next steps together. At the first parent conference of the school year, caregivers should inform parents that legally and for each child's protection, it is part of their job to report child abuse. If your center has a written statement about this mandate, this conversation is easier to have. Ask the parents to read the statement and sign it, and then it is clear that they have been informed of the policy.

Communicating With Families of Children With Special Needs

When communicating with families of children with special needs, the same communication skills apply as you would use with parents of typically developing children. What is important for caregivers to understand is that families of children with special needs come into a conversation or conference with you with an extra set of feelings. These family members may:

- Be in denial about their child's condition
- Carry a heavy burden of guilt
- Be angry
- Not have any unresolved issues at all

Regardless of these factors, it is important to be sensitive to family members' feelings about their child and the specific special needs that exist. Invite them to share their perspective on their child's delay and any observations that they have from home that will help you work with the child. Respect the family members' comfort level with the special need and the discussion of it and work to create a positive conversation of problem solving and hope for the child (Dodge, Rudick, & Berke, 2015; Gonzalez-Mena & Eyer, 2017).

Individual Family Service Plan

When an infant or toddler has a documented disability or special need that requires outside intervention, the center and families create an "Individual Family Service Plan (IFSP)." This plan documents and guides the implementation of the early intervention process for children with disabilities and their families in accordance with the Individuals with Disabilities Education Act (IDEA). An IFSP describes the services necessary to facilitate a child's development and includes information about the family's participation in the intervention services. Family members and caregivers work as a team to plan, implement and evaluate the early intervention services. An IFSP is written with the idea that the family is the child's greatest resource and that the best way to meet a child's needs is to support the family and build on their strengths. The goals are written within the context of the family and have outcomes targeted at both the child and the family members and family as a whole.

The IFSP process begins by assessing the child and family. An effective assessment process addresses each family members' questions and concerns about the child and determines if a child is eligible for services. This determination comes from observations and assessments of the child in a setting that is familiar to the child. The child's strengths; needs; and preferences for activities, materials and environments are documented. The family and the interventionists then create goals for the child. From these goals, strategies and outcomes are developed, and intervention responsibilities are assigned. The intervention strategies should occur within everyday natural environments and work to help the child become more independent in his or her world.

An IFSP must contain the following information:

- The child's present levels of functioning and need in the areas of physical, cognitive, communication, social/emotional and adaptive development
- The family's resources, priorities, and concerns relating to enhancing the development of the child with a disability
- The major outcomes/results that are expected to be achieved for the child and the family
- Specific Early Intervention Services that the child will be receiving, including specific procedures and a timeline
- The natural environments (home, community, childcare center) in which services will be provided (if the services are not provided in a natural environment, a statement must be included justifying why not)
- Number of days/sessions for the services, the projected dates for the services and the anticipated duration
- Whether the service will be one-on-one or as part of a group
- Who will pay for the services
- The name of the service provider who will be responsible for implementing the plan and coordinating with other agencies and persons
- Steps to support the child's transition out of early intervention to preschool or other appropriate services.

An IFSP is reviewed every six months and is updated at least once a year. The families and the intervention team will look at the child's progress and decide how (or if) the IFSP needs to be changed to reflect the child's growth toward the goals that were set or because of other family changes or needs. Questions such as the following are asked and discussed in these review meetings:

- To what extent and at what rate is the child making progress toward attaining outcomes?
- Are the selected intervention strategies and activities promoting gains in development?
- Do changes need to be made in the intervention plan?

(Bruder, 2000)

Incident Report

Child's Name _____
Date of Incident _____
Description of Incident
_____
_____
_____

Place Incident Occurred
_____

Description of injury
_____
_____
_____

Name of Witness _____
Action Taken
_____
_____
_____

Was parent/doctor/other party contacted? What was discussed?
_____
_____
_____
_____

Signature of Caregiver _____
Signature of Family Member _____
Additional Information
_____
_____
_____

Parent Conference Form

Child's Name _____
Teacher's Name _____
Family Members Attending _____
Social/Emotional Development:
Examples:
Physical Development:
Examples:
Language Development:

Examples:
Cognitive Development:
Examples:
Teacher's Observations/Concerns:
Parent's Observations/Concerns:
Goals for the Child:
The Next Steps:

Portfolios give families a visual representation of their children's experiences. As they view the picture of their children playing, exploring and working, they read a description of exactly what the experience looked like. Specific dialogue from the child is included in this description. They then read specific information about their children's development. This is a wonderful way to represent a child's experience in care and also shows just how much learning and development is happening! Below is an example of what one page of a child's portfolio could look like. Hayleigh is 18 months old.

Portfolio Page Example

Hayleigh spent time exploring the sensory bottles during free play time. She used both of her hands to pick them up, examined them with her eyes and shook them. She often turned her head with the direction of the water and materials inside the bottles to watch it from different angles. When the bottles made noise as she shook them, she smiled, made noises of her own and widened her eyes. She said the words "blue, red and green" to show her recognition of the colors of the water and "loud" to show her recognition of the sounds the materials inside made when she shook the bottles. When asked by a caregiver what she was doing, she replied, "I shake bottles." She then held up a bottle to her caregiver, and her caregiver approached her and began to play with the bottles next to Hayleigh.

Hayleigh's Development and Learning:

Cognitive Development:

Hayleigh was learning about *cause and effect* as she explored the bottles. When she turned the bottles around or shook them, the materials inside made noise and the water moved. She also identified the *colors* of the water and *action words* such as "loud."

Language Development:

Hayleigh used her *expressive language* to verbally say different color words and action words. She also engaged in a dialogue with her caregiver by responding, "I shake bottles" when asked to describe what she was doing.

96   *Partnering With Families*

Figure 4.5 Toddler Exploring Sensory Bottles

Physical Development:

Hayleigh practiced her *gross motor skills* when she shook the bottles and her *fine motor skills* to pick up each individual bottle.

Social/Emotional Development:

Hayleigh's *dialogue* with her caregiver about her experience is an important *communication*. She answered her caregiver's question by *making eye contact* and *describing* exactly what she was doing. She then held up the bottle to *show* her caregiver what she was doing, which was an *invitation* for the caregiver to approach Hayleigh and engage in play with her.

Important Family-to-School Communication Forms

On the next few pages are examples of infant and toddler daily sheets and a family questionnaire that you would ask family members to fill out prior to their child entering care. The daily sheets summarize the information that should be provided by both the families and the caregivers on a daily basis. The family questionnaire provides a wide range of questions that you can ask the families to answer that will help you to understand their child and the environment that they live in outside of school. Remember—the more questions you ask, the more you will learn. You can always tell the families that if they do not feel comfortable answering a question, they can leave it blank.

Infant Daily Sheet—Example
FAMILY SECTION (filled out upon arrival):

Child's Name _____
Today's Contact Person's Name _____
Today's Contact Person's Phone # _____
Time Child Woke Up _____ Hours Child Slept _____
Time Child Last Ate _____ Amount Child Last Ate _____
Mood of Child Today _____
Sleeping Schedule: (Times)
Eating Schedule: (Time/Food/How Much)
Is there anything we should know about your child for today?

CAREGIVER SECTION (filled out throughout the day and a copy is given to family member who picks up child):

Eating Log:

Time   What food/drink & How much was eaten

Sleeping Log:

Time periods child slept

Diapering Log:

Time   Wet/Loose Stool/Solid Stool

Today your child:
Write short descriptions of experiences, play and explorations that the child participated in. This is also the area where caregivers can document any concerns or changes in eat/sleep/diapering patterns that the families should be aware of.

Toddler Daily Sheet—Example
FAMILY SECTION (filled out upon arrival):

Child's Name _____
Today's Contact Person's Name _____
Today's Contact Person's Phone # _____
Time Child Woke Up _____ Hours Child Slept _____
Time Child Last Ate _____ What Child Last Ate _____
Mood of Child Today _____
Is there anything we should know about your child for today?

CAREGIVER SECTION (filled out throughout the day and a copy is given to family member who picks up child):

Eating Log:

Meal	What food/drink & How much was eaten
Breakfast	
Morning Snack	
Lunch	
Afternoon Snack	
Other	

Sleeping Log:

Your child napped from: _____ to _____
(_____ total hours)

Toileting/Diapering Log:

Time	Used Potty With Help/Without Help	Diapered

Today your child:
Write short descriptions of experiences, play and explorations that the child participated in. List any books the child read either alone or with the group. This is also the area where caregivers can document any concerns or changes in eat/sleep/diapering patterns that the families should be aware of.

Family Questionnaire

Before a child enters your care, a family questionnaire should be given to the parents. This questionnaire gives you an opportunity ask for as much information as possible from the families so that you can better understand and care for their child. I recommend asking all types of questions about every area of the child's life at home. You can always tell families that if they don't feel comfortable answering a question, they can leave it blank. In general, this questionnaire should cover the following areas:

- Who the child lives with and sees on a daily basis
- The primary caregivers for the child
- The secondary caregivers for the child
- The child's siblings and their ages, sexes and names
- The child's religion/culture and any religious/cultural beliefs that must be known and attended to

- Child's habits
- Child's special needs
- Child's way of communication (and examples if necessary)
- Child's daily schedule/routines at home, complete with times
- Child's sleeping habits and routines
- Child's eating habits, routines and schedule
- The ways that the child likes to be soothed/comforted
- Any comfort objects that should be with the child at sleeping or waking times
- Any health issues or recent health incidents that is important for the caregiver to know and understand. If the child has a severe or recurring health issue that will require more information, a separate form should be provided that allows the family to thoroughly explain the condition and the care that is necessary for the child
- Ask the families to complete the following sentences:
    o The activity I most enjoy with my child is _____.
    o Three hopes I have for my child are _____, _____, and _____.
    o The kinds of play/learning activities my child enjoys most are _____.
    o What upsets my child the most is_____.
    o To comfort my child, I _____.
    o My goals for my child are _____.
    o The kinds of experiences I want my child to have in care that can help to reach these goals are _____.

Bibliography

Bove, C. (2001). Inserimento: A strategy for delicately beginning relationships and communications. In L. Gandini & C. Edwards (Eds.), *Bambini: The Italian approach to infant/toddler care*. New York, NY: Teachers College Press.

Bruder, M. B. (2000). The individual family service plan (IFSP). *ERIC Clearinghouse on Disabilities and Gifted Education*, E605, 1–8.

Dodge, D., Rudick, S., & Berke, K. (2015). *The creative curriculum for infants, toddlers and twos: The foundation* (3rd ed.). Washington, DC: Teaching Strategies.

Edwards, C. P., & Raikes, H. (2002). Extending the dance: Relationship-based approaches to infant/toddler care and education. Faculty Publications, Department of Child, Youth, and Family Studies. Paper 16. *Young Children*, 57(4), 10–17.

Elicker, J., & McMullen, M. B. (2013, July). Appropriate and meaningful assessment in family-centered programs. *Young Children*, 22–27.

Gonzalez-Mena, J., & Eyer, D. (2017). *Infants, toddlers, and caregivers: A curriculum of respectful, responsive, relationship-based care and education* (11th ed.). New York, NY: McGraw Hill.

National Association for the Education of Young Children. (2013). What to look for in a program. Retrieved from http://families.naeyc.org/what-to-look-for-in-a-program

For additional material, visit:
www.parentphd.org/infantandtoddlertext/ch4/

Reflection Questions

- What are some feelings and desires that families might have for their children when they put them in childcare?
- How can the environment be welcoming for all families?
- What is an example of an Active Listening behavior?
- Why is it important to document a child's day for their families?
- What should you do if you suspect that an infant or toddler in your care is being abused? What type of documentation will you need in order to pursue an investigation?
- How is your classroom/field experience welcoming to all families?
- Listen to a parent-caregiver dialogue when a child arrives in the morning or when a parent comes to pick up the child in the afternoon and write down the conversation. Categorize the conversation under three categories: information seeking, questions or affirmation. Explain why you chose the category you did.

Introduction to the Development and Learning Chapters

Chapters 5 through 12 will focus on the development and learning of children ages 0–3. Each chapter is dedicated to one area and will provide the information you need to understand it and respond to it appropriately. It will first provide a definition of the area of development/learning and what it looks like for infants and toddlers. It will then describe developmentally appropriate responses, materials and learning experiences/explorations that you can create in your home or classroom to respond to the area of development/learning.

While all the areas of development/learning are connected and intertwined, the order of chapters five through twelve is purposeful. Learning about them in this order allows you to build your knowledge base effectively and truly see the connections between the concepts.

>Chapter 5: Perceptual Development and the Five Senses
>Chapter 6: Physical Development
>Chapter 7: Play as Learning
>Chapter 8: Attachment
>Chapter 9: Social Development and Interactions
>Chapter 10: Emotional Development
>Chapter 11: Language and Literacy Development
>Chapter 12: Cognitive Development

Both individual differences and life circumstances affect how children develop and learn. Individual differences can be observed on a daily basis by caregivers. Life circumstances, on the other hand, must be shared by the children's families. It is important for caregivers to be aware of each individual child's life circumstances so they can plan accordingly to respond to them as well as consider them when assessing an infant or toddler's development and learning. The following life experiences should be known and considered:

1. The family the child comes from: Number and gender of parents, adults and siblings/other children in each child's household. This includes where in the birth order the child falls
2. Any health problems or disabilities of family members
3. The child's expose to violence, abuse or neglect
4. The home language of the child and if English is spoken in the home
5. Family cultural practices
6. The community in which the child lives
7. The careers/jobs of family members
8. Age of the parents at the time of the child's birth
9. The family's socio-economic status
10. The family's living situation as well as history of moving

11. The primary caregivers' (parents or guardians) education and job history
12. Any special family circumstances (divorce/separation, addition of a new family member, absence of a family member)

Bibliography

Dodge, D., Rudick, S., & Berke, K. (2015). *The creative curriculum for infants, toddlers and twos: The foundation* (3rd ed.). Washington, DC: Teaching Strategies.

5 Perceptual Development and the Five Senses

Human beings experience life through their senses, and all sensory experience is authentic and real. While this is true for people of all ages, think about it in terms of an infant or a toddler. Infants and toddlers rely on their senses to experience life, and their sensory experiences are major factors in the formation of their being. In order to begin to understand the learning and development of infants and toddlers, you must first learn about perception.

In your journal, answer the following self-awareness questions before learning about perception. Your opinions about your own sensory awareness will help shape your perspective on it when working with infants and toddlers:

1. How do you use your senses on a daily basis?
2. Do you find yourself using one sense more than another?
3. What do you learn from using your senses?
4. What if you did not have the use of one of your senses? How would that change your life?

Perception is *the interpretation of sensory input through the five senses* (touch, taste, smell, sight, and hearing) as well as temperature and pain. It is *the ability to take in and organize all of these sensory experiences*. Perceptual abilities begin in utero and continue well into the toddler years. Perception is an "active" term; when infants and toddlers perceive, they are taking in, organizing and interpreting what they are experiencing.

Perception gives infants and toddlers the foundation for interpreting the events of the world around them. It also involves infants and toddlers learning to discriminate differences and perceive similarities. Stimuli from the environment induce sensory experiences, which promotes brain growth and development. Each sense is located in a specific area of the brain, and repetitive early experiences foster neural pathways. You cannot separate perceptual development from other developmental domains because what infants and toddlers perceive in their brains can only be deduced by their behaviors. Sensory experience links to motor development and early sensorimotor experience provides the basis for cognitive development.

104 Perceptual Development and the Five Senses

Children's integration of sensory skills is a particularly important marker in their development. *Sensory integration* is the process of combining and integrating information across the senses. It is critical to the development of perception and helps young children apply information learned from one sense to another sense. Appropriate developmental progression in infants and toddlers is highly dependent on their access to sensory information and experiences in the environment. Every time infants experience new stimuli, their brains are wired to interpret and process similar experiences. As perceptual development proceeds in infants, they learn to associate stimuli with specific activities and events and can anticipate them. This is the foundation for interpreting and making sense of the world (Berk, 2012, 2015, 2018a, 2018b).

Infants' perceptual development is focused solely on direct and physical sensory interactions. The mouth is their primary learning tool during the first months of life and is the hub of these direct and physical interactions. As infants grow, they extend their perceptive experiences to include their other senses. This all happens in the brain, and this neurological process allows infants to tune into an experience and concentrate on certain parts of it.

By the time children reach the toddler years, they have learned to use their senses—particularly hearing, seeing and touching—to help them understand the world around them. Now, perceptual development is focused

Figure 5.1 Infant Exploring His Spoon During Mealtime

on the development of attention. When toddlers are developing their attention, they are developing their ability to focus on a person, object or task. In the toddler years, children's attention spans become longer, they are more selective in what they attend do and they are better able to use their senses to achieve their goals. By age 2, a toddler's attention is more selective, and he can decide what to focus on and what to ignore. By age 3, a toddler's attention span is around 18 minutes, but he is still more easily distracted than adults.

By the time children are 3 years old and are moving out of the toddler years, they are learning to integrate the senses and, in doing so, to be able to do such combined activities as sing while scrubbing in the tub, or draw a picture while listening to music. Caregivers can heighten children's awareness of the world around them by stimulating the senses.

We will now explore each of the five senses that infants and toddlers use to explore and learn about the world. They will be discussed in a particular order: from most direct and developed at birth to most distant and undeveloped at birth. You will notice that there is more information about infants than toddlers. While perceptual development is far from fully developed at the end of the infant year, a great deal of critical development occurs in this first year of life.

Figure 5.2 Toddler Exploring Beads With a Caregiver

Smell

Infants

Infants arrive into the world with an acute sense of smell. Beginning around 28 weeks in utero, infants can detect odors from the foods their mothers eat and aromas they inhale through the amniotic fluid. After birth, there are many behaviors that indicate that infants are guided by their sense of smell.

At the time of birth, infants can recognize the scent of their mothers, particularly their breasts and underarms. Infants placed on their mother's chest after birth will latch onto a nipple and nurse within a short period of time. If a breast is washed and its natural scent is removed, the infant will move toward the unwashed breast. When infants smell their mothers, they might turn their head toward her breasts in an attempt to eat or simply just stop crying. Because breastfed babies are held to their mother's bodies more often, they may be able to recognize the scent of their mothers quicker than bottle-fed babies.

All newborns prefer the smell of a lactating woman over formula or a non-lactating woman. Breastfed babies will prefer their own lactating mother to other lactating women. Bottle fed babies will prefer any lactating woman over formula or non-lactating women. This guidance through the sense of smell allows infants to locate a food source and distinguish their mother from other people.

Infants will also recognize specific smells and connect it to familiar experiences. For example, a smell of a certain food cooking at the same time each day tells the infant that is time for a specific meal. When the infant smells the familiar scent, they will begin to "prepare themselves" for the familiar experience by crawling toward their highchair. Infants also prefer sweet smells to sour ones and can detect the location of a smell and turn their head toward or away from it. Infants will turn their heads away from strong smells, such as vinegar.

Toddlers

Toddlers are continually exploring their sense of smell and are connecting familiar smells to familiar experiences. Familiar smells are an important part of finding comfort in the toddler years. This may be why toddlers grow so attached to a comfort object that might smell awful to an adult, such as a blanket or stuffed animal. Have you ever told a toddler you are going to wash her special blanket, and she vehemently protests? That is because the strong (and probably awful to you) smell emanating from the object is comforting and familiar to her. True recognition of good and bad smells takes many years. This may be why toddlers barely react to smells that would catch an adult's attention immediately (such as a very dirty diaper).(Berk, 2012, 2015, 2018a, 2018b).

Taste

Infants

Infants also arrive into the world with an acute sense of taste. About 10,000 taste buds develop around 7 weeks gestation; by the beginning of the second trimester (around 13 weeks), fetuses can taste the flavors in their mother's amniotic fluid, which comes from everything that mothers eat.

Infants are born with the ability to communicate their taste preferences to their caregivers. From birth, infants have a strong sweet tooth; they have hundreds more taste buds for sweet tastes than do adults. Breastmilk and formula are sweet and contain sugar, which is why infants immediately eat either one when offered to them. The sweet taste of breastmilk or formula is preferred in the first four months. At 4 months, infants will accept a salty taste, which is their preparation for accepting solid foods. A taste that is disliked can become preferred when it is paired with relief of hunger. Hence the reason why infants who are allergic to cow's milk formula and are given alternative formulas (which tend to be more bitter) soon prefer it and readily drink it.

Infants' natural taste preferences vary depending on what foods they are exposed to. Breastfed infants are continually exposed to the flavors their mothers ingest, so these babies may be open to a wider range of flavors. The milk that breastfed infants drink changes every day depending on what their mothers eat and drink. A varied diet will expose infants to a variety of flavors and help them to become less picky eaters. As infants begin to eat food, a varied diet should continue in order to continue to promote non-picky eaters. In general, though, sour and bitter flavors are less attractive to infants.

Toddlers

As infants move into the toddler years, they are becoming more active participants in both the selection and ingestion of their foods. Toddlers are feeding themselves and will turn their heads away from foods they do not want to eat. Feeding is an exploratory experience for toddlers, and they love to squish, taste, and lick different foods. Food and flavor preferences are emerging, and toddlers should be exposed to new flavors multiple times in order to give them a full opportunity to determine if they like them or not. If a toddler rejects a particular flavor, introduce it to him again a few weeks later. This may have to happen more than once, but it is important to not remove a rejected flavor permanently. Taste preferences will change and grow with your toddler (Berk, 2012, 2015, 2018a, 2018b).

Touch (Tactile Perception)

Infants

Tactile perception and the sense of touch directly relates to a person's motor abilities. Motor skills are how infants and toddlers explore and figure out the

108 *Perceptual Development and the Five Senses*

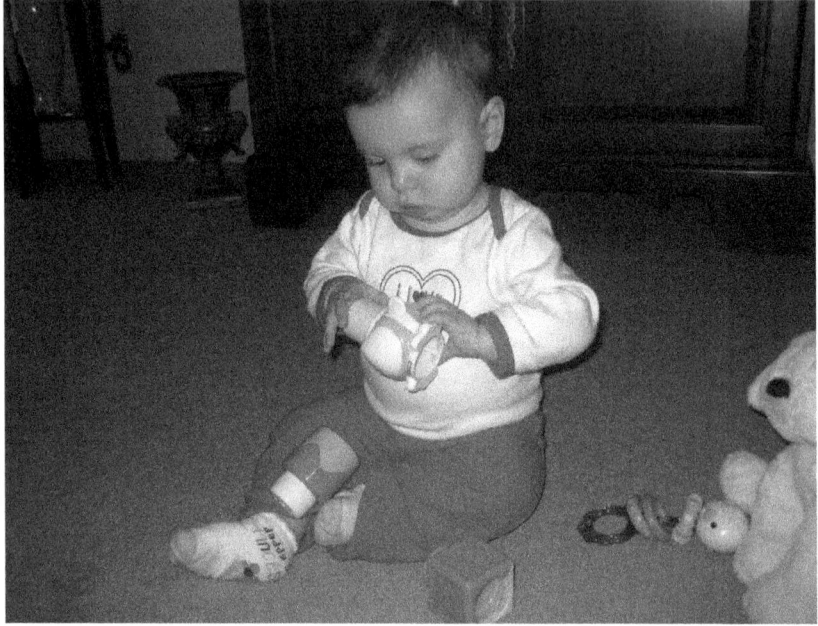

Figure 5.3 Infant Exploring a Toy

world. As motor abilities increase in infants and toddlers, they gain more and more information about the world.

Sensitivity is a human's capacity to respond to stimulation. Sensitivity to touch is well developed at birth. Touch affirms an infant's presence in and mediates his experience of the world. A fetus's mouth begins to develop feeling at about 7 weeks gestation, and by 14 weeks much of his head is sensitive to touch.

A newborn baby responds to touch most strongly around the mouth, on the palms and on the soles of the feet. Skin-to-skin contact is heavily enjoyed by infants, and it is recommended that infants lay on the bare chests of their mothers often. Both full-term and pre-term infants have been shown to breathe better, cry less and breastfeed longer when they share bare-chested moments with their mothers.

Much of the infant years are spent exploring everything by mouth. At around 6 *months*, infants begin to actively grab at anything within their reach. After grabbing, the first place each object goes is in the mouth. This preference for mouth exploration will exist for much of the rest of the infant year. Around 6 *to 9 months* when infants begin to crawl, they are more able to choose what they want to touch (versus having to touch whatever is in their immobile reach), and their tactile explorations will expand and become more complicated. As infants approach *1 year old*, you will begin to see sight and touch exploration last longer before the mouth is used.

It is important to ensure all infants get lots of loving "touch time" throughout the day. Infants who are rarely touched have brains two-and-a-half times smaller than infants who are touched a lot. Think about that for a second! The simple act of holding an infant has an enormous effect on brain development.

Touch contributes to development by providing stimulation, although it is important to remember that each infant has a preference for how he likes to be touched. It is important for caregivers to learn an infant's preference and respond appropriately. Some infants are very sensitive to touch and must be handled with care. For those who can tolerate a light touch, lightly stroking their arms and legs is fine. For those who cannot tolerate even this light touching, gently laying them in a soft surface and gradually building up to lightly stroking them is appropriate.

Infants who are sensitive in any way to touch may not respond well to being picked up and "snuggled," and this type of physical interaction could cause a stressful response. Be cognizant of this and refrain from lifting and snuggling until you have worked up to it with the strategies you just read about. It is also important to be sensitive to different cultures' perspectives on touch. Some cultures will not want parts of a baby's body touched (the head for example), so be aware of this and adhere to it.

Sensitivity to discomfort or pain increases rapidly after birth. Exposing infants to severe or repeated pain overwhelms their nervous system with stress hormones, which can result in difficulty handling common and everyday stresses in their lives. Infants could develop heightened pain sensitivity, sleep disturbances, feeding issues and difficulty calming down when they are upset.

Toddlers

Toddlers are exploring their sense of touch constantly. If you spend time in a toddler room, you will see the children move all over the classroom in an attempt to physically interact with whatever and whomever they can. They will seek out textures that they enjoy and avoid those that are uncomfortable for them.

Toddlers are sensitive to different touch experiences. For example, they may be sensitive to the texture of the clothes they wear, sticky fingers and soiled diapers and find these tactile experiences unpleasant to feel. On the other hand, calming back rubs can be a pleasant tactile experience and often help toddlers settle down for rest time (Berk, 2012, 2015, 2018a, 2018b).

Hearing (Auditory Perception)

Infants

Infants enter the world very prepared to acquire language. They are sensitive to the sounds of human speech and are biologically equipped to detect the

Figure 5.4 Toddler Squeezing Paint Onto Paper

sounds of human language. Infants begin to hear sound at around 20 weeks gestation. In the womb and especially after birth, infants can recognize their mother's voice and prefer to hear it. During the third trimester (beginning at 28 weeks), infants begin to move their bodies in response to external sounds such as music or familiar voices.

Infants are very sensitive to making sense of sounds. Newborns respond to high-pitched, expressive voices that have rising tones at the ends of phrases. This type of speech, often called "parentese," encourages very important early language interactions. Infants have also been shown to suck more on a nipple to hear their mother's voice versus a stranger's voice, which may be connected to hearing her muffled voice in the womb. Infants remember sounds from the womb, such as parents' voices and music. Infants soon learn that they can make sounds to communicate needs, such as crying when they are hungry. They are also able to associate sounds with meaningful experiences and ignore sounds that aren't meaningful.

There are significant auditory perceptual development milestones that occur in the first year of life. From *birth to 4 months*, infants have a limited auditory responsiveness, although their eyes will often blink or widen when they hear a loud noise. They have the ability to turn their heads in the general direction of sounds from only a few days old, although identifying the precise location of sounds greatly improves over the first six months. Infant response varies to soft sounds, though they will typically have a physical reaction similar to loud noises. Around *3 months*, infants have the ability to duplicate sounds they hear (ahhh and ehhh) by cooing.

Perceptual Development and the Five Senses   111

In *the fourth month*, infants will turn their head in the direction of sounds that are at their eye level and can discriminate their name from similar-sounding words. From *4–7 months*, infants prefer speech with natural breaks, such as music and reading. At *five months*, infants begin to babble. They babble because they are now able to recognize their own voices and are excited when others respond to it. At this point, infants can also discriminate between two

Figure 5.5 Infant Responding to Familiar Sounds

languages. By *six months*, infants can ignore sounds not used in their own language. By *7–9 months*, this preference extends to individual words, and infants can detect a simple word-order pattern. This may help them to figure out the basic grammar of language. Infants understand the meaning of many words they hear. During this time period, infants can also turn toward sounds below their eye level. By the *end of the first year*, infants respond to sounds from anywhere and can associate sounds with specific events and people. Infants will also begin to say many of the words that they hear, although they usually aren't perfectly articulated. They are also able to recognize the same melody when it is played in different keys.

Toddlers

As an infant transitions into the toddler years, the ability to hear and hear clearly is a critical part of her development. Hearing affects cognitive, language and social/emotional development. Therefore, it is important that a toddler responds to ALL sounds (loud noises, voices, music, etc.). If a toddler does not react to particular sounds, it is important to test for a hearing loss. Hearing loss affects speech development most profoundly. Speech development will be discussed in detail in chapter eleven. Symptoms of hearing loss include difficulty paying attention, not reacting to sounds or delays in speech development. Hearing loss can be caused by injuries or illnesses, particularly ear infections; head trauma; genetic conditions; a buildup of ear wax in the ear canal; or exposure to loud noise.

Toddlers are usually able to change the way they speak according to their audience. They pick up cues when listening that help them to figure out how to speak differently to a friend, a younger child or a parent. For example, toddlers who encounter infants will often change their tone of voice to mimic parentese. They will have a completely different interaction with the infant than they do with the infant's parent (Berk, 2012, 2015, 2018a, 2018b).

Sight (Visual Perception)

Infants

Vision is the most immature of the senses at birth. The development of visual perception in the first year of life is a complex and detailed process. By the third trimester (around 28 weeks), a fetus can detect bright light inside the womb. Depending on the thickness of her mother's fat, muscle and clothing, enough natural light may come through in during the final two months in utero for a fetus to see her own hand and leg movements.

As an infant's ability to differentiate and isolate visual stimuli grows, she comes to understand the environment and the meaning behind her experiences. Infants can distinguish light and dark at birth. They can focus on a face eight or less inches away in a few hours, although is very blurry. This blurry picture does not hinder their preference for the familiar face of their mother or primary caregiver, though. While they cannot see well, newborns can actively explore their environment by scanning for interesting people and objects and tracking moving objects.

Laying newborns on the floor on their backs to view and explore the world is the most important experience you can provide for them. While their eye movements may be slow and inaccurate, they are learning about the world around them continuously when given this "viewing" opportunity. Newborns also focus on one aspect or feature of an object instead of the object as a whole with many characteristics (for example, the bright color of a shirt).

Black-and-white patterns and primary color pairings are the most interesting to newborns and young infants. A *few weeks after birth*, infants prefer warm colors (red, orange, yellow) to cool colors (blue, green). In the *first month*, infants enjoy large, bold patterns. By the *end of 2 months*, they can focus their eyes on objects and discriminate colors; by the *end of 4 months*, they can see objects clearly; and by the *end of 6 months*, they have nearly 20/20 vision.

For infants, the human face is the most interesting thing to look at because they innately want to form attachments with people. By *3 months*, an infant can recognize a photo of his mother, recognize color, recognize patterns and view three-dimensional objects. At *5 months*, shape, texture and color contribute to an infant's identification of objects. At this point, he is developing eye-body coordination, which enables him to reach for things and grab them. Around *6 months*, infants can focus on any distance and are developing depth perception.

Depth perception is the ability to recognize the relative distance of objects from one another and ourselves. Depth perception guides motor activity, particularly the ability to reach for objects, and helps infants understand the layout of their environment. Around the time when infants crawl (typically between *6 and 9 months*), they have the depth perception to not bump into furniture or fall down stairs. Stairs should still be guarded though, because infants' curiosity will still cause them to reach over the stairs and possibly fall. As infants have more crawling experience, they will be more cognizant of the dangers of drops such as stairs. Infants gradually figure out how to use depth cues to detect any danger of falling.

Between *7–10 months*, interactions with caregivers determine how infants interpret events. They can perceive emotional expressions and have the ability to differentiate between a happy and a sad expression. They can then interpret the experience based on that facial expression. By *8 months*, infants track objects as they move and will avoid drops at stairs or other visual cliffs. By *1 year*, infants associate patterns of movement with specific meanings, such as a mother opening the refrigerator meaning that she will be getting food or drink out to consume. As infants move into the toddler years at age one, their vision is typically the same as an adult's.

Toddlers

Visual worlds for toddlers are larger, and they have a better understanding of what they are seeing. While the majority of vision develops in the infant years, the following aspects of vision development strengthen in the toddler years: hand-eye coordination, eye teaming and depth perception. Hand-eye coordination allows toddlers to accurately handle, grasp and throw objects. Eye teaming is the ability to move both of their eyes at the same time. Depth perception is the ability to recognize when objects are near or far away without having to look at them (Berk, 2012, 2015, 2018a, 2018b).

Promoting Perceptual Development

Now that you understand the development of each of the five senses, it is important for you to know what types of experiences and explorations help to promote perceptual development in infants and toddlers. It is important to be cognizant of how an infant or toddler's day allows for the use and development of their five senses.

Smell

In order to help infants and toddlers continue to develop their sense of smell, expose them to a variety of scents from both food and non-food items. Fill containers with different scents for toddlers to sniff and explore. Herbs, fruits, vegetables and aromatic flavorings and seasonings such as cinnamon, vanilla and paprika are all food items that have distinguishable scents. Be careful with irritating spices such as chili powder or pepper, because they can create a burning sensation in the back of the nose if inhaled too strongly. Flowers, clean diapers and baby shampoos are examples of non-food items that can be explored with infants and toddlers. Simply place the item underneath the child's nose, being careful not to be close enough to inhale into the nose. Tell the child what scent she is inhaling and talk about the characteristics of it (sweet, sour, strong). As infants progress into the toddler years, they can start to identify these characteristics with you.

Toddler classrooms should have many different things to smell. Be sure to draw toddlers' attention to the wonderful aromas of foods prepared for snack and mealtimes. If possible, grow bulbs indoors in a pan of water with pebbles so toddlers can sniff the perfume of hyacinths and narcissus flowers in bloom. It is important to be careful not to make things smell good that they cannot eat. This will confuse toddlers. For example, do not make playdough smell like food, and do not finger paint with food items (such as chocolate pudding).

Taste

In order to foster infants and toddlers' sense of taste, expose them to many different foods and tastes at different types of consistencies. Give infants and

Figure 5.6 Toddler Planting Flowers

toddlers the opportunity to taste food at its purest (no flavorings or seasonings) and separate the different foods/flavors on a plate and serving spoon. As their taste repertoire increases, mix flavors and slowly add seasonings.

Infants and toddlers should be seated at the dinner table so that they can watch adults eat. Infants can be in a bouncy seat until they are able to sit up, and then you can move them to an eating chair that is more inclusive of the eating experiences. Tell them what food or flavor you are eating and show pleasure by saying "yum" as you eat. This modeling will help infants and toddlers to be more open to trying new foods. Introduce spices/strong flavorings slowly, and their palates will become broader and more accepting of adventurous foods and flavors.

Provide foods with different and interesting colors and textures. If an infant or toddler is reluctant to eat a particular food, eat some of it in front of him to show that the food is, in fact, tasty. When in childcare, infants' families indicate what they eat, so each child will have different foods and consistencies in front of them. You will also have different levels of caregiver involvement in the eating process. Some families may want the caregiver to feed their infant, other families may ask that the caregiver allow the infant to feed himself as much as he can, while still others may ask for the eating experience to be a dual partnership between caregiver and infant. Whatever the family's preference, it is important for caregivers to follow it in order for the infant to experience consistency in this caregiving routine.

As infants move into the toddler years, toddlers eat the same foods and eat as a group. Toddlers also take responsibility for feeding themselves. As soon as this begins to occur, it is important to provide a well-balanced meal that is the same for every child (except for those with food allergies or religious restrictions of course). When every child has the same food in front of them, they will be more apt to eat it and even try something new. One child with a different food detracts the other children's attention from the food in front of them, and they may be less apt to trying something unfamiliar. It is helpful if childcare centers have a "no food from home" policy for children beginning in the toddler years because it encourages the children to try the nutritious meal provided for them.

Touch

Infant and toddler classrooms should be totally touchable. Infant classrooms should also be mouthable (most objects can be put in the mouth without harm) since that is the sense that they use the most and is the most developed. Provide different textured objects for the children to explore such as carpet squares, foam blocks, squishy toys and mild sandpaper. Give infants and toddlers words for what they are feeling (soft, hard, rough, etc.). Infants will listen and toddlers will be able to respond and soon give you the word for the sensation that they are experiencing. These experiences teach infants and toddlers to discriminate how different textures feel.

Hold infants and toddlers with a soft and loving touch. Massages can also encourage positive interactions with caregivers and can improve an infant's mood, a toddler's sociability and infants and toddlers' attentiveness to stimuli. Bathing infants and toddlers is also another tactile experience that promotes the sense of touch in a calm and comfortable way.

The use of slings and baby carriers also help to promote tactile perception and provide the comfort of a close physical connection with

Figure 5.7 Young Toddler Exploring Musical Instruments

caregivers. While many slings and carriers are meant for infants, there are some such as the Ergo carrier that can carry children through the toddler years. As children grow from infants to toddlers, they will want to be on the ground crawling and eventually walking on their own when exploring the world. For the times when they want a close physical connection with a caregiver or wish to see the world from the caregiver's perspective, a baby carrier is an excellent resource. Some even allow the placement of a child on the back of a caregiver versus the front, which provides a different perspective of the world.

Hearing

Talking to infants using parentese (high pitched sounds, different tones and drawn out vowels) attracts them to your face and encourages them to look at you while you are talking to them. As infants enter the toddler years, this talk shifts to normal speech with the use of inflection and animation to communicate emotions, feelings and tone.

It is also important to determine optimum noise level for each infant and toddler. Startled and strained physical reactions and/or facial expressions are signs that an infant is overstimulated. Hands over ears, crying or startled/strained physical reactions are signs that an infant or toddler is overstimulated. Reduce the noise volume or amount of noises until the child relaxes and calms and make contact with the child to calm him down.

While paying attention to the level of stimulation, it is also important to provide experiences and explorations that allow infants and toddlers to use their sense of hearing in different ways. First and foremost, give infants and toddlers time to themselves to listen to, take in and appreciate the noises around them. They need opportunities to find and interpret the sounds around them. Talk and sing to infants so they can hear the human voice and respond to it. Talk and sing with toddlers so they can hear your voice and participate in an interaction. Be cognizant of the toys you choose for infants. Toys that make noise should not substitute for the human voice. The human voice and its inflections contribute to the beginning of language development. The less toys that make noise, the better.

Music and reading are important experiences to provide for infants and toddlers. Play music each day and alternate between new and familiar music. Infants and toddlers will enjoy swaying and clapping to easy rhythmic nursery rhyme chants. You can also make music together using toy instruments or anything that makes noise when shaken. Along with providing musical experiences, it is imperative that caregivers read to infants and toddlers often. Picture books are ideal because they allow caregivers to point to the pictures and tell the children what they are looking at. These reading experiences give infants and toddlers more opportunities to hear the human voice, as well as allow them to associate words with objects. If exposed to reading experiences on a daily basis, older infants and toddlers will eventually participate in the reading experience with their caregivers by pointing to specific objects when they hear the name.

Sight

Hold infants close to you so they can study the contrasts in your face and allow them to touch your face as they visually explore it. Look closely at infants

Figure 5.8 Toddlers Reading Together

when you interact with them and communicate with them with happy eyes. Along with the human face, infants should be given many things to look at both inside and outside, and these things should be as natural as possible. Large open spaces in classrooms surrounded by toys and objects to pick up and explore are appropriate. Colorful mats with mirrors and objects to reach for give infants interesting things to look at and examine during tummy and play time. Too much visual stimulation can be overwhelming, though, so be aware of how much is around infants for them to look at. This balance might be different for each infant, but overall the classroom should not resemble an "amusement park" of blinking lights and toys. This overstimulation will not only overwhelm infants, but it will also teach them to be a passive rather than an active participant in their explorations. If a toy is meant to light up or blink, it should only do it when an infant makes it happen (for example, a toy butterfly only lights up or plays music when an infant touches or squeezes it).

A toddler classroom environment is less open and is organized in more of a "center-based" way. Low barriers in the classroom can divide areas and have a calming (versus overstimulating) effect. Strengthen toddlers' eye-hand coordination by playing rhythmic hand games such as pat-a-cake and "open, shut them." Give toddlers experiences with two-dimensional visual images by providing storybooks with colorful pictures. Classroom walls should be decorated with pictures and artwork placed at toddler eye levels. Point to and talk about the different colors and images in these different pieces. Pictures should be of realistic objects (photographs), and caregivers should bring nature and the outdoors into the classroom as often as possible. Labels for centers are very appropriate at this age and give toddlers a visual indication of what belongs where.

Take infants and toddlers on outdoor walks so they can see grass, flowers and other interesting sights. Point out these interesting things as you walk and describe them in detail. As you walk, ask toddlers to identify and describe everything that they can see.

Developmentally Appropriate Practice

When discussing perceptual development in infants and toddlers, it is important to remember that these young children need to be interacting with people and objects in order to learn and develop appropriately. Learning to talk and play is critical for future learning. Unstructured play time is more valuable for an infant or toddler's developing brain than any electronic media. Through this play, infants and toddlers learn to think creatively, problem solve and develop reasoning and motor skills. They also learn how to entertain themselves because they are left to manipulate and learn about objects using their senses.

The American Academy of Pediatrics (AAP) recommends no television for children under the age of 2 and very limited viewing for children over the age of 2. The AAP emphasizes that a child's brain is developing rapidly in these first years, and young children learn best by interacting with people, not staring at screens. Television is overstimulating and provides a passive (versus active) experience for young children. If you observe an infant or toddler watching television, they are typically sitting completely still and staring blankly at the television. No learning is occurring. Many videos and television programs that are labeled "educational" for infants and toddlers are misleading, and there is no evidence that they have a positive learning effect on young children.

Frequent television viewing has been linked to attention problems and language delay. This connection may be because television provides quick and frequent stimulation, which a child may become accustomed to and expect in his daily lives. These children may lose attention quickly in daily life experiences if the stimulation does not come as fast as the television typically provides. And, if an infant or toddler is watching television, he is not interacting with people. This lack of interaction means that he is not being exposed to language and engaging in interaction with adults and other children. This lack of experience can lead to language delay (AAP, 2011).

There are many ways to help infants and toddlers develop their senses that do not involve media of any kind. All of these activities can be done in just about any care setting, whether it is in the home or in a childcare center. Here are three "quick lists" of experiences that promote perceptual development in infants and toddlers, along with short videos that provide further information:

Multisensory Experiences Indoors:

- Dress up area with many textured cloths
- Sensory tub (cloth, yarn, shaving cream, shredded paper—anything that the children can move their hands through and explore)
- Sandboxes
- Water table
- Playdough
- Finger painting
- Cooking activities where they need to use their hands (rolling cookie or pizza dough)
- Paint on bubble wrap (infants in diapers, toddlers use hands)

Multisensory Experiences Outdoors:

- Nature walks and explorations
- Low- and high-activity areas
- Wet and dry areas
- Soft and hard areas
- Loud and quiet areas
- Large motor physical experiences (moving sticks and rocks)

Perceptual Development and the Five Senses 121

Figure 5.9 Outdoor Infant/Toddler Play Area

- Hands-on activities exploring things from nature (pinecones, leaves)
- Plant a garden and have the children maintain it (learn about bugs, plants, caring for plants and cultivation of flowers, fruits and vegetables)

(Spencer & Wright, 2014)

Daily Activities and Explorations:

- Play music often and dance to it
- Sing songs, fingerplays and verbal games
- Continuously point out objects and verbalize their names, ask questions and discuss their characteristics
- Identify animals and the sounds they make
- Read, read, read every day—indicate specific objects on the pages and ask the children to point them out to you
- Explore art—drawing, coloring and painting using art manipulatives and the children's hands and feet
- Provide puzzles and blocks for play
- Teach "hot" and "cold" by giving children items to touch that are both hot and cold and say the words as the item is touched
- Provide a variety of items to smell and verbalize the names of them
- Take the children outside and encourage them to observe nature and how it changes
- When outside, provide sensory-motor experiences like crawling over, moving and building with rocks and other hands-on activities using natural materials

Sensory Processing Disorder

About SPD

Sensory Processing Disorder (also known as sensory integration dysfunction) is a condition where sensory signals are not organized into appropriate responses. Put simply, it is the way that a child responds to what she tastes, smells, feels, hears and sees. Sensory Processing Disorder (SPD) can affect one sense or multiple senses and can be visible as an "over response" to a stimulation or an "under response" to a stimulation. An example of an "over response" is a child screaming and putting his hands over his ears at the sound of a door slamming. An example of an "under response" is a child showing little or no reaction to his hand touching something extremely hot. Another type of SPD is when a child's processing of messages from his muscles and joints is impaired, so his posture and motor skills are underdeveloped and weak. A final type of SPD is a child that has an extreme need for sensation to the point where he has limited attention and control over himself and his body. Unfortunately, this final group of children can be misdiagnosed as having attention disorders, when in fact it is a sensory disorder.

The causes of SPD in children are likely the combination of environmental and genetic factors. Because of their sensory impairments, children with SPD are at higher risk for social, emotional and educational problems. Their difficulty with motor skills, making friends and becoming part of a group often results in a poor self-concept and being labeled as uncooperative, disruptive, clumsy or belligerent. This negative social status can result in behavior problems such as aggression, anxiety and depression.

Most children with SPD are just as intelligent as their peers, and many are gifted. The difference between SPD children and typically developing children is that their brains are wired differently. Once the sensory delay is identified, these children must be taught in ways that recognize their delay and then adapt to how they process information. These children must be taught to recognize and compensate for their delay so that they may function appropriately in society. It is also important for SPD children to have leisure activities that suit their own sensory processing needs (www.spdstar.org/)

Identifying and Diagnosing SPD

The sooner SPD is diagnosed in a child and he starts treatment, the better their chances for improvement. Parents should tell their pediatrician about any concerns the have about their infant or toddler's behavior. Pediatricians may also identify concerns during well visit check-ups. Caregivers should be fully aware of the signs of any type of sensory processing disorder and document any concerns they have for the children that they care for. Whenever there is a concern, especially one that has been documented frequently, the families should ask their pediatrician for a referral to a developmental specialist and their state's early intervention program. These trained professionals can evaluate the child and determine if there is, in fact, a sensory impairment.

Perceptual Development and the Five Senses 123

When working with infants and toddlers, it is important to recognize and document any early signs of sensory impairments. If these signs are identified early, they can be addressed early, and the chances of the child feeling many of the negative effects discussed above can be limited. Below is a list of signs of sensory impairment. Many of them can be considered "early" signs because they can be seen in infants and toddlers, while others may become more obvious as the children progress through the toddler years:

- Frequently rubs eyes or complains eyes hurt
- Chronic redness or tearing in eyes
- Poor focusing or visual tracking (ability to follow objects)
- Abnormal alignment of eyes
- While pupils instead of black
- Avoids eye contact
- Talks very loudly or very softly
- Gets extremely agitated or overstimulated by loud sounds or bright lights
- Easily distracted
- Often bumps into things or falls frequently
- Constantly head banging
- Spins around frequently
- Has trouble with balance
- Shies away or from touch or even strongly dislikes being touched OR
- Seems to be unable to resist touching everything
- Uses one side of the body more than the other
- Usually turns the same ear toward a sound to hear
- Reacts strongly to the feel of certain substances or textures
- Rarely plays with toys
- Very irritable when being dressed
- Finds it unbearable to wear clothes made of rough fabrics or with tags
- Seems insensitive to extreme cold or heat
- Has extreme aversions to certain foods (not just a dislike for one type of texture)
- Becomes extremely distraught when his face or hands are dirty
- Needs excessive help to fall asleep (long periods or rocking or noise machines)
- Has trouble being gentle with animals
- Refuses to go to anyone but one particular primary caregiver
- Resists cuddling; arches away when being held
- Cannot calm self
- Floppy or stiff body
- Has motor delays

(www.spdstar.org/)

Treating SPD

Children with SPD typically receive a combination of occupational, physical, listening and language therapies. These therapies are given by specialists in the field; in the case of infants and toddlers, it is given through early intervention services. The work that the specialists do with children who have SPD is created to feel more like fun and games and less like therapy and typically occurs in a sensory-rich environment.

The activities are structured so that children constantly feel challenged but are always successful. The specialists work through interactions and games to teach children how to appropriately respond to sounds, lights, touching of textures and any other area where there is a processing disorder. The goal is to teach the children to respond to sensations in a more active, meaningful and fun way in order to behave in a more functional manner. The children learn how to become more comfortable when sensations bother them or become more aware of sensations that they do not typically notice because of their delay.

These treatments help children with SPD handle many different kinds of situations and give them coping mechanisms for the sounds, smells and touch experiences that they encounter in life. Effective therapy also allows the child to participate in the normal activities of childhood such as school, friendships, eating, dressing and sleeping. Some examples of the therapies include:

- Swinging
- Jumping on trampolines
- Games with
    - Sand and water
    - Light
    - Scent
    - Sound-play
- Chances to try different foods

(www.spdstar.org/)

Many SPD children need therapy into adulthood, especially when encountering new environments.

Families are typically involved in the SPD therapy so that they can learn more about their child's sensory challenges. It also gives them methods and activities that they can do at home to address their child's SPD. The therapist will also communicate this information to the child's caregivers if they are in childcare. It is important for caregivers to request this information and make sure they understand it and how to appropriately implement the therapies. Families and caregivers should also have the opportunity to communicate their ideas, concerns and priorities for treatment.

The STAR Institute for Sensory Processing Disorder (www.spdstar.org/) provides a plethora of information about Sensory Processing Disorder. They provide guidance and resources about treatment and research about SPD and strive to educate people about the disorder. One important part of the website that is particularly helpful for parents and caregivers is the page containing information about signs and symptoms that a child might have SPD (www.spdstar.org/basic/red-flags-for-spd). They suggest that parents and caregivers contact their child's pediatrician if they have any of the symptoms listed, especially if they are ongoing issues. Symptoms such as eating and sleep struggles, motor and sensory problems, under- or overstimulation by touch and sound or lack of control of the body are some of the concerns that should be addressed.

Sensory Bottles and Sensory Bags

Making sensory bottles and sensory bags for your infants and toddlers to explore are excellent additions to your sensory materials in your home or classroom. They provide an opportunity for the children to use all of their senses. You can make the bottles and bags for the children or have the children make them with you. Here is how you do it:

Sensory Bottles

Materials:

- Empty water bottles or any clear bottle
- Water
- Glitter, beads, sequins, small bells, etc. (basically anything that can float in water, be visually appealing while floating and may or may not make noise when shaken in the bottle)
- Food coloring

Choose what materials to put in the bottle to float around or make noise. Glitter and sequins provide a purely visual experience, while adding beads or bells provide a visual and auditory experience. Once the materials are in, fill the bottles about two-thirds of the way full of water. This will provide enough room for the water and materials to move around as the children move the bottles around with their hands. You can also use the food coloring to make the bottles different colors. You only need one to two drops of the food coloring—any more will make the water too dark, and it will be hard to see the materials inside. Seal the tops with superglue to ensure that they cannot be opened by the children.

Sensory Bags

Materials:

- Ziploc bags
- Water or hair gel
- Glitter, beads, sequins, foam pieces (basically anything that can move around with your hands in the bag when filled with water or hair gel)
- Food coloring

Fill the bag about halfway with either water or hair gel. Each one provides a different tactile sensory experience for the children. The water is thinner and flows more freely, while the hair gel is thicker and requires more manipulation

126 *Perceptual Development and the Five Senses*

Figure 5.10 Sensory Light Table With Homemade Sensory Bottles and Sensory Bags
Source: www.parentphd.org/2012/03/sensory-bottles-and-sensory-bags-lets-talk-perception/

of the bag with your hands. Next, choose what types of materials you want to mix into the water or gel. Glitter and food coloring alter the visual experience, while beads or foam pieces alter the visual and tactile experience. I also suggest putting an extra seal of protection around the top with duct tape. Toddlers can figure out how to open the bags!

Both the bottles and bags provide a great sensory experience for infants and toddlers. As they move the bottles and bags around with their hands (touch), they will be looking at the visual changes and movement of the materials (sight). Some materials will make noise, which will allow them to use their auditory sense (hearing). Try it and watch the children's senses at work!

For additional material, visit:
www.parentphd.org/infantandtoddlertext/ch5/

Reflection Questions

- Review the additional articles about media use with infants and toddlers AND the additional articles/posters in additional materials for this chapter. You should begin to develop (or already have developed and it is evolving) your position on media use with 0–3 children. In one paragraph, state your personal position on the topic based on the research and information you read. *Be specific as to what information from all of the documents you are using to support your stance on media use with 0–3 children.*

- Observe experiences where children are fostering their perceptual development. Cite one example for each of the five types of perception for both an infant and a toddler (ten total).
- Compare the two experiences (infants versus toddlers) for similarities and differences.

Bibliography

American Academy of Pediatrics. (2011). Media use by children younger than two years. *Pediatrics, 128*(5), 1–6.

Berk, L. (2012). *Child development* (9th ed.). Boston, MA: Pearson.

Berk, L. (2015). *Infants and children: Prenatal through middle childhood* (8th ed.). Boston, MA: Pearson.

Berk, L. (2018a). *Exploring child development.* Boston, MA: Pearson.

Berk, L. (2018b). *Exploring child and adolescent development.* Boston, MA: Pearson.

Davies, J. (2002). Perception in infancy: How babies experience their world. Retrieved from http://adoptmed.org/static/5109a7bee4b000ead7df669b/5109af55e4b00b7548b8fc4a/5109af58e4b00b7548b8ff6a/1117067292357/Perceptual World of Infants.pdf

DeCasper, A. J., & Fifer, W. P. (1980). Of human bonding: Newborns prefer their mothers' voices. *Science, 108,* 1174–1176.

Elliot, L. (2000). *What's going on in there? The brain and mind development in the first five years of life.* New York, NY: Bantam Books.

Gonzalez-Mena, J., & Eyer, D. (2017). *Infants, toddlers, and caregivers: A curriculum of respectful, responsive, relationship-based care and education* (11th ed.). New York, NY: McGraw Hill.

Honig, A. (2013). Infants and toddlers: How children develop sensory awareness. Retrieved from www.scholastic.com/teachers/article/infants-toddlers-how-children-develop-sensory-awareness

Kaywork, J. (2012, March 19). Sensory bottles and sensory bags: Let's talk perception! Retrieved from www.parentphd.org/2012/03/sensory-bottles-and-sensory-bags-lets-talk-perception/

Nothern, J. F., & Downs, M. P. (2002). *Hearing in children* (5th ed.). Baltimore, MD: Williams & Wilkins.

Pollack, D., Goldberg, D., & Caleffe-Schenck, N. (1997). *Educational audiology for the limited-hearing infant and preschooler: An auditory verbal program.* Springfield, IL: Charles C. Thomas Publisher, Ltd.

Proctor, R., & Compton, M. (2004). Perceptual development. *Collaborative Early Intervention National Training E-Resource.* Retrieved from www.inclusivechildcare.org/resourcesWeb2/details.cfm/GetRecID/518

Rones, N. (2013). Your baby's developing senses. Retrieved from www.parents.com/baby/development/physical/babies-developing-senses/

Spencer, K. H., & Wright, P. M. (2014, November). Quality outdoor play spaces for young children. *Young Children,* 28–34.

What to Expect. (2013). Top questions about sensory processing disorder in children. Retrieved from www.whattoexpect.com/developmental-delays-in-children/sensory-processing-disorder-in-children.aspx

6   Physical Development

> While physical development is *predictable*, always remember that each child is *unique*.

This chapter will focus on the gross and fine motor skills of infants and toddlers. It will explain the general progression of motor skill growth that all humans move through as they grow and how reflexes, large motor skills and small motor skills change and refine themselves through the first three years of life.

Physical development is perhaps the most "prescribed" area of development. Most humans progress through motor skills in the same general order and in the same general age range. It is very important for parents and caregivers of infants and toddlers to understand the progression of large and small motor skills so that they can recognize what the children are doing, what they should already be able to and what they will be doing next. Again, there is a range of motor skills and an age range that children perform them in, so there definitely is flexibility. The more understanding you have of the skills and the order they appear, the more flexible you will be when observing and assessing infants and toddlers' motor skills.

Physical development occurs in a predetermined order and progresses from gross motor control to fine motor control. Stability (sitting and standing upright), locomotion (crawling, walking and running) and manipulation (reaching, grasping, releasing and throwing) all develop in the first three years of life. Physical development is also very observable: We can see infants and toddlers refine and perfect specific physical skills as they grow. There are particularly sensitive periods for development, but it is never too late for a child to benefit from quality experiences.

Body and Brain Growth

Before understanding specific motor skills, it is important to understand how the body and brain grows. The average newborn is just over 7 pounds and 20 inches long. By 5 months, an infant's birth weight has doubled, and by 1 year it has tripled. The pace of weight gain then slows down as the infant moves into the toddler years.

130 Physical Development

Figure 6.1 Sensory Exploration With a Light Table

Different parts of the body grow at different rates. At birth, an infant's head is 1/4 of her body, and by age 2 it is 1/5 of her body. This rapid growth requires infants to coordinate and refine body movements that are continually changing. The first muscles that develop are those that control head movements, which is why a newborn has no control over his head and neck. He will gradually gain strength and control to a point where he can hold his head up on his own. This happens over the first month or so of life and shows great strength and muscle coordination.

Overall physical development starts from the head and chest and then moves to the trunk and lower extremities. This directional growth is clearly observable as infants gain control of their head, chest, trunk and then legs in order to turn over. In order to crawl, infants must gain control of their lower back and leg muscles. In order to walk, infants must gain control of their neck, shoulders, back, legs, feet and toes. They develop control of their arm movements as they move from irregular waving to precise reaching. Hand control develops as they move from accidentally bumping and hitting things to purposefully reaching out and touching something. Infants reach with an open hand grip first, and then the fingers slowly shift from reflexive pinching, grasping and releasing to controlled opening and closing.

This stability in motor development is explained by two key growth principles: the *cephalocaudal* principle and the *proximodistal* principle. Cephalocaudal development explains that growth begins from the head and moves down the rest of the body. Hence the fact that infants can control their heads and necks before they can sit up. Proximodistal development explains that growth starts at the center of the body and moves out. Hence the fact that infants can control and move their arms before they can do the same with their hands and fingers.

An infant's brain is 25% of its adult weight at birth and 90% of its adult weight by age 3. Quite a large amount of growth in the first three years of life! *Myelinization* is when brain fat coats and insulates the neural fibers of the brain. This is the rapid growth in the brain's size after birth. The neural fibers can then transmit the synapses easier, and more stable learning connections are made. Cells in the brain become more mature and interconnected, and children move from reflexes to more complex motor skills.

Physical growth occurs as the brain grows. The brain matures and grows from the brain stem at the base of the neck to the cortex in the frontal area. As this growth occurs, movement moves from reflexive to more voluntary, and large and small motor skills are refined. As this refining occurs, infants and toddlers gain and perfect more and more motor skills that allow them to explore the world. In infancy, neurons in the brain move around and become arranged by function. The subcortical levels of the brain are fully developed at birth. The subcortical levels are responsible for reflexes and fundamental activities like breathing and heart rate.

Current brain research emphasizes the importance of free movement and the growth of motor skills. Experience helps form brain circuitry and is essential in fine tuning the young brain's ability to respond to the environment. An interesting environment that encourages active exploration and movement with people and objects may improve the quality of brain functioning and increase myelinization. More neural connections and experience foster more coordination and stronger muscles. Increased myelinization influences development of fine motor skills. To put it simply, physical movement helps children's brains grow (Gonzalez-Mena & Eyer, 2017).

Gross and Fine Motor Development

Gross motor skills include the large muscles of the arms, legs and abdomen. The large muscles in the body work together to allow infants and toddlers to move up and down and side to side freely. Growth and strength start with the head and move down the body. Therefore, the first large muscles to strengthen are

132 *Physical Development*

Figure 6.2 Toddler Kicking a Soccer Ball

the neck and head muscles. Once the infant has this control, his shoulders strengthen, then arms and so on. Eventually an infant will be able to sit up on his own; this isn't something that can be taught or practiced. It comes with increasing strength. Infants and toddlers are only then able to move when they have a strong solid base from which to move. If left alone, infants will learn to roll over, creep, crawl, sit, stand and walk all on their own.

Figure 6.3 Toddler Painting With Popsicle Sticks

Fine motor skills include the small muscles of the hands and wrists, as well as the mouth, bladder, rectum, feet, toes and eyes. The development of the hands and fingers is called *manipulation* and will be the focus of the fine motor discussion of this chapter. It is a set of organized skills that progress and combine in an increasingly sophisticated way. Infants begin by holding their hands in tight fists. They hold on tightly to anything in their hands and cannot control the grasp or release. Hand and arm movements gradually become more voluntary, and they begin reaching for and eventually grabbing objects. They will also explore their own hands and fingers and the movements they slowly can make with them. Along with manipulation, children gradually begin to have control of the small muscles in their mouth, bladder, rectum, feet, toes and eyes.

Reflexes

Reflexes serve as the basis for later movement; infants progress from reflexive movements to voluntary movements. There are reflexes that are protective (blinking, swallowing and clearing the face for breathing), those that are present at birth and those that appear after birth. Knowing what these reflexes look like and what they mean is a key set of knowledge for infant and toddler caregivers. The appearance and delay of certain reflexes help us learn about infants' development.

Reflexes at birth:

- Rooting—head turns toward things that touch the cheek
- Sucking—suck things that touch the lips

134 Physical Development

Figure 6.4 Infant Working to Pick Up Food

- Stepping—legs move forward when held upright with feet touching floor
- Palmar grasp—hands curl around object placed in them
- Babinski—toes fan out if sole of foot is touched
- Moro—if head support released, arms fling out and seem to grasp
- Startle—arms fling out in response to sudden noise
- Tonic neck (fencing)—head turns to one side and arms extends while other arm flexes
- Swimming—swimming movements occur when infant placed in water

Reflexes after birth:

- Reciprocal kicking—if infant held outward, kicks legs alternately (bicycling)
- Neck righting—if head turns, body follows
- Parachute—if infant is falling, arms go forward

- Landau—if infant placed on stomach, arms and legs extend in a "U" position

(Dodge, Rudick, & Berke, 2015; Gonzalez-Mena & Eyer, 2017)

The Progression of Physical Development, Caregiver Strategies and Appropriate Materials

Infants and toddlers are explorers. Given the chance and the ability, they move constantly. Numerous factors influence the rate of motor development, and developmental charts describe the specific milestones for each age group of children. These charts are not exact for every child, but they do offer a general progression of motor skills at the approximate time a child should exhibit them.

Caregivers can facilitate motor development by valuing it and giving children natural everyday experiences; freedom to move in safe environments; and interesting, appropriate choices of objects and happenings. Allow children to move into and get themselves out of positions on their own. Some children may require more time and practice for motor skills to develop. Don't push them! Usually, teaching is not necessary except in cases when individual children may need caregivers to take a more active role.

Since infants and toddlers learn through physical exploration, everything that you provide for them to play with and explore will help develop their physical skills. When infants and toddlers explore materials in their home or classroom, they refine the small muscles in their hands and fingers, cultivate their large muscle growth and develop hand-eye coordination.

Table 6.1 provides physical development milestones for children ages 0–3, specific caregiver strategies to promote physical development, and specific materials and explorations that allow children to develop physically. Use it as a guide when caring for infants and toddlers.

Children With Physical Development Delays

As with all areas of development, it is important for parents and caregivers of infants and toddlers to be aware of the progression of physical development so that they are able to identify any delays. Caregivers should provide nurturance and support to families of children with physical delays, as well as offer resources and connections to Early Intervention specialists. When working with children with physical development delays, parents and caregivers should give the children some direct instruction or prompting when needed, provide a way for them to explore and play with other children, and emphasize use of the senses.

Parents and caregivers of infants and toddlers should seek assistance if a child:

- Has stiff arms or legs
- Has floppy or limp body posture

Table 6.1 Physical Development Milestones and Corresponding Caregiver Strategies

Physical Development Milestones (Milestones have emerged by the end of the age period)	Caregiver Strategies
0–4 months **Reflexes:** Grasp, Startle and Tonic neck **Muscle Control:** Develops from head to feet Head and Neck – Turns head – Holds head upright with support and eventually without – Lifts/holds up head when on stomach and back and can turn it side to side Trunk – Holds up chest – May attempt to raise self up/sit up – Holds up chest and shoulders **Muscle Control:** Develops from mid-body to limbs Arms – Moves around randomly – Reaches for people and objects Hands – Opens and closes – Plays with hands – Uses hands to grasp and move objects – Uses thumb and fingers/forefinger to hold objects Hand-Eye Coordination – Will move arms and hands toward objects and may either grab or miss it	**Reflexes** – Place objects in palm of hands – Calm by touching/holding – Place objects on sides of infant **Muscle Control** – Place infant on back to explore arms and hands – Place infant on stomach to work on lifting head, shoulders and trunk – Tummy time—put toy in front or to the side of infants; get on floor in same position; try your stomach if he refuses the floor – Support head when holding infant – Place infant in reclined sitting position (bouncy seats) – Place objects within reach – Place objects slightly beyond reach and give to infant when she reaches for it – Place toys in hand and help infant close fist around them – Use your body to stimulate infants: grab infant's hands and lift them upright, hold your hands in different places and snap your fingers so infant will turn their heads to locate the sound – Move for infant through exercise: cross arms over chest, lift knees to stomach, stretch out legs
4–8 months **Muscle Control** Head and Neck – Holds head up independently when sitting up, on back and on stomach Trunk – Holds up chest and shoulders – Arches back and hips	**Muscle Control** – Keep hand near head as infant lifts it – Place infant where he can look around; lay against pillows for a better view of everything – Provide space for infant to move freely and safely: Sit and eventually lay, crawl, creep along furniture, roll and push with arms and legs to sit up

- Pushes self into sitting position
- Sits with support and eventually without

Legs
- Lifts legs when on back
- Rolls from stomach to back/back to stomach
- Straightens legs when held in standing position
- Stamps feet when held in standing position
- Raises hands and knees
- Pulls self to standing position
- Stands with support

Locomotion
- Kicks against surface to move
- Rocks on hands and knees
- Creeps on stomach
- Uses legs to pull and push self when sitting

Arms
- Throws objects
- Visually directs hitting and reaching

Hands
- Picks up objects with thumb and forefinger (pincer)
- Clutches objects with whole hand/fingers against thumb
- Picks up objects with one hand and can pass it to the other hand
- Holds objects in both hands
- Drops objects

8–12 months

Muscle Control

Trunk/Legs
- Can move self into sitting position and can sit alone
- Can stand holding onto hand/furniture
- Squats and stands without assistance
- Can sit from standing

Locomotion
- Crawls on flat surface and up steps
- Climbs on furniture

- Dress infant in clothes that allow free body movement
- Hold infant's hands and allow him to pull himself up to a standing position
- Hold infant in standing position and allow him to bounce
- Provide different floor surfaces (carpet, tile, wood) and furniture to push against/pull up on
- When infants inevitably fall down, praise them and give them an opportunity to get themselves back up again
- Place a toy slightly out of reach and encourage movement toward it; praise and encourage efforts
- Provide toys that infants can pick up, hold with hands, hit and safely throw
- Ask for a toy from one hand and give toys to each hand
- Make sure toys cannot be swallowed; EVERYTHING will go in his mouths
- Bang/play with ball, bells and blocks
- Play games where infant has to imitate your actions (put a toy in the same place, drop toy into a container)

Muscle Control
- Allow infant to stand alone or against furniture; remove furniture that can tip over
- Be aware of sharp-cornered furniture and toys that will hurt infant if he falls on them
- Allow crawling, cruising, walking with assistance (hold their hands) and climbing (walk behind them on stairs)
- Model how to get down stairs backward; allow infant to crawl down things hands first if he can safely do it

(Continued)

Table 6.1 Continued

Physical Development Milestones (Milestones have emerged by the end of the age period)	Caregiver Strategies
– Walks with help – Steps forward and sideways Hands – Uses thumb and forefinger/two fingers – Can "poke" with fingers – Brings both hands to middle of body – Reaches for and touches objects and can carry them in hands – Holds pen/crayon and can use them – Will hold an object in one hand and will explore/reach for things with another – Uses dominant hand to stack blocks – Can take off clothes	– Barricade stairs you do not want infants crawling up or down – Be aware that infants will climb into areas where they do not fit (not aware of how much space body takes up) – Provide objects that infants can use pincer grasp to pick up – Provide objects that can be picked up and carried – Provide soft and hard objects to bang and poke – Provide objects of different textures to explore – Provide markers/crayons and model how they are used; remain with infant when he is using them – Allow infants to choose which hand to stack blocks with – Allow infants to play with buttons and zippers

Infants will use all of their senses to explore materials, and everything typically ends up in their mouths. They will look at, bat at and eventually reach and grab for objects and then begin their exploration. The following blocks/toys/manipulatives/explorations are appropriate for infants:

- Play mats (with toys hanging above an infant laying down)
- Materials to grasp and mouth (rattles, key rings, cloth toys)
- Balls
- Puzzles
- Push/pull toys
- Foam, rubber and plastic blocks
- Stacking/nesting cups and rings
- Shape sorters
- Large snap beads
- Measuring cups and spoons
- Activity boxes, trays or cubes (with doors to open, dials to turn, knobs to pull, buttons to push)
- Soft and board books
- Water play: Small bin on the floor with plastic cups and/or rubber toys (or nothing at all—splashing and feeling the water is enough)
- Sand play (older infants): Small bin on the floor with scoops and pails for scooping, filling and dumping (Bins for water and sand can be raised as infants begin to pull themselves up and eventually stand on their own)

12–18 months
Muscle Control
Trunk
- Is active/full of energy, and will move quickly from one activity to another
- Pulls self up to stand

Locomotion
- Walks alone
- May still crawl instead of walk
- Climbs up and down stairs and over objects
- Carries containers of objects around

Hands
- Shows hand preference, though will carry/exchange objects in both hands
- Uses thumb against fingers
- Points with fingers
- Rolls, catches and throws objects
- Likes to push/pull/dump things

Hand-Eye Coordination
- Accurately reaches for and grabs objects
- Scribbles
- Participates in dressing and undressing (removes socks/hats/mittens; tries to/can put on shoes)
- Lifts cup to mouth and drinks
- Begins to use utensils
- Stacks 2 blocks

18–24 months
Muscle Control
Locomotion
- Walks forward, backward and sideways
- Runs and can stop/start
- Jumps with both feet
- Kicks objects
- Climbs

Muscle Control
- Provide a variety of materials, explorations and experiences for toddlers to change activity/play often
- Have a designated clean up time at the end of play time to put away toys with toddlers
- Provide space for safe standing
- Allow toddler to walk or crawl when she wishes; offer hand as assistance when requested
- Provide low equipment for safe climbing (foam pieces, low lofts with stairs and slide), stools, cardboard boxes
- Provide toys to reach for, grasp, lift, carry and move
- Ask toddlers to point to specific objects or pictures in books
- Provide room to throw and roll objects
- Provide markers/crayons and paper and a good place to work with them; encourage all explorations and manipulations
- Allow toddler to dress herself as much as possible; assist and encourage her

Muscle Control
- Provide adequate space to walk in different ways
- Provide different spaces/inclines to walk and flat spaces to run
- Provide adequate room to jump, kick and push/pull toys
- Provide safe equipment for climbing and riding
- Provide a safe space to throw objects at targets
- Provide toys/objects that stimulate manipulation, digging/scooping and picking up/dropping

(Continued)

Table 6.1 Continued

Physical Development Milestones (Milestones have emerged by the end of the age period)	Caregiver Strategies
– Can walk up and down stairs holding a railing – Pushes and pulls objects while walking – Bends over to pick up toy without falling over – Pedals a cycle **Arms** – Toss/roll large ball – Can throw and object at a specific target **Hands** – Fingers: Can grasp and release objects, pull zippers, and turn book pages – Can scribble and make individual marks with a crayon, marker or pen – Helps dress and undress self – Turns wrist to turn an object – Is establishing right or left handedness – Digs with a tool – Builds a tower of three or four blocks – Opens cabinets/drawers/boxes	– Provide zippers, drawing tools and books to manipulate; model where and how to turn pages of books
24–36 months **Muscle Control** **Movement** – Walks, runs, climbs, jumps (in place and forward), bends at waist and stands on one foot – Dresses and undresses self with assistance – Uses fine motor coordination (turning pages one at a time) **Arms** – Throws **Hands** – Touches – Twists – Establishes handedness – Can turn doorknobs – Washes and dries hands	**Muscle Control** – Provide adequate and safe space for all movement – Make a texture box where toddlers can pull out different objects to touch and see; talk about what they feel and label the objects – Provide objects that twist off easily – Demonstrate different dressing actions

Toddlers will continue to explore and play with all of the blocks/toys/manipulatives/explorations listed for infants but in different and more complex ways. They also benefit from materials that stimulate their understanding of themselves and how they connect to the world around them. The following blocks/toys/manipulatives/explorations are appropriate for toddlers:

- Push/pull toys
- Transportation toys
- Animal figures
- Puzzles
- Matching games
- More complex shape sorters, stacking rings and snap beads (unifix cubes)
- Plastic, cardboard, wooden, alphabet or large interlocking blocks
- Lacing cards
- Dramatic play clothing and props
- Soft, board and paper books
- Gross motor equipment such as climbers, shopping carts, tricycles and ride on toys
- Sand and water bins at standing height and with the following additional materials: Plastic/rubber animals and people; rakes; shovels; sieves; cookie cutters; small watering cans; slotted and unslotted spoons; squeeze bottles; ladles; scoops; strainers; straws; muffin tins; bubbles and supplies; natural collectables (rocks, shells, etc.)

Source: (Dodge et al., 2015; Gonzalez-Mena & Eyer, 2017).

- Walks on toes
- Has poor coordination or moves in a clumsy manner compared to other children of that age
- Uses one side of the body more than the other
- Shows signs of pain during exercise
- Seems very clumsy
- Is constantly moving
- Has troubling grasping and manipulating objects
- Drools and has difficulty eating
- Motor skills are regressing
- By *age 1*—has difficulty reaching for objects or picking up objects
- By *age 2*—has difficulty walking without help, kicking a large ball or building a tower with two or three blocks
- By *age 3*—does not walk up or down stairs, run without falling frequently or turn pages of a book

(Babycenter, 2018; Gonzalez-Mena & Eyer, 2017; www.cdc.gov;)

Music and Movement

Children typically don't need to be encouraged to move around to music. They are usually uninhibited and creative in their movement and dance. Music and movement help children develop their large and small muscles and gives them opportunities to exercise, use their bodies and brains together and expend energy.

Children engage in music and movement by listening, singing, moving to music, playing instruments and imitating/representing movement. Infants will bob their heads and torsos to music. Toddlers move their hands and fingers to fingerplays and their whole bodies as they dance. Infants and toddlers love to hear and sing the same songs over and over again and like to make music by hitting just about any material against another.

Both fine and gross motor skills are practiced when infants and toddlers respond to music. As they are more and more exposed to music, they practice gross motor skills by learning to move their legs, feet, arms, hands, heads, hips and torsos to the music. They learn to move quickly, slowly, up, down, in, out, over and under. They practice fine motor skills by opening and shutting their hands and fingers to fingerplays.

Music and Movement Environment

- Open area to move around and dance (both inside and outside)
- Storage and labels for materials:
    - Musical instruments
    - Props
    - Music

Music and Movement Materials

- Wrist and ankle bells
- Manipulatives on play mats that must be touched/batted to play music
- Balls with bells
- Toys that play music when touched or moved
- Store-bought musical instruments (wooden or plastic): drums, bells, cymbals, maracas, tambourines, clackers/shakers, wood blocks
- Make your own musical instruments: boxes as drums; pie pans as cymbals; containers full of rice, beads, and beans; pots and spoons
- Parachute to dance under and move around

Interacting With Infants and Toddlers During Music and Movement

- Join their music and movement activities and follow their lead
- Enjoy music together by moving with the children to the beat
- Encourage children to respond to music physically
- Teach simple fingerplays
- Vary speed of songs and rhymes to change their physical movement and response
- Describe what children are doing
- Ask open-ended questions about tune, words and movements
- Group singing and movement activities
    - Simple songs with lots of repetition
    - Songs with fingerplays
    - Singing games and action songs
    - Songs with funny sounds or silly lyrics
    - Songs and dances of different cultures
    - Movement games without music
- Strategies for introducing a new song:
    - Relatively short, simple words; melody that is easy to remember
    - Make sure you have practiced the song and know it by heart
    - Tell the children a story about the song
    - Sing the song to the children with animation
    - Sing the song again and again and invite the children to join
    - Use props (puppets, flannel board figures, pictures) to help children remember the words of the song
    - Add motions to the song

In your journal, document different songs and movement activities that you could share with infants and toddlers from each of the following categories:

- Songs with repeating phrases and/or rhythms
- Songs that use fingerplays
- Singing games and action songs
- Songs with funny sounds or silly lyrics

- Songs and dances of different cultures
- Movement activities with or without music

(Parlakian & Lerner, 2010)

Gak

"Gak" is a manipulative that you can make with and for infants and toddlers. It is mess-free (once it is finished) and promotes fine motor exploration. It can be colored and colored on with markers and molded into different shapes and sizes. This was a common manipulative in my toddler classroom, and I encourage you to make some and watch the children explore! Click the additional materials QR code at the end of this chapter for a recipe I created for children to complete with caregiver assistance. In my classroom, I printed and laminated the recipe and the pictures so that the children could collect the ingredients using the picture cues and visually follow the steps in the recipe with me. Enjoy!

Yoga for Children

Yoga practice with children has become quite popular in schools, childcare centers and studios. Children can start as early as infancy with their caregivers and then practice with a small group when they reach toddlerhood. Yoga with children has been shown to have social/emotional, cognitive, and physical benefits for children of all ages. Children are able to get in touch with their bodies, feel love and energy for themselves and others and can find a quiet space to think, question and find answers. Many schools are incorporating yoga in the classroom in order to give children a chance to focus and feel calm, which will help them attend and learn better (Parents, 2013; PBS Kids, 2011; www.yogakids.com).

> I absolutely love teaching yoga to young children and am truly convinced of its benefits. I make my classes fun and include a lot of music and movement, non-competitive games and group and partner poses, which help children build social skills. Balancing poses can be taught to children as young as two and research has proven that these help with focus and concentration, ultimately leading to better academic performance. I also encourage a lot of creativity and self-expression to develop confidence and build self-esteem—very important lifelong skills. The simple breathing and meditation exercises that I teach the children help them to relax and get in touch with their emotions, ultimately leading to stress reduction. I wish all young children could get the benefits of yoga and meditation and am thrilled to be able to do whatever I can to enhance and positively affect the lives of my young students!"
>
> (Marsha Silverstein, MSEd, Certified YogaKids Teacher)

Marsha teaches kid's yoga in Rockland County, New York, and the surrounding area. She teaches at my children's school and each year comes to my early childhood education courses to teach my preservice teachers. She is a fantastic kid's yoga teacher!

For additional material, visit:
www.parentphd.org/infantandtoddlertext/ch6/

Reflection Questions

- Read the articles "Development of Movement" by Emmi Pikler AND "Rocking and Rolling: Learning to Move" in the additional materials for this chapter and answer the following questions:
  - What are your thoughts about leaving infants to develop on their own without ever being put into a position they can't get in themselves? Were your thoughts different before/after reading this article?
  - What are your thoughts about adults using caregiving times to interact with infants and toddlers and leaving them to explore and move on their own the rest of the day?
- Read the two articles, "Rocking and Rolling: Learning to Move" AND "HAPPE: Toddlers and Physical Play" in the additional materials for this chapter. Explain what new knowledge you now have about the importance of physical movement and play for infants and toddlers?
- Read the article "Beyond Twinkle Twinkle: Using Music with Infants and Toddlers" in the additional materials for this chapter and answer the following questions:
  - In what ways does music promote growth in the various developmental domains?

- o How can infant/toddler professionals use music experiences to support children's early learning?
- Based on all that you have read in this chapter, describe the brain's role in infant and toddler physical development.
- Mapping Assignment. Draw a brief map of the environment that you are observing. Choose one child and draw a path he/she takes during a particular time period.
  - o Indicate on the map when the child stops, picks up an object, interacts with other adults or children, etc.
  - o Document the child's *specific* motor skills and actions each time s/he stops.

Bibliography

Babycenter Medical Advisory Board. (2018). Warning signs of a physical developmental delay. Retrieved from www.babycenter.com/0_warning-signs-of-a-physical-developmental-delay_6720.bc

Blessing, M. (2012). Physical development guidelines for early childhood. Retrieved from www.brighthubeducation.com/infant-development-learning/122222-early-childhood-physical-development/

Bronson, M. B. (1995). *The right stuff for children birth to 8: Selecting play materials to support development.* Washington, DC: NAEYC.

Casaer, P. (1993). Old and new facts about perinatal brain development. *Journal of Child Psychology and Psychiatry, 34,* 101–109.

Cosmato, D. (2012). Gross motor skill development for infants and toddlers. Retrieved from www.brighthubeducation.com/infant-development-learning/62391-gross-motor-activities-for-infants-and-toddlers/

Dodge, D., Rudick, S., & Berke, K. (2015). *The creative curriculum for infants, toddlers and twos: The foundation* (3rd ed.). Washington, DC: Teaching Strategies.

Douville-Watson, L., Watson, M. A., & Wilson, L. C. (2003). *Infants and toddlers: Curriculum and teaching* (5th ed.). New York, NY: Thomas Delmar Learning.

Fomon, S. J., & Nelson, S. E. (2002). Body composition of the male and female in reference to infants. *Annual Review of Nutrition, 22,* 1–17.

Gallagher, K. (2005, July). Brain research and early childhood development – A primer for developmentally appropriate practice. *Young Children, 60*(4), 12–20.

Gonzalez-Mena, J., & Eyer, D. (2017). *Infants, toddlers, and caregivers: A curriculum of respectful, responsive, relationship-based care and education* (11th ed.). New York, NY: McGraw Hill.

Ireton, H. (1995). Child development inventory: Teacher's observation guide. Retrieved from www.childdevrev.com/page15/alltools.html

Parents. (2013). The benefits of yoga for kids. Retrieved from www.parents.com/fun/sports/exercise/the-benefits-of-yoga-for-kids/

Parlakian, R., & Lerner, C. (2010, March). Beyond twinkle twinkle: Using music with infants and toddlers. *Young Children*, 14–19.

PBS Kids. (2011). Why yoga and kids go together. Retrieved from www.babycenter.com/0_warning-signs-of-a-physical-developmental-delay_6720.bc

Wittmer, D. S., & Peterson, S. H. (2017). *Infant and toddler development and responsive program planning: A relationship-based approach* (4th ed.). Boston, MA: Pearson.

7   Play as Learning

Play interacts and overlaps with all areas of children's development. Parents and caregivers can easily determine where a child is on a developmental continuum by observing him play. Play development and experience progresses from simple to complex, from concrete to abstract and from focusing on the self to interacting with other people.

Based on these statements, consider the following questions:

1. What do you need to know and understand about play?
2. How does this knowledge influence how you work with infants and toddlers?
3. How does this knowledge affect how well you can assess infants and toddlers' learning and development?

Now, answer the following questions in your journal before reading this chapter. Document your current ideas and understandings. After reading this chapter, add your new and/or changed knowledge to your notes:

1. How do infants and toddlers learn?
2. What is the connection between how infants and toddlers learn and their play?
3. How are materials chosen for infants and toddlers to play with?
4. What is the adult's role in an infant and toddler play environment?

Understanding Infant and Toddler Play

Play has long been recognized by early childhood educators as an important part of children's development and learning. Many of the knowledge and skills that are important in childhood (and in life) are advanced through play. This is especially important for infants and toddlers. Infants and toddlers are learning about themselves and the world every day, and much of this learning occurs through play in and active exploration of their environment. When infants and toddlers play, they are working on their large and small motor skills; self-regulation; verbalizations and vocabulary; imagination and

Figure 7.1 Toddler Unwrapping Toy

creativity; memory, concentration and attention span; curiosity and problem solving; and empathy and cooperation with others. If you read over that list again, you realize that it covers every area of infant and toddler development. Play influences it all. Caregivers help to create a curriculum out of play by giving children the freedom to play and explore however they wish, pursue their interests in whatever way is available and by providing the resources for all of this to happen. Caregivers can observe children in play and become aware of their competences, skills and understandings.

It is important to understand, though, what play truly is for infants and toddlers. *Free play and exploration* should encompass the majority of infants and toddlers' days. Free play and exploration means undirected play where children have the opportunity to pursue their interests without any adult control or expected outcomes. Infants and toddlers learn best through active involvement with materials that is initiated and guided by them. These self-initiated play experiences are times for thinking, language, problem solving and investigating. Through this play, infants and toddlers use their mind and body to respond to the stimuli in front of them. They plan, investigate and organize their thoughts and explorations. The experiences are completely open-ended. There are no expected processes or outcomes for play. Ever.

Play is truly empowering for children. When children play, they have the power over the experience in their hands. Play offers children opportunities that they cannot get anywhere else or with any other type of experience. When children play, they are participating in an open-ended experience where there are no rules, procedures or expected outcomes. They make discoveries, problem solve and make choices about their explorations that come only from their own minds.

The more children practice and master new skills in their play, the more often they will take on new challenges. This promotes a continuous cycle of learning. As children roll, then crawl and then walk, they are exploring and testing their environment. You will find that infants and toddlers will climb on furniture, climb into small spaces, open cabinets/drawers/containers and take everything out, touch everything they can and play with water anywhere they can. Their interest in the world encourages them to use their senses to explore, which helps to grow their intelligence. They will eventually ask questions about their explorations and experiences (beginning with "why?"), which helps them to make sense of their experiences (Zero to Three, 2010).

Play changes its look and its complexity as children progress through the first three years of life. Each child explores and learns about the world in different ways, although there is a definite progression in play participation. *Infants* participate in what Piaget called "practice" or "functional" play, where they repeatedly practice actions with objects and their bodies. *Young infants* will mouth toys almost immediately and then proceed to bang, shake and hit materials to learn about them. These very young children will also intently watch others play. *Mobile infants* will extend this viewing of others play to imitation and will physically explore objects more. They will pull, push, kick, turn around in their hands, and place objects in and out of containers to figure out what they do with them. *Toddlers* try these same strategies repeatedly and at a more complex level. They can change and adapt their strategies for play and collaborate with other children in their play. Toddler play is more advanced and extends to what Piaget called "symbolic play." In this play, toddlers participate in make-believe or pretend play with objects and themselves (Piaget, 1962).

Vygotsky also provided us with some understandings about children's play. He agreed that play was a central source for development and emphasized play as a learning process. He said that play behavior is influenced by the conditions in which it takes place, such as the materials available and other people involved. Therefore, he focused on the social aspect of play and how it promotes learning in the children involved. Vygotsky believed that humans learn through social interactions with others, and play experiences were no different. To Vygotsky, children observing each other play, playing near each other and eventually playing with each other are all learning opportunities. Play promotes language and learning, as well as fosters important social skills and interactions (Vygotsky, 1967).

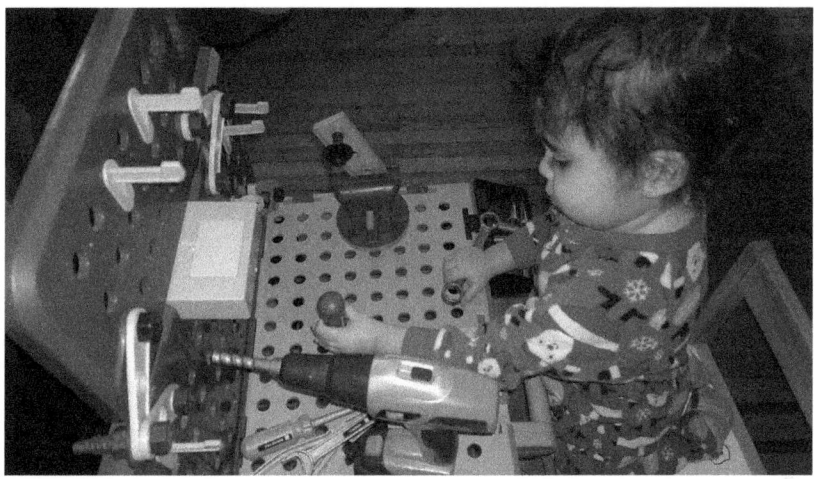

Figure 7.2 Toddler Playing With Tools and Tool Table

The Play Environment

The play environment is as important as the play materials in it. It must continuously support free play and exploration. Remember from chapter three that the infant/toddler environment is comprised of the physical set-up and the social/emotional atmosphere. Constructing the play environment in your classroom is no different. Specifically, the play environment should follow these guidelines:

- Be separate from caregiving areas
- Everything is touchable
- Provides for both gross and fine motor activity
- Provides both hard and soft materials and surfaces
- Allows children to find unique ways to combine toys and materials
- Provides the right amount of choices and toys
- Provides environmental limits such as shelves, tables and chairs
- Provide familiar experiences along with new ones that are appropriately challenging (ideally, the challenging experiences are ones in which the children need no adult interference, scaffolding or intervention)

In order for free play and exploration to happen, caregivers must not restrict infants and toddlers' activity. By restricting *infants*, I mean placing them in seats, playpens and cribs. Infants should only be placed in these apparatuses for safety and comfort purposes. When it is time to explore and play, take them out. Infants should be placed on the floor with room to move and explore. Materials should be within reach or at a distance that the infants can reach on their own. Caregivers can use toy and bookshelves to outline the large and open play area.

By restricting *toddlers*, I mean gating them or closing them into specific areas of rooms. This goes for both classrooms and homes. In classrooms, low standing bookshelves/toy shelves provide appropriate barriers between different types of play and should be enough. Toddlers should be free to move about the room, and no area should be off limits. In homes, there is no need to "gate" your child into a specific corner of a room for play. Most often, this is done to keep toddlers in a certain area and out of other areas of the house. Usually, simply putting a toddler's toys in one area will keep them there; if they want to leave that area and explore other places in the house, they should be allowed to do so. It is their home, too, after all.

For both infants and toddlers, gates should only be used at the tops and bottoms of stairs for safety reasons. If there are unsafe materials within reach of where an infant or toddler is playing, either move them or close the door to that room. You can also teach your child not to touch certain materials by continually redirecting them to things they can touch or placing these touchable materials nearby to attract their attention. Regardless of the presence of gates, parents and caregivers should always be keeping an eye on children while they are freely playing. If you are constantly doing this, numerous gates and barricades are not necessary, and children will freely and safely explore the environment.

The Role of the Caregiver in Play

As a caregiver for infants and toddlers, I structured the majority of my curriculum around the children exploring materials and objects on their own. As I observed their play and talked with them about what they were doing, I got new ideas for new explorations. I also watched the children continually learn new skills. As a parent of infants and toddlers, I often placed my children on the floor with materials and objects within reach and left them to explore and play. I started this practice very early on (within the first few months of life) and saw the benefits almost immediately. My children could play on their own easily and without needing me to "entertain" them, and they slowly grew into toddlers and then preschoolers who immediately looked at a new material or object with the question, "I wonder what that does?" versus "Mommy what does this do?" Approaching life with the desire to explore, play and figure out everything new they encountered also benefited their learning, and I found that they were communicative at an early age and exhibited cognitive skills of older children in their play.

Caregivers can create a curriculum of play by providing children with materials and objects to play with, helping children pursue their interests and giving children freedom to explore freely and without restraint. Caregivers should provide long periods of free play time where infants and toddlers can make choices about what materials to play with and how they want to play with them. Infants and toddlers will build a sense of confidence, competence and motivation to learn if given numerous opportunities to play freely. An infant-toddler environment promotes free play by providing a rich selection of materials in a well-organized and appropriately structured environment.

Therefore, the role of an adult in a child-centered environment is that of a facilitator and supporter, not of a teacher. Adults set up the environment for children's exploration and then support and encourage the children's self-initiated explorations. They provide resources when necessary but refrain from taking over and directing any of the children's actions in their play. The focus should be on the children's self-discovery during free play. Free play is just that—free!

This free play time where a child is rolling, crawling or walking around and playing with different materials is a time for the caregiver to learn about his interests and abilities. As the child plays, the caregiver closely observes and follows the child's actions and explorations. Caregivers can also be responsive to a child by joining him in his play. Caregivers can engage *with* the child by playing alongside in a similar manner, adding dialogue about his play or asking questions as they play together. This dual play experience is open-ended, stress free and completely guided by the child.

Happenings are child-initiated explorations or play experiences with an object or material. They can be explorations or play that just "happens" when an infant or toddler chooses to explore a material, or they can be simply what a child does with a material that is given to her to explore and play with. Happenings completely focus on the child's experience and can be simple or complex. They are often quite satisfying for the children because they are in complete control of the entire experience.

Happenings are very different from activities. *Activities* are planned experiences. Children are given materials, and there is some expectation for an outcome or a product. Happenings have no such characteristics. An example of a happening is a child taking playdough out of a container, rolling it into balls and rolling the balls across a table. The playdough was available for play, but no direction was given. The child decided what he wanted to do with it on his own and performed the task how he thought it should be done (Gonzalez-Mena & Eyer, 2017).

Caregivers should take advantage of happenings either created by children or from their own spontaneous ideas. For example, if it snows, put snow in the sensory table for the children to play with and explore. If a child brings in different leaves collected from a tree in their yard, use this opportunity to explore the leaves and go outside to find more with the children.

With all of this in mind, it is important for caregivers to remember that they do not need to push children to make choices out of fear of children's boredom. Boredom is actually educational because it encourages children to push from an internal motivation. A "bored" child is actually a child actively using his brain to figure out what to do next. Caregivers should not interfere with this thought process unless the child exhibits a high level of stress (remember optimum stress level?). If this occurs, a caregiver can offer materials for play or play opportunities as a way to engage the child and lower the level of stress.

A question I often hear is, "What happens when a child 'gets stuck' and can't figure out what to do next?" This is an important question. Caregivers can step in and intervene with a small amount of help. It is important for caregivers to wait to intervene until it is absolutely necessary or requested by the child. While they might show the child how a toy works, they should refrain from doing this each time. Provide just enough help or modeling to keep frustration to a minimum but allow the child to try it on his own. This behavior will motivate him to try new skills. It is also important to read a child's signals. Infants and toddlers cannot always verbally tell you when they have had enough or are frustrated. Be cognizant of non-verbal cues such as facial expressions and gestures and shift attention to a new activity if necessary.

Here are some important specific roles for adults in infant and toddler play. Use these bulleted guidelines as reminders of what exactly you should be doing while the infants and toddlers in your care play freely.

- Make sure the play area is completely safe
- Provide free play time, space and appropriate materials
- Observe the children at play
- Encouraging interactions between children and then step back
- Intervene in children's play only when it is absolutely necessary (safety and high levels of stress)
- Always be present and available to the children but do not interrupt their play
- Supporting problem solving by encouraging children to figure something out and providing dialogue and questions to help in this process
- Scaffold the children in their play if requested by placing their hands over yours as you manipulate the objects

(Zero to Three, 2010)

Developmentally Appropriate Play Materials and Experiences for Infants and Toddlers

This section will provide you with information about how infants and toddlers play and how you can create appropriate play environments for children ages 0–3. This section was written from my own experiences caring for infants and toddlers along with information provided by Zero to Three (www.zerotothree.org). Zero to Three provides information that promotes the health and development of infants and toddlers. They are an excellent resource for any type of information about infants and toddlers and how to care for them.

Infants: Birth to 12 Months

Magda Gerber's life work focused on infants and infant care. Her RIE approach was discussed in chapter one and extends into this chapter's discussion of play. When discussing infants and play, Gerber emphasized that the following occur

Play as Learning 155

Figure 7.3 Toddler Playing With Felt Board and Felt Pieces

in order to support play and exploration in infants. I have always considered her ideas to include both infants and toddlers and have summarized her ideas below to include all children ages 0–3:

1. Infants and toddlers should be active participants in their routines
2. Caregivers should observe and understand what each infant and toddler needs
3. There should be consistency and clearly defined limits
4. Caregivers should trust the infant or toddler to be an initiator, explorer and self-learner
5. Environments should be safe, emotionally nurturing and cognitively challenging
6. There should be a large amount of time for uninterrupted play where infants and toddlers can play at their own pace
7. Infants and toddlers should be given the freedom to explore and interact with other objects and infants

(Gerber & Weaver, 2002; Gerber & Greenwald, 2013)

With Magda Gerber's ideas in mind, let's explore infants and toddlers and their play. Always remember that as a caregiver for infants and toddlers, you have a significant impact on how much the children in your care learn through play. Remember these strategies:

- Join in with their play with happiness and excitement
- Observe children's play carefully in an attempt to understand what they are trying to do or figure out

- Provide the support that is needed to accomplish a goal or continue a play experience. This might mean providing additional materials or helping in the manipulation of a material.
- Provide challenges when you see that the children are ready. Children should have play experiences that are both familiar and new to them. New experiences challenge their thinking and stretch their knowledge and skills
- Be spontaneous and have fun. Play is not work—it's play! Relax and enjoy yourself

An infant's five senses are his learning tools. Infants use their whole body to make discoveries and learn about everything they can get near. This helps them to develop the necessary muscle strength, balance and coordination needed to explore the world around them. Infants have an innate curiosity about the world, and a caregiver's job is to provide the resources and the space to build on that curiosity.

In the first three months, infants' play is guided by their reflexes (automatic actions like grasping an object put in their hand). Around 3 months, the reflexes disappear, and infants move their bodies with purpose. This is when sensory exploration really kicks into high gear. Around 6 months, the joy in repetition emerges. These infants enjoy repeating actions over and over again. They do this to perfect a skill and to begin to understand cause and effect (a certain action will lead to a certain response).

At 9 months, infants understand cause and effect and that things out of their sight still exist. Verbalizations about their explorations will slowly increase as this first year progresses; as infants reach 12 months, those verbalizations will be used to communicate to others what they are doing. Infants watch others play, play alone and begin to play alongside others toward the end of the first year. The ability to play cooperatively with another person has not emerged yet, although infants will sometimes engage in interactions and communicate verbally and non-verbally with others during their play.

How to Play With Infants (Birth—6 months):

- Verbal and non-verbal communication
    - Gaze into infants' eyes, smile and talk to them. Infants will return the gestures. Babies will physically and verbally communicate their needs through cries and strong body movements. Respond to their communications by meeting their needs. These first interactions help infants feel connected to their caregivers and are the first play experiences they have.

Play as Learning 157

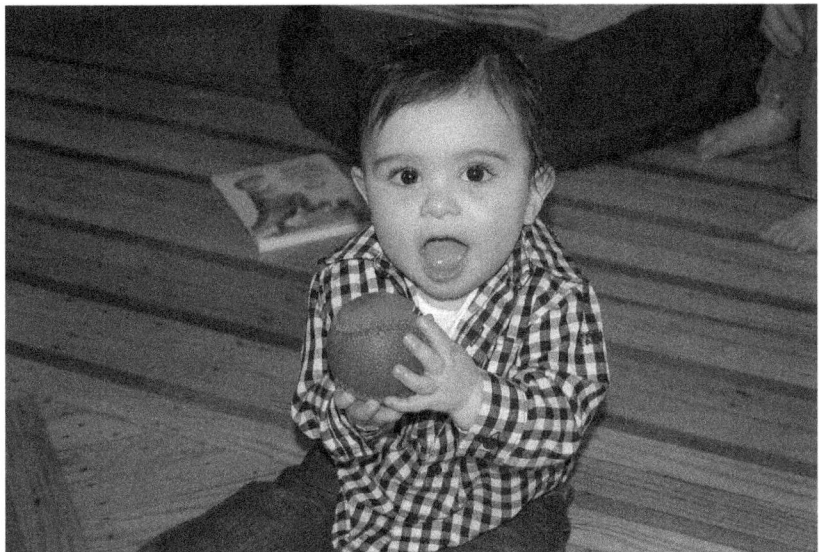

Figure 7.4 Infant Exploring a Ball

- Looking at your face and colorful objects
  - Infants prefer to look at your face, so make eye contact and watch them follow you with their eyes. Show them colorful objects and move the objects to allow infants to track them with their eyes. Lay infants on the floor so they can gaze at the environment around them. Place them in an elevated infant seat in areas of activity so they can watch.
- Grasping
  - Hold objects such as rattles or your finger in front of infants so they can reach and grab them. Hold two and see which object infants choose to grab. Give infants something to hold in each hand and then offer a third item. They will drop one of the original items to grab the third and eventually learn to hold all three objects.
- Objects to mouth
  - Provide objects with different textures that infants can safely put in their mouths. The mouth is their preferred body part for exploration.
- Tummy time
  - Place infants on their stomachs for a different way to explore the world. Tummy time also helps to strengthen infants' neck, trunk

and arm muscles. Place a mirror in front of them to look at and toys within reach to grab. Lay on your stomach in front of their faces and talk/sing to them. Infants become more tolerant of tummy time if you gradually increase the time period. Start with a minute or two and increase the time as their tolerance increases.

How to Play With Infants (6–12 months):

- Toys that encourage repetition
    - o Provide rattles, musical instruments, pop up trays and hammering benches that allow infants to repeatedly perform the same action. Allow infants to try to figure out the toy before intervening. If you do participate, place your hand over the infant's hand and perform the action together. Blocks that can be stacked and knocked over repeatedly are also popular and is a play experience caregivers can actively participate in with infants.
- Pincer grasp practice (using pointer and finger and thumb to pick up small objects)
    - o Lay Cheerios on a table or tray for infants to eat for snack. Start with a small amount so that infants can concentrate on each one individually. Toys that have strings attached, puzzles with handles and books make of cloth and boards are all opportunities for infants to practice their pincer grasp.
- Problem-solving toys
    - o Shape sorters, stacking cups, ring stacks and blocks are all materials that encourage infants to problem solve. Allow infants to explore the materials first, and then slowly join their play. Stack the cups or rings and put the shapes in the appropriate holes while infants hold your hands, the objects or just watch. Then allow them to work through the problem-solving experience on their own.
- Toys and furniture that can be pushed, pulled or allow infants to stand up against
    - o Push/pull toys, activity cubes and furniture such as chairs and tables are all play materials for older infants. They enjoy pulling themselves up while leaning on them, and then eventually maneuvering their way around them to play and explore. Push/pull toys can be played with while infants are sitting or standing and then eventually will move along with them as infants' mobility increases.

Below are play experiences that can be provided to all infants in the first year. The level of physical exploration and cognitive understanding strengthens as the infant moves through the first 12 months of his life.

How to Play With Infants (0–12 months):

- Talk to infants often
  - Narrate what you are doing and identify objects and actions that infants observe. Imitate their sounds and wait for them to respond. You will find that you are quickly engaged in a conversation of sounds that is very pleasurable to them.
- Play "peek-a-boo" behind your hands, objects or a mirror
  - Infants will simply pay attention to your movements at first. Soon they will smile, make happy sounds or move their arms and legs in excitement. Eventually they will move your hands or the object away from your face to "find you." Stand in front of a mirror with infants or place mirrors on the floor where they can sit or lay in front of it. Allow infants to look at their image and then move them away from the mirror and then back again. They will delight at the baby that keeps appearing and disappearing in front of them.
- Listen to, dance to and sing all different types and volumes of music
  - You will learn infants' preferences for types of music and volume, and they will learn to move their bodies in different ways depending on what type of music is playing. Move your body and theirs to music to promote physical play and rub or massage their bodies to appropriate music to help them feel the different rhythms they are hearing.
- Offer objects of different shapes, textures, sizes and colors such as balls, blocks and stuffed toys
  - Allow infants to explore each object with all of their senses (it will probably go right in the mouth—that's OK!). Talk with infants about the characteristics they are experiencing. Toys that "crinkle" when grasped especially grab infants' attention, and they will work to make the noise happen again.
- Toys that make noise
  - Infants should be given toys that make noise *only* when the infant manipulates them. Once infants discover that they can make a toy "work" with their own hands, they will repeat the act over and over again. Toys that make noise without any manipulation necessary make infants passively sit and watch; you want them actively engaged.
- Sensory experiences
  - Provide well-supervised sensory experiences for infants, such as water and finger paint. If possible, undress infants down to their diapers so that they can feel the sensory materials on as much of their body as possible. Place trays of paint (or put it right on the table) and allow

160 *Play as Learning*

infants to first explore with their hands. They will then decide what other body parts to add to the experience. If infants begin to put their hands in their mouth, slowly guide their hands back down to the table or their bodies. Small, low water bins on the floor provide another sensory experience. Infants don't need anything to play with in the water; the simple act of running their hands back and forth and making motions in the water is enough for them. In this instance, you can allow infants to place their hands in their mouth if they choose; the droplets of water on their hands are not harmful. Another alternative to these sensory experiences is to put water, paint or hair gel in different-sized Ziploc bags and let infants manipulate them. This non-messy version gives infants sensory experiences without the mess. You can even tape the bags to the floor and allow infants to crawl over them or roll on them, giving them a whole-body sensory experience.

- Read to infants often
    - It is never too early to expose children to books and reading. Hold infants on your lap and place the book in front of them. Read using animation and inflection (this will engage the infant in the story). As you read, point to pictures and identify what you see and let the infant grab, hold or even mouth the book. Infants are listening to your voice as they manipulate the book, so keep reading and talking. Read short books, books with few words or books with just pictures.

Figure 7.5 Infant Playing With Picture Blocks (Zero to Three, 2010, 2012a; 2012b).

Toddlers: 12 to 24 Months

The five senses are still strong learning tools as infants move into the toddler years. They are now used in a more complex way. Toddlers have goals for their actions now. Toddlers are learning how objects are used together and are discovering the connections between objects. Their play teaches them about the similarities and differences, sizes and shapes of all of the objects they explore.

As the toddler years begin, children are using their fingers and hands to explore and play in a more complex way and have developed preferences for this play and exploration. They are communicating better with gestures, sounds and words. They learn to stand on two feet, walk forward and backward and run. Toddlers also imitate what they see in real life in their play and use their imagination to begin to participate in dramatic play. Toddlers under age 2 are still watching others play, playing alone and playing alongside others. The ability to play cooperatively with another person is beginning to emerge.

How to Play With Toddlers (12–24 months):

- Movement and Action
    - Music-based action games like "Ring Around the Rosie," "Teddy Bear Teddy Bear," "Listen and Move," "Animal Action" and "Tooty Ta" encourage toddlers to move, sing, listen, cooperate and take turns. Outdoor play experiences such as playing on playground structures and even just running around give toddlers opportunities to run, climb and play with other children. If you are unable to go outside, create a safe obstacle course inside where children can crawl and climb.

- Repetitive Actions and Explorations
    - Repetition gives toddlers an opportunity to figure out how things fit together and work. Repetition also allows toddlers to know what to expect, which is comforting. They feel a sense of security and control of their world. This comforting environment helps them to master new skills and boosts their self-confidence. Provide sensory bins filled with sand and water and watch toddlers fill and dump over and over again. Read familiar books to them when they request it.

- Music with Rhyming and Repetition
    - Words are easier to learn when they rhyme or are put to music. Toddlers can imitate words and melodies and will enjoy singing along with you to songs with rhyming words. They will also enjoy "reading"

a familiar book with you. Pause before a word in a song or book and see if toddlers can tell you what it is. Dance to music to get their bodies moving and provide musical instruments so they can make their own music.

- Busy Hands
    - o Toddlers enjoy making toys "work." They use their fingers and hands to push buttons, open boxes and turn pages of books. They also enjoy using these body parts to actively explore mediums such as paint, playdough and water. Sensory bins (filled with sand, water, shaving cream, snow, etc.) are favorites for toddlers because of the active sensory experiences they provide.
- Manipulatives
    - o Provide toys and objects that toddlers can use their hands and fingers to manipulate. Many of the toys provided for infants still apply to young toddlers, such as stacking cups, nesting cups, shape sorters and pop-up boxes. Add chunky puzzles, plastic spoons and cups, pop-beads and chunky interlocking plastic blocks to the play scene for increased manipulative experiences.
- Communication tools
    - o Young toddlers communicate using words, sounds and gestures. Provide toy telephones to "talk" with toddlers and puppets and dolls to converse with. Model these conversations and encourage toddlers to join you.
- Large muscle movement
    - o Give toddlers opportunities to walk, run, climb structures and stairs and throw balls. This active play time builds strength, balance and coordination. Tunnels and simple obstacle courses are enjoyable to crawl through. Toys that can be pushed, pulled or ridden provide an array of large muscle experience. It is important to allow this play to be free and without rules or guidelines. Young toddlers need to explore in their own way.
- Read to younger toddlers often
    - o Continue to read board books, short stories, books with few words and picture books. Encourage younger toddlers to "read" with you by saying words or phrases with you and anticipating what is coming next. Ask them to identify specific objects in the books with gestures, sounds and words.

Toddlers: 24 to 36 Months

Older toddlers are still continually practicing and mastering their physical abilities, language and problem-solving skills. Now, though, they are interested in playing with a friend. Up to about 2 years old, children watch others play (onlooker play), play alone (solitary play) and play alongside other people (parallel play). Around age 2, they begin to gain the ability to play *with* other people (associative and then cooperative play), which are huge milestones! Older toddlers' imaginations are bigger and more complex as well. Pretend play dominates in this final stretch of the toddler years. Detailed pretend play with friends is a common practice, and as toddlers approach the end of the third year, stories and rules for games and play begin to emerge. Pretend play helps children to understand their real lives and work through experiences in their lives that bring up positive and negative emotions. They act out steps of a familiar routine and use symbols in their play (such as a block for a phone).

How to Play With Toddlers (24–36 months):

- Play with others

    o   Provide numerous opportunities for toddlers to play together both inside and outside. Observe the play and coach children about how to cooperate, share and take turns.

- Musical Games and Songs

    o   Play musical games and songs that ask toddlers to listen and follow directions such as "Freeze Dance," "Body Is an Instrument," "Simon Says" and "Hokey Pokey." These physical musical experiences teach toddlers about words and sounds while giving them a much-needed opportunity to move their bodies. Add musical instruments to strengthen the physical experience and ask toddlers to identify the type of sound each instrument makes as all of you play with them.

- Quiet Play

    o   Give toddlers opportunities to play quietly, and when you observe them making this choice on their own, leave them to their play. Reading books, listening to stories, playing with manipulatives and participating in art experiences builds imagination, concentration and language skills. Provide sensory experiences like sand and playdough for toddlers to explore on their own, and art supplies like crayons, paint and paper to create on their own. When you see that they are reaching the end of their solitary experiences, ask them to tell you about their play. Or, ask if you can join them in their play to extend the experience.

- Dramatic/Fantasy Play
    - Provide dress up clothes, props and prop boxes (boxes filled with materials focused on one specific play theme) for toddlers to participate in dramatic and fantasy play. Dolls, stuffed animals, accessories and play kitchens are all enticing play experiences for older toddlers who want to act out what they see in real life. Ask older toddlers if you can join in their play – they might even let you! Your participation will help expand their ideas and help you to learn about their life experiences, thoughts and ideas as they act them out in their play.
- Problem solving/manipulative toys
    - Add to the infant and young toddler manipulative toy collection with puzzles without handles (but still have large, chunky pieces), memory games and toys that can move on their own with simple pulling/pushing motions. Stringing beads, bristle blocks, Legos (large and small), and different sized crayons give further manipulative practice. Sorting trays give older toddlers an opportunity to sort manipulatives by type, size, shape or color.
- Take a walk outside
    - Take a walk with older toddlers and talk about what you see and hear. Ask questions and allow them to ask their own and talk about what they see. A simple walk around the school, the block, the woods or the playground can provide an exploratory play experience for toddlers.
- Read to older toddlers often
    - Extend your reading experiences to include longer and more complex books, and those with repeating phrases. Encourage older toddlers to "read" with you by predicting words and phrases that are coming up in the story and reading them for or with you.

(Zero to Three, 2010, 2012a; 2012b).

How to Choose the Right Toy

I am often asked what toys and materials are best for infants and for toddlers and what the difference between the two is. Almost all toys and materials can be used by infants and toddlers. They are just used differently based on the age of the children. Small pieces should be kept away from infants because they could choke, but any toy that cannot be swallowed or ingested can work for all children in the first three years. But as you have just read, there are specifics that relate to young infants, mobile infants, young toddlers and older toddlers.

It is very important to remember when purchasing toys and materials for infants and toddlers that the more a toy does, the less the child has to (and will) do with it. Toys that are constantly blinking and playing music or have numerous levers and buttons that also blink and make noise are inappropriate. Companies may even proclaim that these toys and materials are developmental and will help infants and toddlers learn. This is false, and they actually tend to have the opposite effect on the children. These types of toys are overstimulating and turn infants and toddlers into passive viewers instead of active players. The most useful toys are those that require infants and toddlers to actively play with and manipulate them. The more infants and toddlers have to use their brains and bodies to play with something, the more they learn.

Toys that engage the five senses are most appropriate for infants, such as rattles, chew toys, soft blocks and board or cloth books. Around 9 months, toys that imitate real life can be integrated into the play area, such as plastic animals, food and tools. Shape sorters, nesting cups and simple puzzles provide beginning problem-solving experiences. Push and pull toys and balls give opportunities to move bodies and be active. As infants reach the end of their first year and move into the toddler years, the same toys and materials apply, but you can now integrate push and pull toys and different-sized and textured balls. Provide materials that allow toddlers to use their hands and fingers to create such as playdough, paint and crayons. Materials that encourage the use of their imagination such as dress up clothes and props, dolls, stuffed animals and animal figures will also integrate nicely into their desire to participate in dramatic and pretend play.

It is also important to remember that your own home is a play experience for infants and toddlers. Kitchen cabinets filled with bowls, cups and spoons as well as baskets of magazines, newspapers and books provide a simple play experience for the children and will occupy their bodies and their minds for long periods of time. There is always a cabinet or two in my kitchen just for infants and toddlers to open, empty and fill up again. In my bathroom and living room, there are baskets of magazines to explore, take out and put away. And a cardboard box can provide hours of fun and exploration! Many materials can also be brought outside, giving the children a different environment to play in.

Here are some toy/material categories that are appropriate for infants and toddlers. You want to look for toys and materials that:

- Are open-ended and can be used in a variety of ways
    - Blocks
    - Nesting blocks and cups
    - Cups and bowls
- Grow with children
    - Cars
    - Trucks
    - Toy animals
    - Toy houses/farms

- Stuffed animals
- Dolls

- Encourage exploration and problem solving
  - Puzzles (handles, no handles, chunky pieces)
  - Shape sorters
  - Blocks
  - Nesting blocks and cups
  - Art materials such as paint, playdough, and different-sized crayons
- Spark imagination
  - Dress up clothes and accessories
  - Play kitchen and kitchen materials (food and tools)
  - Toy tools
  - Cardboard boxes and tubes to turn into any dramatic play object or accessory
- Are real-life materials
  - Dress up clothes, including community workers
  - Pretend food and kitchen tools
  - Brooms, mops and dustpans
  - Toy phones and keys
- Are emergent literacy materials
  - Books
  - Plastic and/or magnetic letters
  - Writing materials and paper
- Encourage activity
  - Different-sized and shaped balls
  - Tricycles and scooters
  - Pull toys
  - Child-sized sport equipment (bowling, basketball, etc.)
  - Child-sized gardening tools
- Require adult participations
  - Board games
  - Memory games

As a caregiver for infants and toddlers, you should ask yourself these questions when choosing toys and materials for the children to play within your classroom:

- Does it meet the needs and strengths of one or more of the children?
- Is it interesting to one or more of the children?

- Can infants, mobile infants and toddlers and children with special needs play with it?
- Is it safe and durable? Washable? Non-toxic?
- Does it support learning in numerous areas of development (cognitive, language, motor, social)?
- Can the children do many different things with it?
- Can it be played with or without adult intervention?

(Guyton, 2011; Zero to Three, 2010, 2012a; 2012b).

What Infants and Toddlers Learn Through Play

Play provides a meaningful context for children to learn new skills and acquire new knowledge. Children explore and learn on their own and with others and are able to extend their learning in any way that their explorations allow them to. Through play, children practice skills, learn new skills, experiment and take risks. It is clear that play affects every area of an infant and toddler's development. In the coming chapters, you will learn about each these areas of development. The chart below summarizes how each area of development is touched upon when children play (Guyton, 2011; Honig, 2007).

Table 7.1 Connecting Development and Learning

Area of Development	What Infants and Toddlers Learn
Emotional Development	Self-control and self-regulation of feelings and behaviors
	Expression of feelings in socially appropriate ways
	Sense of self and identity as a person of worth who deserves to be treated kindly and fairly
	Ability and desire to relate to others
	Security and trust in a community and in relationships
	A fun and enjoyable way to relax, release energy and express themselves
Social Development	Balancing their needs with those of others
	Expression of affection and kindness toward others
	Ability to play with peers cooperatively
	Empathy toward others
	Conflict resolution
	Perspective-taking
	Self-confidence and self-esteem
	Cooperation/sharing/turn-taking
	Leadership
Language Development	Desire and ability to exchange ideas and feelings with others
	Desire and ability to communicate with others (verbally and non-verbally)
	Communication skills
	Vocabulary

(Continued)

168   *Play as Learning*

Table 7.1 Continued

Area of Development	What Infants and Toddlers Learn
Cognitive Development	Curiosity about what "things can do"
	Intentionality in their actions
	Success and failure, and that adults can help
	Knowledge that they can contribute ideas and make decisions (that they are capable and competent)
	Knowledge that they will become more proficient at something in each day of practice
	Creativity and imagination
	Problem solving
	Abstract thinking
	Attention/Concentration
	Persistence
Physical Development	Ability to use both small (fine motor) and large (gross motor) muscles to accomplish tasks
	Stability in their bodies and the ability to use their bodies more effectively
	Physical challenges
	Self-help skills

Source: (Zero to Three, 2010, 2012a; 2012b).

The Concept of "Sharing"

I am often asked by parents and caregivers: "How do I make my kid share?" My answer is always, "You can't *make* him share, but you can show him how it is done. And he still won't really understand the concept until he reaches the end of the toddler years." Toddlers are concerned with their own needs and interests. This "me, me, me" focus is why it is difficult for them to understand the concept of sharing with others.

As children move into the toddler years, they develop attachments to things and people. This attachment is healthy and an important part of a child becoming an emotionally healthy person. It soon translates to certain toys or objects. Toddlers will not want to share these very important objects with others. And they do not understand why someone else wants to play with them. Sharing requires a child to see someone else's viewpoint and have true empathy for another person's desires. This is nearly impossible for toddlers, and caregivers should not expect a child under the age of 2 to have these understandings and easily share. Children at this age and younger engage in *parallel play*, where they play *alongside* someone else but not *with* someone else. Toddlers engaged in parallel play care only about themselves and the materials that they are manipulating and do not acknowledge the other person playing near them. This play soon shifts to associative and then cooperative play with other children, and only then can they see the value of sharing and engaging in play with another person. But do not expect a child to understand the concept of sharing immediately when they turn 2. It is still a learning process and does not happen overnight.

There are ways to foster cooperation between toddlers instead of requiring them to share. Caregivers should not force toddlers to share but rather through guidance and generosity model a cooperative interaction with each other and materials. In doing this, caregivers create attitudes and an environment that encourage children to share. Here are some tips for promoting cooperation and eventually sharing:

- Encourage and model sharing materials with other children and even simply playing together with another child using the same materials. Do this while still respecting the normal possessiveness of a child and either his own toys or the toys in a classroom that he deems valuable and important
- Watch how each toddler operates in a group-play setting. This will help you to learn about each child's play behaviors and preferences, as well as determine what type of guidance he needs in the cooperation/sharing department. A positive and strong self-image are also connected to a child's ability cooperatively play with others
- Model generosity and cooperation. If the children are constantly surrounded by this type of behavior, they tend to do it as well. Teach toddlers to communicate their needs and encourage them to take turns
- Use a timer for materials that are continuously popular and often become the object of sharing disagreements between children. If the timer doesn't work, it may be time to put the object away until everyone calms down. Or, you may need to get more of this object so that more children can enjoy it at the same time
- Play simple "share games" with toddlers to show that objects can be used by everyone. Games hold a toddler's attention and allow them to fully synthesize lessons and concepts. Gather children together and practice giving objects to each other, all along verbalizing "share with ___" as the objects are passed. These are fun and stress-free learning experiences
- Read books to groups of children and encourage individual children to participate throughout the reading. Place a child on each side of you as you read and have them take turns participating
- Encourage simple actions and activities that require two children to participate, such as rolling a ball back and forth or drawing/painting on a large surface together. Each child should have their own art supplies in these cooperative art experiences, but they are creating a work of art together. Two-sided easels are one way to create this experience
- Sit with the children at mealtimes and encourage them to ask each other for materials or food, help each other pour, scoop or serve food, or just simply take turns talking.

(Sears, 2013)

170 Play as Learning

Figure 7.6 Toddlers Shopping Together

For additional material, visit:
www.parentphd.org/infantandtoddlertext/ch7/

Reflection Questions

Read the article "Using Toys to Support Infant-Toddler Learning and Development" in the additional materials for this chapter. Based on the italicized excerpt below, give a specific example of a play experience and indicate which of the bolded skills the children can learn from it.

  "*A child's cognitive development involves thinking skills—the ability to process information to understand how the world works. Toys and play naturally* *provide opportunities for practicing different thinking skills, such as **imitation, cause and effect, problem solving, and symbolic thinking**.*"

- Describe any "happenings" that you have seen in your classroom/field experience.
- Observe a child in an engaged self-chosen task. Describe what the child is doing. What might the child's goals and objectives be?
- Observe and time children's attention spans. What was the longest one? The shortest? What were the children occupied with during these two instances?

Bibliography

Copple, C., & Bredekamp, S. (2010). *Developmentally appropriate practice in early childhood programs: Serving children from birth through age 8* (3rd ed.). Washington, DC: NAEYC.

Gandini, L., & Edwards, C. (2000). *Bambini: The Italian approach to infant/toddler care.* New York, NY: Teachers College Press.

Gerber, M., & Greenwald, D. (2013). *The RIE manual: For parents and professionals.* Los Angeles, CA: Resources for Infant Educarers.

Gerber, M., & Weaver, J. (2002). *Dear parent: Caring for infants with respect.* Los Angeles, CA: Resources for Infant Educarers (RIE).

Gonzalez-Mena, J. (2008). *Diversity in early care and education* (5th ed.). Washington, DC: NAEYC.

Gonzalez-Mena, J., & Eyer, D. (2017). *Infants, toddlers, and caregivers: A curriculum of respectful, responsive, relationship-based care and education* (11th ed.). New York, NY: McGraw Hill.

Guyton, G. (2011). Using toys to support infant-toddler learning and development. *Young Children*, 50–56.

Honig, A. S. (2007, September). Play: Ten power boosts for children's early learning. *Young Children*, 72–78.

Hymes, J. (1981). *Teaching the child under six.* Columbus, OH: Charles E. Merrill.

Lerner, C., & Dombro, A. (2004). *Bringing up baby: Three steps to making good decisions in your child's first years.* Washington, DC: Zero to Three.

Lerner, C., & Greenip, S. (2004). *The power of play.* Washington, DC: Zero to Three. Retrieved from http://main.zerotothree.org/site/DocServer/ThePowerofPlay.pdf

Mooney, C. G. (2009). *Theories of attachment: An introduction to bowlby, ainsworth, gerber, brazelton, kennell, and klaus.* St. Paul, MN: Redleaf Press.

Piaget, J. (1962). *Play, dreams and imitation in childhood.* New York, NY: W.W. Norton and Company.

Rogers, C., & Sawyers, J. (1988). *Play in the lives of children.* Washington, DC: NAEYC.

Sawyers, J., & Rogers, C. (1988). *Helping young children develop through play: A practical guide for parents, caregivers and teachers.* Washington, DC: NAEYC.

Scholastic. (2013). Helping toddlers play together. Retrieved from www.scholastic.com/parents/resources/article/social-emotional-skills/helping-toddlers-play-together

Sears, W. (2013). 11 ways to teach your child to share. Retrieved from www.askdrsears.com/topics/discipline-behavior/morals-manners/11-ways-teach-your-child-share

University of Illinois Extension. (2013). Toddlers exploring the world. Retrieved from http://urbanext.illinois.edu/toddlers/exploring.cfm

Vygotsky, L. S. (1967). Play and its role in the mental development of the child. *Soviet Psychology, 12*, 62–76.

Vygotsky, L. S. (1978). *Mind and society: The development of higher psychological processes*. Cambridge, MA: Harvard University Press.

Wittmer, D., & Peterson, S. (2017). *Infant and toddler development and responsive program planning* (4th ed.). Boston, MA: Pearson.

Zero to Three. (2010). The power of play. Retrieved from www.zerotothree.org/resources/311-the-power-of-play#downloads

Zero to Three. (2012a). Development of play skills. Retrieved from www.zerotothree.org/child-development/play/development_of_play_skills.html

Zero to Three. (2012b). Tips for choosing toys for toddlers. Retrieved from www.zerotothree.org/child-development/play/tips-for-choosing-toys-for.html

8 Attachment

When infants and toddlers have reciprocal and consistent relationships with adults, they feel a sense of security in their life and a trust in the world. Secure attachment relationships teach these children that the world is a responsive place where they can explore safely. They feel power over their lives and a sense of comfort that they are cared for and safe.

These words should seem powerful to you as an infant/toddler caregiver. How amazing is it that the relationships someone has so early in life can set the groundwork for how she approaches the world for the rest of her life? These first relationships with adults are the foundation of attachment, and attachment is the foundation for the rest of life. Infants are born with the ability and desire to attach to their primary caregivers. It is the nature of this attachment (whether it is healthy and secure or unhealthy and insecure) that makes the difference in the life of the child.

What Is Attachment and Why Is It Important?

Attachment is the bond or connection with another person. It is a biologically based behavior system that allows people to experience pleasure and joy with those they are attached to when they interact with them and feel comforted by their nearness during times of stress. The bond of attachment is deep, strong, affectionate and enduring.

In your journal, respond to the following questions, and then keep them in mind as you learn about attachment:

1. What do the words *deep, strong, affectionate* and *enduring* mean to you?
2. What feelings do you have when you read those words out loud?

The formation of attachment relationships begins at birth. Infants are born equipped with a repertoire of behaviors such as crying and certain reflexes that are meant to keep the primary caregiver and some secondary caregivers in close proximity. These behaviors represent infants' desire for attachment. In the beginning these attachment behaviors simply occur and are not always directed at a specific person. This changes quickly, though, to be directed at a specific person. Behavior slowly becomes more intentional, and infants use these behaviors as a means for communication.

Principal attachment is typically formed with the mother or whomever is the primary caregiver. Attachment is shown through comfort when she is close and distress when the infant is separated from her. Attachment behavior can be seen when a child is tired, ill, hungry, alarmed, when he has moved too far away from an attachment figure or when an attachment figure leaves and then returns.

Infants' cries indicate that they need to be cared for in some way and that they are asking a caregiver to come for them and meet that need. They also make eye contact, wrap their hand around your finger if you place it in their hand and turn their heads to the sound of your voice. All of these behaviors are their way of making an attachment and initiating some social interaction. The key to the formation of attachments between parent and infant is the parent's response to the infant's needs and communications. Infants need to know that their parents understand what they need and will respond appropriately. To infants, these primary attachments are as essential to their lives as breathing and eating.

Therefore, it is important to be responsive and emotionally available to infants and work continuously to form a healthy and secure attachment with them. The idea that a caregiver can "spoil" an infant and reinforce needy behavior by attending to all of his needs is a myth. The opposite is, in fact, true: research shows that infants whose needs are met and who are consistently soothed and comforted emerge with stability and independence. The emotional connections established between an infant and caregiver in the first year of life are incredibly important and have lifelong effects on the child.

As infants begin to trust caregivers as those who will care for them and respond to them, they might become distressed when the caregivers leave their sight and may even try to move toward them. These behaviors are clear signs of attachment. The "dance" between caregiver and child as they send signals to each other and interact with each other is the basis for a trusting relationship built on attachment and comfort. This should be the goal of the primary caregivers (parents) of infants, as well as the secondary caregivers (childcare caregivers). Trust brings comfort, and this comfort brings a desire for autonomy (independence) in the toddler years. Autonomy is what drives young children to explore and figure out the world (Benoit, 2004; Zero to Three, 2010).

Different Attachment Relationships and Their Outcomes

Early life experiences play a crucial role in a person's psychological, social and neurological development. The quality of the relationships infants have with their primary caregivers influence the rest of their lives, specifically their sense of selves and their relationships with others. Throughout the first year, infants are building up expectations of the regularity and consistency of what

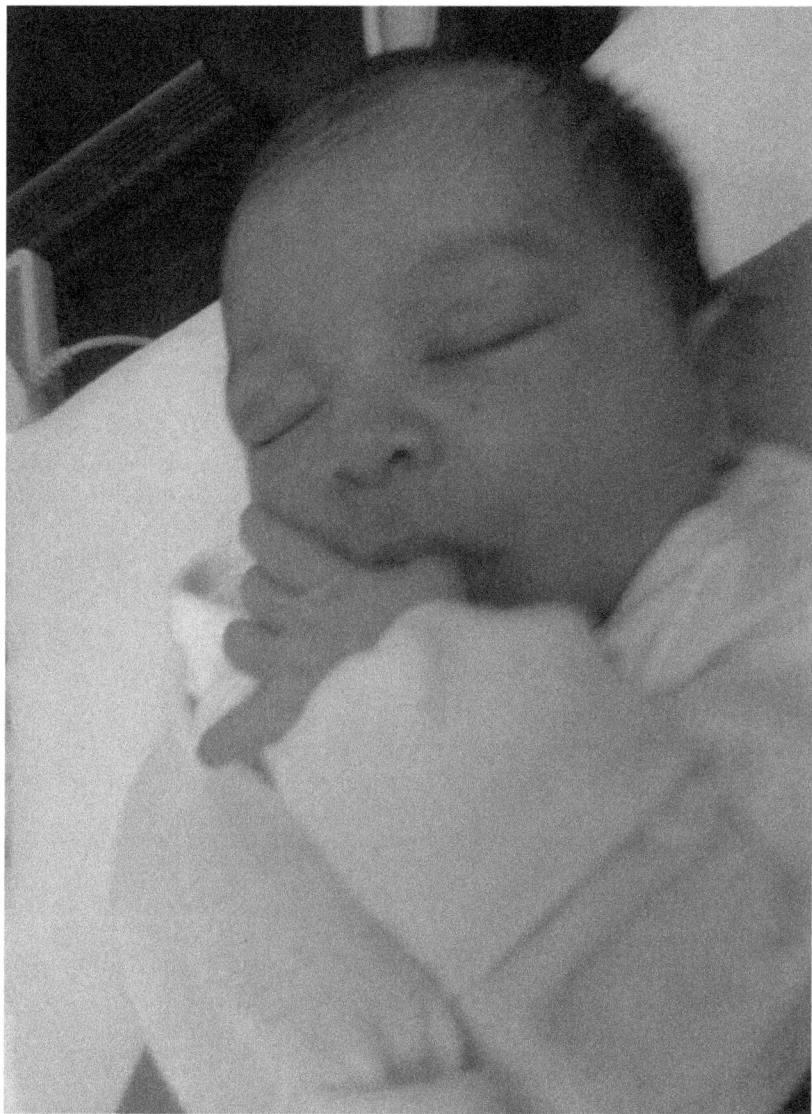

Figure 8.1 Infant Relaxed and Sucking his Thumb

happens to them. What infants feel, know and experience create the "map" by which they navigate the world. Parents who are consistent in their care and react sensitively and reassuringly to their infants create a secure and healthy attachment. Parents who are inconsistent in their care and ignore or reject an infant's needs will create an insecure and unhealthy attachment.

These different attachments have different outcomes for infants. They determine the quality of all of their relationships, how they view the world and the deepness of their lives. Infants who have positive and healthy early relationships will gain key developmental advantages, including a healthy overall psychological health and well-being.

Secure, Healthy Attachments

Infants who have healthy and secure attachments to their parents and/or caregivers know that these people are a source of comfort for them. These infants will explore and play with the knowledge that these caregivers are always nearby. Their caregivers are available for comfort and support while at the same time give them the freedom to be curious and explore the world in safe ways. These infants miss their caregivers when they leave and are relieved when they return. This trusting and secure relationship sets the stage for a confident, competent and caring adult. Their initial dependence on their caregivers for comfort teaches them that the world is a safe place. This leads to their independence and desire to explore and play on their own.

Children who had sensitive, responsive and loving caregivers who consistently met their needs when they were infants have a stronger chance of leading a well-balanced and fulfilling life. These children are more able to

Figure 8.2 Mother Closely Interacting With Infant

skillfully and happily negotiate their presence in the world. Specifically, these children are shown to have higher self-confidence and a keen sense of independence and self-management skills. They manage stress easier, are able to form and maintain healthy relationships and perform better in school (Ainsworth, 1973, 1985; Bowlby, 1969).

Insecure, Unhealthy Attachments

Infants who have unhealthy and insecure attachments to their parents and/or caregivers are unsure if these people are a source of comfort or if they will respond to their needs. Their caregivers are often either uncomfortable with too much closeness and neediness or too much distance and independence. Initially, these infants will still often try to maintain some connection with their unresponsive caregivers and attempt to get their attention. But eventually they will give up. Infants in these types of relationships are either overdependent (frightened when their caregivers leave) or inappropriately independent (barely notice when their caregivers leave). In general, they tend to act scared or chaotic around their parents or primary caregivers. This insecure relationship sets the stage for future anxiety, anger and depression.

Children who had inconsistent, unpredictable and unloving caregivers tend to have difficulty managing their emotions and relationships with other people. They may become unmotivated children who exhibit social problems such as acting out and disobedience. They cannot easily identify and communicate their feelings and have a difficult time establishing and maintaining social relationships. These children are at risk for a myriad of social and emotional problems including depression, anxiety, addiction and aggression.

So far in this chapter, you have read about what attachment is and why it is important and what the difference is between secure/healthy attachment and insecure/unhealthy attachment. You might be wondering how we know all of this and how we have figured out what these different attachments look like in both process and result. John Bowlby and Mary Ainsworth are two key attachment theorists and researchers, and their work has determined much of the information you have read. Along with their work, brain research has also led to some conclusions about attachment. The next sections will summarize all of this information and provide you with a clear understanding as to why early childhood educators are so in favor of establishing secure and healthy attachments with infants, toddlers and young children (Ainsworth, 1973, 1985; Benoit, 2004; Bowlby, 1969; Bretherton, 1992; Brodie, 2012; Cherry, 2013).

Bowlby's Theory of Attachment

John Bowlby was a psychoanalyst who believed that all mental and behavioral problems could be attributed to experiences in early childhood. Bowlby's *theory of attachment* proposed that children are born biologically pre-programmed to form attachments with others in order to survive. Infants are born with the ability to display innate behaviors such as crying, smiling, reaching for/crawling to their caregivers as ways to ensure proximity and contact with the mother or mother figure (primary caregiver). Bowlby believed that attachment behaviors are instinctive and are activated by conditions such as separation, insecurity and fear. Fear of strangers is a survival mechanism instilled by nature. He hypothesized that *both* mothers and infants have a biological need to stay in contact with each other.

Bowlby believed that infants have an innate need to attach to one main attachment figure. While he did not rule out the possibility of other attachment figures, he did believe that there should be one primary bond that is more important than any other. This primary bond is typically with the mother and is completely different from all other relationships that a child will have. This attachment relationship leads to the development of an *internal working model*, which is a child's framework for understanding himself, others and the world. This model is a representation of others as trustworthy, the self as valuable and the self effectively interacting with others. It guides further social and emotional behavior.

Bowlby argued that children should be continuously cared for by this primary attachment figure for at least the first two years of life, calling this period in a child's life a *critical period*. If this care is disrupted or broken during this critical period, Bowlby believe that there would be long-term negative consequences for the child. His *maternal deprivation hypothesis* stated that this disruption could be separation from or loss of the mother, or simply a failure to develop an attachment. The long-term consequences of maternal deprivation could include delinquency, lower intelligence, aggression, depression, antisocial behavior or lack of ability to show affection or concern for others.

Bowlby believed that there are four distinguishing characteristics of attachment:

- Proximity Maintenance—the desire to be near the people we are attached to
- Safe Haven—returning to the attachment figure for comfort and safety in the face of a fear or threat
- Secure Base—the attachment figure acts as a base of security from which the child can explore the surrounding environment
- Separation Distress—anxiety that occurs in the absence of the attachment figure

Bowlby believed that attachment to a caregiver has profound implications for the child's feelings of security and capacity to form trusting relationships. He stated that attachment develops in four phases, and that each person moves through these phases when forming attachments.

In the Preattachment phase (birth to 12 weeks), infants use their built-in signals of grasping, crying and gazing into eyes to communicate and bond with their caregivers. Caregivers should remain close to infants as often as possible and provide nurturance and comfort when necessary.

Infants then move into the Making the Attachment phase (10 weeks to 6–8 months), where they respond differently to a familiar caregiver than to strangers. Infants will coo, smile and babble for their familiar caregiver. They will give a long stare, show fear and show distress to a stranger. It is in this phase that a sense of trust in infants' caregivers develops.

Next, infants progress into the Clear Attachment phase (8 months to 18 months–2 years). Infants will also become toddlers during this phase. It is in this phase that an infant/toddler's attachment to his primary caregiver is evident. Infants/toddlers will use their primary caregivers as a *secure base* from which to explore the world that they can return to for a "check in" or for comfort. Infants/toddlers will also display *separation anxiety*, where they display attachment behaviors as a way to show they are distressed at their caregivers leaving them.

Finally, toddlers reach the point where this is a Formation of a Reciprocal Relationship (18 months to 2 years and on). In this phase, toddlers show a rapid growth in their representation and language. This progression in their development enables the children to understand their caregivers coming and going, and they are able to predict their return. The children's separation protest declines, and they are better able to handle time away from their attached caregivers.

According to Bowlby, after progressing through these four phases, children construct a lasting and loving tie to their primary caregiver. They are then able to use this bond as a secure base in that caregiver's absence. It becomes a large part of their personality and becomes their set of expectations about the availability of attachment figures, how likely they are to provide support during stressful times, and their overall interaction with those figures. This becomes the guide, or *internal working model*, for all future close relationships for the rest of their lives (Bowlby, 1969; Bretherton, 1992; Brodie, 2012; Cherry, 2013).

Mary Ainsworth and Attachment Theory

Mary Ainsworth worked closely with John Bowlby and developed a procedure for observing and assessing the quality of attachment between caregivers and children, particularly mothers and children. This procedure, called the *Strange Situation*, allowed Ainsworth to develop three categories of attachment relationships: Secure, anxious-ambivalent and anxious-avoidant. The *Strange Situation* is a sequence of episodes that are meant to activate the attachment system at a progressively higher intensity (unfamiliar environment, arrival of a stranger, separation from mother and reunion with mother). It involves a child playing for 20 minutes while caregivers and strangers enter and leave the room. The procedure then examines the balance between attachment behavior and exploratory behavior, specifically when the balance is shifted away from exploratory and toward attachment.

Specifically, the sequence of events is as follows:

1. Caregiver and infant enter a room and are alone
2. Infant plays and explores; caregiver does not participate
3. Stranger enters the room, converses with caregiver and the approaches the infant
4. Caregiver leaves the room (first separation)
5. Stranger attempts to play with/interact with the infant
6. Caregiver returns and comforts the infant (first reunion); Stranger leaves
7. Caregiver leaves again (second separation)
8. Infant is left alone
9. Stranger returns and again attempts to play with/interact with and comfort the infant
10. Caregiver returns, greets and picks up infant (second reunion); stranger leaves

Throughout the procedure, the infant's behavior is observed. Specifically, the infant's amount of exploration and reactions to the departure and return of the caregiver are observed. Based on these behaviors, infants are categorized into one of the three groups. Ainsworth stated that a successful outcome of the procedure is a secure attachment, while an unsuccessful outcome is either anxious-ambivalent or anxious-avoidant, either of which are insecure attachments.

Securely attached infants will explore and play freely while their caregiver is present. They will engage with strangers while their caregiver is in the room but not when the caregiver is not present. These infants become upset when their caregiver leaves and are happy to see her return. *Anxious-ambivalent (resistant) attached infants* are anxious of strangers and of exploration even when their caregiver is present. They are distressed when their caregiver leaves, and although they will seek closeness with her when she returns, they will also be resentful or resistant of that attention. *Anxious-avoidant attached infants* will avoid their caregivers and show little or no stress when they come and go. Strangers are treated no differently than their caregivers, and they will not explore a great deal no matter who is in the room. The following chart delineates each of the behaviors of the three types of attached infants:

Table 8.1 Three Attachment Relationships and Their Corresponding Behaviors

	Secure Attachment	*Anxious- Ambivalent (Resistant) Attachment*	*Anxious-Avoidant Attachment*
Separation Anxiety	Distressed when mother leaves	Signs of intense distress when mother leaves	No sign of distress when mother leaves

	Secure Attachment	Anxious-Ambivalent (Resistant) Attachment	Anxious-Avoidant Attachment
Stranger Anxiety	Avoidant of stranger when alone but friendly when mother is present	Avoids stranger and shows fear of stranger at all times	OK with stranger present and plays normally
Reunion Behavior	Positive and happy when mother returns	Approaches mother but resists contact (may push her away)	Shows little interest when mother returns
Other Behaviors	Uses mother a safe base for exploration	Cries more and explores less than secure and avoidant infants	Both mother and stranger can equally comfort the infant

Source: (Ainsworth, 1973, 1985; Bretherton, 1992; Brodie, 2012; Cherry, 2013).

Ainsworth further suggested that secure attachment is associated with sensitive and responsive primary care, while insecure attachment is associated with inconsistent or unresponsive primary care. Her findings provided the first evidence for Bowlby's attachment theory. Securely attached children have a positive working model of themselves and high self-esteem and look positively upon others and themselves. These children are socially and emotionally stable. They have the ability to establish and maintain trusting and lasting relationships and will seek out social relationships and support from others. They tend to be comfortable sharing their feelings with others.

Ambivalent/resistant children have a negative view of themselves and do not express emotions appropriately. They are reluctant to become close to others, worry that others do not love them, and become distraught when relationships end. Avoidant children think of themselves as unworthy and unacceptable. They may have problems with intimacy and invest very little emotion into social relationships. These children have a great deal of difficulty sharing their thoughts and feelings with others. Both of these groups of children have social and emotional problems.

As children approach their second birthday, the Strange Situation would be less stressful because attachment behaviors are aroused less intensely at this age. Children may be distressed when separated from their attached caregivers, but the reunion changes to more recognition and less physical seeking of contact or comfort.

Ainsworth conducted other research studies of mother/infant attachment along with developing the Strange Situation procedure. Her studies of mother/infant attachment revealed that the mothers of securely attached infants are more accessible and positively responsive to their infants. They were able to accurately read the signals of their infants and respond promptly and appropriately. They were less rejecting, interfering and ignoring. These positive responses included picking up the baby when she cried and giving the baby close physical contact. Sensitive responsiveness to infants' signals fostered cooperative obedience with demands.

Ainsworth concluded that securely attached infants are able to form the "working model" that Bowlby emphasized and see their mothers as someone they could rely on to be accessible and responsive. They could leave her to explore and play, and, when separated, they knew she was still available for comfort and contact. Ainsworth emphasized that cultural context must be considered when assessing attachment and that individual differences in maternal behavior have different effects on infant behavior.

Ainsworth's Strange Situation procedure has been criticized for not taking other factors into account when analyzing infants' behaviors, such as the short timeframe of the procedure, the fact that the study was primarily with mothers and their children only and that many variables such as the mood of the mother and child and cultural variation can alter the infants' behaviors. But support for the basic concepts delineated from the procedure remains (Ainsworth, 1973, 1985; Bretherton, 1992; Brodie, 2012; Cherry, 2013).

Brain Research and Attachment

Brain research has allowed us to come to understand how infants learn and, consequently, how important early experiences are. It is important for parents and caregivers of infants and toddlers to be aware of the specifics of brain development for infants and toddlers and how to provide the experiences and environments to promote brain growth.

Figure 8.3 Caregiver Reading With Toddlers

There is a direct relationship between the care an infant receives and his or her brain growth. Responsive and positive experiences are very important in an infant's early development. It is these early experiences that influence social and emotional brain functions. It is in the first year that infants' emotion-focused right brain is growing rapidly, and this growth will slow down in the second year of life. While infants will not remember specific experiences from this first year, they will rely on those experiences to retrieve emotions. This finding provides further evidence of the importance of secure early attachments beginning at birth. A lack of nurturance in infancy and frequent stress has been shown to affect brain functioning, and it is hypothesized that these negative experiences can lead to depression, loss of impulse control and heightened aggression in later life (Zero to Three, 2010).

Brain Growth and Development

The basic building blocks of the brain are called *neurons*. Each neuron has an *axon* that sends energy and impulses to other neurons. Neurons also have many *dendrites* that receive the impulses from other neurons. The dendrites grow and branch out to receive signals from other neurons. These connections are called *synapses*. Synapses that are used often and are reinforced then mature and become part of the brain's circuitry. Early life experiences help to form these stable connections.

In the early years, the brain produces about twice as many synapses as it will need. By age 2, the number of synapses is similar to an adult. By age 3, the child has twice as many synapses as an adult. This stays stable for about ten years, at which point about half of the synapses have been eliminated. The brain will eliminate all unnecessary (unused or undeveloped) synapses.

Mirror neurons are neurons that fire when a human acts and when that human observes another human performing the same action. This is similar to an infant imitating the mouth movements of a caregiver. This behavior is an early attachment behavior that infants use to either get food or to socially interact. When infants experience secure attachments, *neurotransmitters* are released in the brain and induce a sense of well-being.

Brain development research indicates that if quality and positive early experiences are repeated, the brain forms stable *neural pathways*. These stable neural pathways get stronger as young children have experiences where they need to use their brain (such as exploring a new toy and figuring it out). Strong neural pathways allow signals to travel quickly, and the child can solve problems quickly.

In general, brain research shows that nature (genes) and nurture (environment) are constantly interacting. Infants and toddlers participate in their own brain development by signaling their needs. Parents and caregivers of infants and toddlers participate in the children's brain development by consistently responding to those needs. Strong neural pathways are created by stable experiences and reciprocal and responsive relationships. Therefore, secure and

184 *Attachment*

healthy attachment relationships lead to healthy brain growth (Berk, 2012, 2015, 2018a, 2018b).

Toddlers and Attachment

While the majority of attachment research and information focuses on the first year of life, toddlers are still actively involved in their attachment relationships. These relationships are still with their caregivers, and also extend to comfort objects.

Toddlers will have strong attachments to comfort or transitional objects such as blankets, stuffed animals and other snuggly items. These provide a sense of comfort and security to them. And as you read in chapter five, these objects also have a particular scent that is comforting. Toddlers' dependence on the objects for comfort will reach its peak in the second year. Comfort objects are like an extension of home and a little part of Mommy or Daddy (or another primary caregiver) that travels with the toddler into unfamiliar territory. The objects offer comfort, reassurance or support when the toddler needs it. Do not expect toddlers to give them up and definitely do not pressure them to do so.

Toddlers will also continue their attachment relationships with their caregivers. Toddlers who have secure attachments to their caregivers may have

Figure 8.4 Toddler Attachment Object

difficulty with separation. They have a desire to stay close to these important people as they navigate the world with their new toddler skills and abilities. It is important to always allow toddlers to have separation feelings. If they show distress, sadness or even anger at the fact that they must separate from their important caregiver, allow them to express these feelings in a safe way. Non-primary caregivers should stay close to show the toddler that they are also safe and comforting people and be ready to engage the child in something of interest as a way to transition them into the classroom or any new environment. Encourage parents to make eye contact and physical contact with their toddler to say goodbye and then promptly leave so that the toddler can begin his transition. Parents should be discouraged from "sneaking away" in order to avoid getting their toddler upset. It is far worse for a distressed toddler to look up and realize that her parent has disappeared than to deal with the fact that the parent has just said goodbye and walked out of the room.

When teaching toddlers, I had a few who had difficulty transitioning into the classroom. One girl would cry and hold on to her parent, while the other would stand silently in the doorway and refuse to enter. My daily approach was always the same with both girls; I would walk up to them, say hello and welcome them to our classroom. I would then tell them about the explorations we had available to start the day. During the first few months when we were working on their transitions into the classroom, I made sure to have something each day that both girls would be interested in. One loved the sensory tub, and the other loved paint. After my greeting, the parents would then begin their transition out of the classroom. I would take over their children's care by sitting near them. I would stay physically present through any emotions. When the first girl calmed and the second girl took her first step into the classroom, I would remind them of the explorations and then engage myself in them. I would continue to check back with both girls while still playing. Eventually both girls transitioned into the room easily. Sometimes this would take five minutes. Sometimes it took 20 minutes. But I was consistent every day. I will never forget the day that the first girl said goodbye to her parent first and went to play, and other girl walked right into the classroom, not even stopping in the doorway (Briody & McGarry, 2005).

Attachment Issues

While the theories and conclusions about attachment primarily focus on relationships with parents and primary caregivers, the concepts can and should be translated to childcare settings. Children who spend time in childcare need caregivers who understand them and respond to them. This continuity of care provides stability and comfort for the children. Utilizing a Primary Caregiving System in a childcare setting can help to promote secure attachment. Infants have one caregiver who knows their communications and needs and will appropriately and consistently respond to them.

Caregivers in infant/toddler settings may encounter an infant who has either no attachment to a primary caregiver or one of the negative attachments described in this chapter. This may have occurred because the parent or primary caregiver does not know how to effectively respond to or form secure attachment relationships with her infant or because the infant was exposed to something in utero that is affecting his attachment behaviors. Whatever the reason, it is important for infant/toddler caregivers to understand attachment theory so they can work to remedy these delays. Caregivers can work with families to promote attachment by teaching them how to read and respond to infant's cues. Together parents and caregivers can spend time with the infant and learn about them. Together they can form secure attachments with the infant.

Caregivers should be supportive and persistent with these infants to help them attach and should work diligently with those whom they do not "naturally" attach to. You must find way to reduce stimulation for infants who are too active and enhance stimulation for those who are too passive. Hold infants who reject you and work daily on communicating with them and forming a secure relationship. Without help, children with no secure attachments or negative attachments may fail to thrive, become passive or lack trust in the world. As you have read, these negative effects have strong implications for the rest of the child's life. If infants have been exposed to a lack of consistency in care, they may have already given up on forming any secure attachments with anyone. Infants who have been exposed to alcohol or drugs may not exhibit attachment behaviors or have other attachment problems. This makes the job of a caregiver even harder but not impossible. These children need individually designed care and require caregivers to spend time "teaching" the infants how to attach using attachment behaviors.

If you find that the child does not respond to your interventions or your desire to form a secure attachment, outside help might be necessary. In chapter four, you read about communicating with families and creating an IFSP. These collaborations lead to Early Intervention Services. Early Intervention services are available to all children ages 0–5. It is the process of identifying young children with disabilities or who are at risk of developing disabilities. After identification, early intervention specialists develop a plan that supports the children and helps them to reach their full potential. The plan is solely focused on the developmental needs of the child.

Early Intervention supports young children with disabilities early in their development. Accurate assessment of children recognizes the difference between temporary and permanent delays. The earlier a disability or delay is identified and a plan is put in place to combat it, the better chance the child has of learning to overcome it. If a disability is temporary, the child can learn to completely overcome it. If the delay is permanent, the child can learn to compensate for it with other abilities. Early Intervention specialists work closely with the families of the children to find the most appropriate resources and develop the most appropriate plan with the most potential for success.

Attachment Disorders

Children who have extreme difficulty forming lasting relationships are considered to have an attachment disorder. These children do not know how to be affectionate with others, fail to develop a conscience and do not trust others. They experience anger and have difficulty experience love or guilt. Any of the following conditions during a child's first three years of life can put them at risk for attachment disorders:

- Unwanted pregnancy
- Exposure to trauma, drugs or alcohol in the womb
- Physical, emotional or sexual abuse
- Extreme poverty
- Extreme neglect (this includes not responding to crying as an infant)
- Severe or prolonged separation from the primary caregiver (illness, death, adoption—this can include forced removal from an abusive home)
- Ongoing pain or prolonged hospitalization from illnesses
- Childcare caregivers who don't bond with them or work toward attachment relationships
- Having a chronically depressed mother or parents with mental illness or addictions
- Frequent moves or placements (foster care or failed adoptions)
- Caring for a baby on a schedule developed by the parents without consideration for the child

The following are some symptoms or complications of attachment disorder:

- Superficially engaging/charming
- Acts entitled
- Lack of eye contact
- Affectionate with strangers
- Not affectionate with primary caregivers/parents
- Primary caregivers/parents seem hostile and/or angry
- Destructive or cruel to self, others (people and animals) and objects
- Lying
- Stealing
- Hyperactive/no impulse control/persistent chatter and abnormal speech patterns
- Delayed learning or physical growth
- Relationship, eating, temper or anger problems
- Anxiety
- Academic problems
- Drug or alcohol addiction
- Low self-esteem
- Delinquent or anti-social behavior

- No conscience
- Abnormal eating patterns
- Lack of or poor relationships with peers
- Preoccupation with fire, blood/gore
- Demanding and clingy
- False accusations of abuse

Reactive Attachment Disorder is when a person has serious problems in emotional attachments. RAD usually presents itself by age 5 but can be noticed as early as age 1. Concerns such as severe colic, feeding difficulties/failure to gain weight, detached/unresponsive behavior, difficulty being comforted, preoccupied/defiant behavior, resistant/withdrawn in social interactions and inappropriate familiarity or closeness with strangers may be a sign of RAD.

Most children with RAD have had severe problems or disruptions in their relationships during the first years of life. Physical abuse, neglect, inadequate care or traumatic loss of or change to their primary caregiver are suggested to be possible causes of RAD. Treatment focuses on understanding and strengthening the relationship between the child and the primary caregivers. Not every child who is exposed to these unfortunate circumstances develops RAD. Many are resilient, and it is not fully understood why some children develop the disorder and others do not (The Mayo Clinic Staff, 2013; Thomas, 2013).

Attachment Parenting

The final section of this chapter discusses the Attachment Parenting style of caring for children. Attachment Parenting is rooted in attachment theory. Attachment theory states that infants instinctively seek closeness to a secure attachment figure from birth. This closeness is important in order for the infant to feel safe emotionally as well as for food and survival. Based on this theory, Attachment Parenting states that infants learn to trust the world and can thrive when their needs are consistently met.

Many of the strategies of Attachment Parenting are appropriate for caregivers. An understanding of this perspective on caring for children will allow anyone who cares for infants and toddlers to create a responsive and caring relationship with the children. You may like or agree with some or all of the Attachment Parenting strategies. As a mother, I chose those that were right for me and my children and believe fully in the philosophy of the parenting style.

William Sears is the "Dr. Sears" who writes frequently online and in books about every aspect of raising and caring for young children. William and his wife Martha coined the term "Attachment Parenting" to describe what they considered to be a highly responsive and attentive style of caring for children. It is the oldest way of caring for infants and focuses on following the infant's cues and responding to them. Parents are attentive to their infant's needs; as the infant grows, parents become more of an expert on reading them.

This expertise allows parents to respond appropriately. Dr. Sears stresses that Attachment Parenting is the best investment a parent could make in their child and themselves as parents.

Attachment Parenting is about balance. Parents are neither indulgent nor permissive but rather attentive. The close attachment that forms between parent and child teaches the child to be independent with the comfort that he is cared for and loved. Parents shape their infant's behavior through this close relationship and appropriate responses. There is a "mutual giving" between parent and child; the more parents give to their infants, the more the infants give back to them. Both parties are active members of the Attachment Parenting relationship, and both influence behaviors and decisions.

Attachment fosters independence, so the fear that Attachment Parenting will make a child overly dependent or manipulative is emphatically wrong. Attachment Parenting implies that parents respond appropriately to their infants. Attachment parents hold their infants often and feed them on demand, and some sleep with them. These behaviors produce positive and secure results for the infants as they grow up and make the parents feel connected to their children. Attachment enhances development.

Attachment Parenting involves both physical and emotional closeness between parent and child. While the mother is typically the parent who becomes the most "attached" to an infant, Dr. Sears urges there to be shared Attachment Parenting with the father and other primary caregivers. Attachment Parenting is about knowing each individual infant well and responding to her using that knowledge and your instincts as a parent. As a caregiver, it is important for you to form a relationship with the parent as well as the infant so you can emulate any Attachment Parenting tools in your childcare environment. Attachment Parenting is an avenue through which you get to know the infant and your own unique and sensitive caregiving style.

Dr. Sears emphasizes that Attachment Parenting is truly the "easiest" parenting style. Attached parents truly know their infants and are strongly connected to them. This connection gives parents the ability to read and respond to their infants. As these infants grow into toddlers, children, teenagers and then adults, parents will be able to see things from their point of view. Parenting is ultimately easier from birth on through the child's life.

Attached parents become increasingly sensitive to their infants. They learn their infants' communications and how each one is a cry for a different need to be met. Their infants' cries bother them; they want to comfort infants. Attached parents gradually become more skilled at anticipating their infants' needs, and their responses become more intuitive and natural the more they bond with infants. This process can be emulated with caregivers in childcare settings.

If caregivers understand the premise of Attachment Parenting and work to emulate the practices that are possible for them, their relationship with the infants whom they care for will be stronger and healthier. While caregivers do not take the place of parents, if they spend a significant amount of time with

190 Attachment

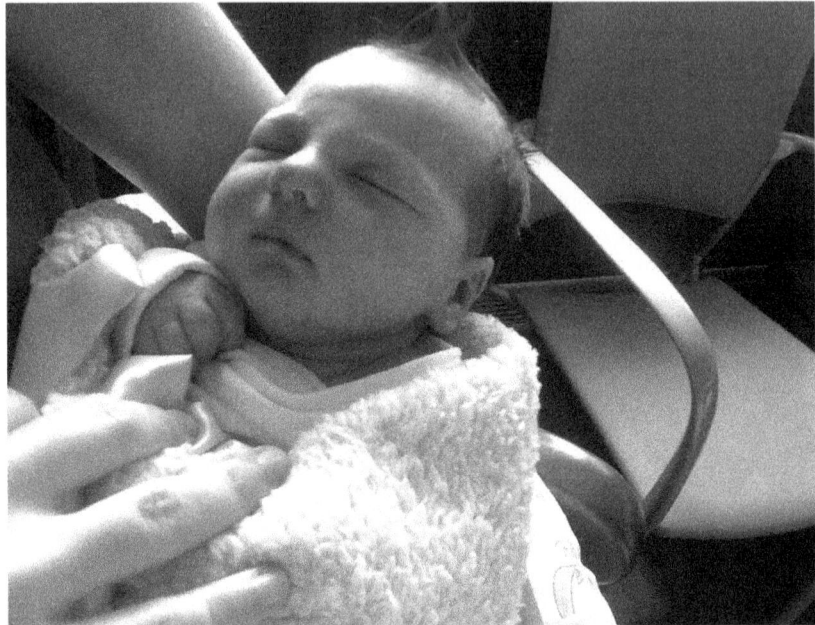

Figure 8.5 Infant Sleeping in Mother's Arms

infants, those infants should feel as though they are bonded to them as well (Sears, 2013a; 2013b).

The Baby B's

Dr. Sears developed seven Attachment Parenting tools called "The Baby B's." All of these tools can be used by parents of infants. Some of these tools can be used by caregivers of infants. The Baby B's are focused on promoting a trusting and intuitive relationship between parents and their infants. It promotes an emotional closeness that allows parents to truly know and understand their infants, so they can appropriately respond to their needs.

The Baby B's are recommended tools that each parent or caregiver should individualize to fit their needs and situation. This next section will describe each tool and then provide additional information about how to alter the tool to fit different lifestyles and situations. The idea is for you to understand the tool and then mold it to fit your own parenting or caregiving situation.

Birth bonding focuses on the important bonding that should occur in the days and weeks after an infant's birth. This is the period of time where both mother and baby want to be close to one another. Dr. Sears emphasizes that a close attachment after birth allows what he considers to be the natural and biological attachment behaviors of the infant and the intuitive and biological caregiving behaviors of the mother to unite. If an infant must be kept apart from the mother in the beginning of life for medical reasons, birth bonding can occur as soon as the two are united.

Breastfeeding is promoted for both its bonding and health benefits for both mother and infant. Breastfeeding helps a mother to read her infant's cues and respond with food and comfort. It also releases hormones in the mother that help her bond to her infant. And as you read in chapter two, breastmilk contains brain-building nutrients that are very beneficial to an infant's growth and development. Breastfeeding promotes a healthy immune system and ensures constant closeness with the mother because of the frequency of nursing. This closeness helps an infant naturally transition into life outside of the womb.

Babywearing focuses on caregivers carrying their infants close to their bodies often. Infants who are carried are less fussy and more alert. This quiet alertness is when an infant is looking at and listening to the world around them. These moments are when they learn about the world. Caregivers who carry infants close to their bodies are more sensitive to infants' needs, behaviors and communications. The infants feel a sense of closeness and comfort as they try to figure out the complicated world around them. While many infants enjoy close physical contact, some may also enjoy sitting in a stroller in certain environments so they can see the world. Adhering to this preference is just as important.

Bedding close to baby refers to co-sleeping with infants. Co-sleeping allows parents to reconnect with their infant at night and teaches infants that sleeping is safe and comfortable. The idea is to promote closeness, and this looks different for every family. Some parents have the infant sleep in the bed with them, while others may have a crib attached to the side of the bed. Still others may have infants sleep in a bassinette or crib in the room near them. When the infant (or toddler) transitions into his own room is based on each individual family.

Belief in the language of your baby's cry focuses on understanding and responding to an infant's cries. Sensitively responding to an infant's cries builds trust and this trust will influence the infant's behaviors for the rest of his life. Infants cry to communicate, and sensitive caregivers learn what different cries mean and how to respond to each one with different caregiving practices (feeding, changing, comforting, etc.).

Beware of baby trainers simply means do not listen to people who tell you to put an infant on a schedule that you as the adult determines. Caregivers should listen to and respond to infants and follow infants' cues for hunger, sleep and comfort. Together you establish a "routine" or "schedule" that works best for the infant. This is done keeping the infant close and devoting time and attention to him in order to fully understand him. In short, watch the infant, not the clock.

Balance refers to the balance you must establish between taking care of yourself and taking care of your infant. Parents and caregivers should respond to the genuine and age-appropriate needs of infants and children and use gentle guidance that is logical and appropriate for each child. Parents and caregivers must also have age-appropriate expectations for infants and toddlers. When you understand every aspect of development for this age group, creating age-appropriate expectations is easy (Sears, 2013a; 2013b).

Benefits of Attachment Parenting

There are many benefits to parent and child when Attachment Parenting tools are used. Attachment Parenting forms a strong relationship between parent and child. There is mutual giving, shaping and sensitivity between parent and child. Attached parents and children enjoy each other and their time together. They smile, gaze and physically connect with each other on a daily basis. Breastfeeding also produces hormones in the mother that make her feel calm and loving, which only increases the bond. Parent and child also shape each other's behavior. They act, talk and think at each other's level and in ways that ensure communication and understanding. A mutual sensitivity to each other's needs forms as well.

Attachment Parenting promotes independence in children. Forming strong and secure relationships with infants teaches them that they can trust the world and that the world is a safe place. This understanding gives them the confidence to go out and explore the world because they know that they are safe. Attached parents almost seem to add energy to their children's explorations. When in unfamiliar situations, the bond with a parent gives children the confidence to explore and handle the situation. The constant emotional availability of the parent provides trust and comfort, which leads to independence and the ability to be alone with the child.

Attachment Parenting has also been shown to improve behavior, development and intelligence. Attached infants cry less because they feel like their cues are read and communications are understood. They feel secure and valued. When infants cry less, they have more time to be quietly alert, where they take in and learn about the world. These infants are more receptive to interacting with and learning about the world. Their energy is focused on growing, developing and interacting with the environment. And since the brain grows more during infancy than at any other time in life, the more time they have to interact with and learn about the world, the more their brain grows. Research has shown that the most powerful enhancers of brain development are the quality of the parent/infant attachment and the response of the caregiving environment to infants' cues and communications. Attachment Parenting "feeds" the brain with the right kind of stimulation at a critical time for brain growth. When caregivers utilize the tools of Attachment Parenting, they are creating the optimal condition for learning to occur.

Here are some specific benefits of utilizing Attachment Parenting tools:
Benefits of Attachment Parenting for infants include:

- Trust
- Competency

- Growth and behavior are appropriate
- Better organized
- Learns language easily
- Healthy independence
- Learns intimacy and how to give/receive love

Figure 8.6 An Example of Babywearing

Benefits of Attachment Parenting for parents include:

- Confidence
- Sensitivity
- Strong ability and intuition when responding to cues and temperaments
- Discipline/guidance is easier
- Become keep observers of people and behaviors
- Know infants' competencies and preferences
- Can clearly and effectively navigate all of the parenting advice out there and decide what works best for them and their family

The relationship between parents and infants also benefits from Attachment Parenting. Both parents and infants experience a mutual trust, sensitivity, giving and shaping of behaviors. They feel strongly connected to each other, which allows them to actively interact and understand each other. Both parties tend to be more flexible with daily life decisions and experiences (Sears, 2013a; 2013b; www.attachmentparenting.org).

Different Perspectives on Attachment Parenting

While no one would argue that close emotional bonding with infants is a negative thing, there are criticisms of some aspects of Attachment Parenting. As I stated earlier, it is important for parents to figure out what is best for them and their children. Understanding the Attachment Parenting tools allows parents to make these decisions. Caregivers of infants and toddlers should also understand Attachment Parenting so that they have knowledge of the importance of closeness and consistent responsiveness to infants and toddlers.

One of the big concerns is bed-sharing or co-sleeping and its link to Sudden Infant Death Syndrome (SIDS). Infants can suffocate in beds with blankets and mattresses made for adults, and there is the possibility of adults rolling onto infants in their sleep. Attachment Parenting International has addressed this concern by providing rules for safe bed-sharing. Check out the section of their website that focuses on safe sleep and infants: www.attachmentparenting.org/infantsleepsafety/.

Attachment relationships have also changed since attachment theory's development in the 1950s. Many children are now in childcare, so they have multiple caregivers in their lives. Think about a child who goes to daycare five days per week for eight or more hours per day. The caregivers who care for him must be considered primary caregivers because of the sheer amount of time they spend with him. But attachment theory is only based on parent/child relationships. The caregiver/child relationship must be analyzed and reflected in the theory as well. Developmental psychologists also argue that the ability to form healthy attachment relationships is affected by school and social relationships just as much as children's early childhood experiences.

Since attachment theory focuses on the critical period of infancy as the time to form secure attachments that affect the child for the rest of his life, there is the threat of severely maladapted children if they don't form these secure relationships early on. Recent research, though, has found that attachment issues can be changed with intervention and therapy. Children who have insecure attachments early on are no longer doomed for the rest of their lives. Based on my own experiences I know this to be true. I have worked with 1-year-old children who never experienced secure attachments, and through intervention, love and time, I was able to teach them that the world is a safe place that they could trust.

For additional material, visit:
www.parentphd.org/infantandtoddlertext/ch8/

Reflection Questions

Read the article "Caring Relationships: The Heart of Early Brain Development" in the additional materials for this chapter. Then, imagine you are approached by a new parent of an infant. This parent doesn't know what to do to help his/her infant's brain grow at the optimal level. S/he has no idea what to do with this baby! What would you say to him/her? Remember that this isn't a practitioner. What you say has to be clear and make sense to a non-ECE-educated person. Be sure to address the following:

- Describe the difference between a secure/healthy attachment and an insecure/unhealthy attachment.
- What are at least two adult behaviors that promote positive adult/child attachments?
- What are at least two adult behaviors that inhibit positive adult/child attachments?

- How do secure and healthy attachment relationships lead to healthy brain growth?

Read the article "Easing the Separation Process for Infants, Toddlers, and Families" in the additional materials for this chapter. Tell me in your own words what developing a "Curriculum of Trust" entails.

- List two to three verbal and non-verbal communications infants and toddlers use to communicate their needs. How do the caregivers respond *to each communication*?
- Choose ONE of these scenarios to observe and reflect on:
  - Observe a toddler (1–2-year-old child) with his/her parent in a setting where there is freedom to move around. List the attachment behaviors that you observe. Note the child's reaction to situations around them and how they respond to strangers and the caregiver. What happens if/when the parent leaves the room?
  - Observe a separation situation between a parent and a child (when the child comes to school in the morning). What attachment behaviors do you see, and how do the parents respond to the behaviors? What are the responses of the caregiver?

Bibliography

Ainsworth, M. D. S. (1973). The development of infant-mother attachment. In B. Cardwell & H. Ricciuti (Eds.), *Review of child development research* (Vol. 3, pp. 1–94). Chicago, IL: University of Chicago Press.

Ainsworth, M. D. S. (1985). Patterns of infant-mother attachments: Antecedents and effects on development. *Bulletin of the New York Academy of Medicine, 61*(9), 771–791.

Albrecht, K., & Miller, L. (2001). *Innovations: Infant and toddler development.* Lewisville, NC: Gryphon House.

American Academy of Child and Adolescent Psychiatry. (2011, March). Facts for families: Reactive attachment disorder. Retrieved from www.aacap.org/galleries/FactsForFamilies/85_reactive_attachment_disorder.pdf

Attachment: Why it is crucial for your baby. (2011, April). Retrieved from www.babycenter.com/0_attachment-why-its-crucial-for-your-baby_10349909.bc

Benoit, D. (2004, October). Infant-parent attachment: Definition, types, antecedents, measurement and outcome. *Pediatric Child Health, 9*(8), 541–545. Retrieved from www.ncbi.nlm.nih.gov/pmc/articles/PMC2724160/

Berk, L. (2012). *Child development* (9th ed.). Boston, MA: Pearson.

Berk, L. (2015). *Infants and children: Prenatal through middle childhood* (8th ed.). Boston, MA: Pearson.

Berk, L. (2018a). *Exploring child development*. Boston, MA: Pearson.
Berk, L. (2018b). *Exploring child and adolescent development*. Boston, MA: Pearson.
Bowlby, J. (1969). *Attachment: Attachment and loss: Vol. 1: Loss*. New York, NY: Basic Books.
Bretherton, I. (1992). The origins of attachment theory: John Bowlby and Mary Ainsworth. *Developmental Psychology, 28*(5), 759–775.
Briody, J., & McGarry, K. (2005, September). Using social stories to ease children's transitions. *Beyond the Journal*, 1–4.
Brodie, R. (2012). Mary Ainsworth and attachment theory. Retrieved from www.child-developmentmedia.com/mary-ainsworth-and-attachment-theory.html
Cherry, K. (2013). Attachment styles. Retrieved from http://psychology.about.com/od/loveandattraction/ss/attachmentstyle.htm
Gallagher, K. (2005). Brain research and early childhood development: A primer for developmentally appropriate practice. *Young Children, 60*(4), 12–20.
Gonzalez-Mena, J., & Eyer, D. (2017). *Infants, toddlers, and caregivers: A curriculum of respectful, responsive, relationship-based care and education* (11th ed.). New York, NY: McGraw Hill.
Kuhn, K. (1999, January 1). Attachment parenting: What is attachment parenting? Retrieved from www.ivillage.com/what-attachment-parenting/6-a-127876
The Mayo Clinic Staff. (2013). Reactive attachment disorder. Retrieved from www.mayoclinic.com/health/reactive-attachment-disorder/DS00988
McLeod, S. A. (2007). Simply psychology; Bowlby | Maternal deprivation theory. Retrieved 16 April 2012, from www.simplypsychology.org/bowlby.html
McLeod, S. A. (2008). Simply psychology; Mary Ainsworth | Strange situation. Retrieved 16 April 2012, from www.simplypsychology.org/mary-ainsworth.html
Mooney, C. G. (2010). *Theories of attachment*. St. Paul, MN: Redleaf.
Schore, N. (2001a). The effects of early relational trauma on right brain development, affect regulation and infant mental health. *Infant Mental Health Journal, 22*(1–2), 201–269.
Schore, N. (2001b). Effects of secure attachment relationship on right brain development, affect regulation and infant mental health. *Infant Mental Health Journal, 22*(1–2), 7–66.
Sears, W. (2013a). 7 benefits of ap. Retrieved from www.askdrsears.com/topics/attachment-parenting/7-benefits-ap
Sears, W. (2013b). What ap is: 7 baby b's. Retrieved from www.askdrsears.com/topics/attachment-parenting/what-ap-7-baby-bsThomas, N. (2013). Reactive attachment disorder. Retrieved from www.attachment.org/parents/reactive-attachment-disorder/
Zero to Three. (2010). Relationships: The heart of development and learning. Retrieved from www.zerotothree.org/resources/73-relationships-the-heart-of-development-and-learning

9 Social Development and Interactions

Now that you have learned about the importance of attachment, we will discuss the natural extension of attachment behaviors and security-socialization. Attachment is the prime factor in the development of social skills, and socialization is a major focus of development in the early years. Socialization starts at birth, when adults recognize and respond to the social behaviors of newborns, such as imitation, facial expressions and non-verbal communication. Remember that these behaviors are meant to attract adults to interact with them, which reveals infants' desire to socially interact with others. Adults socialize infants and toddlers by helping them learn the skills that connect them to others. One of those skills is learning to separate from people to whom they are attached in order to interact with other people.

Social Skills and How We Learn Them

Social skills are the appropriate behaviors for interacting and connecting with others. These skills connect us to and help us be away from other people. As children learn and practice these important skills, they learn the social standards and expectations of the culture they live in. Healthy social skills help infants and toddlers develop skills in cognition, language, emotion and even physical skills. Children also develop self-esteem as a part result of positive socialization.

Parents and caregivers who interact with infants and toddlers have the very important job of modeling and facilitating appropriate skills so that the children adopt them. These important adults are teaching the children from birth how to act and behave appropriately and have healthy social relationships. This process takes time and requires care and attention from adults.

Appropriate socialization begins with secure attachments and opportunities to be social with others from early in life. Socialization with peers is present in the infant and toddler years when it is fostered by a secure child-caregiver bond. When infants interact with sensitive and responsive adults, they learn how to send and interpret emotional signals that they will then use in their first social interactions. Infants who have a warm relationship with their primary caregiver(s) will engage in more extended social exchanges with peers. Toddlers who are in childcare and have a secure attachment to a caregiver

Figure 9.1 Toddler Painting on an Easel

will show advanced social and play behavior with their peers. When these children reach the preschool years, they tend to show more socially competent behavior.

Erikson's Psychosocial Theory

Let's begin with a discussion of a developmental theory that emphasizes the attachment/socialization bond. Erik Erikson's Psychosocial Theory is a theory that shows the connection of attachment and social development. Erikson believed that the foundation of social and emotional development is formed in the early years of life. His theory is a stage theory where a person must overcome a "crisis" or "struggle" before continuing to the next stage. The resolution of the crisis/struggle then influences the way the crisis in the next stage will unfold.

Erikson's theory contributes to an early childhood educator's knowledge of a person's development as cumulative, with each developmental step laying the foundation for the next one. Each step forward is influenced by those that came before it. While Erikson's believed that each stage occurred during a specific age or age range, I urge you to focus on the *progression* and *order* of the stages. The ages are important to know so that you have a general idea of what children are experiencing and when, but they are not absolute. People can also return to the crisis/struggle later in life and, with the help of others, overcome it.

Because this book focuses on ages 0–3, we will only discuss the first three stages of Erikson's theory. And while the third stage begins around age 3 and will move beyond the parameters of this book, it is important for you as a caregiver to know where the infants and toddlers you are moving towards developmentally.

Trust Versus Mistrust (0–1 year)

The title of Erikson's first stage tells you everything you need to know about this point in an infant's life; they are learning whether to *trust* or *mistrust* the world. In the first year of life, infants are learning whether the world is safe or unsafe, predictable or unpredictable. The consistency and quality of a parent or primary caregiver's behavior and attention to an infant's needs is what determines the outcome of this very important first stage. Caregivers must be loving and affectionate and always meet infants' needs in a loving and consistent manner.

If an infant receives reliable, predictable and consistent care, he will develop a trust in the world. He will carry this trust with him into future relationships and feel a sense of security in the world. If a child receives unreliable, unpredictable, inconsistent or even harsh care, he will develop a mistrust in the world. This mistrust will carry on to other relationships as well and may result in anxiety and insecurity.

Autonomy Versus Shame and Doubt (1–3 years)

The focus of this stage is the child's growing *autonomy* (independence) and developing a sense of personal control. This independence and control is shown in the child's choice of what to play with, what to eat, what to wear, etc. Parents and caregivers need to encourage the child to be independent and try new things and always support him when he fails. They must support, not criticize. A certain level of failure is necessary and healthy, and it is the positive and loving support of the parents that makes the failure a natural part of life. Control and independence also refers to physical skills, such as toilet training. As children learn to control their body's functions, they gain more confidence and independence. The key for parents is balance; the goal is for toddlers to gain self-control without losing their self-esteem.

If a toddler is supported and encouraged in her independence, she will become more confident and secure in herself and her ability to survive in the world. She will try new things without a fear of failure, and her independence and self-confidence will grow. If she is overly controlled, overly criticized or not given the opportunity to assert herself, she will feel shameful because of her failures and feel inadequate in her abilities. These negative feelings can lead to her feeling overly dependent on others because of low self-esteem and

Social Development and Interactions 201

doubt in her abilities. Her desire to try new things will decrease because of her fear of negative reactions and consequences.

Initiative Versus Guilt (3–5 years)

This third stage of Erikson's theory begins in the preschool years, which is beyond the parameters of this infant/toddler book. It is important, though, for you to understand where the infants and toddlers whom you are caring for are headed in their social and emotional development, as well as see the connections with the previous toddler stage.

It is in Erikson's third stage that children explore new things and new directions in their lives. They assert themselves more and plan, initiate and participate in activities with others more frequently. They ask many questions as their desire for knowledge grows. If you have ever spent time with a preschooler, you know that this time in his life is a time of action and *initiative*—time to really test out the world. The children crave control and power over their world, which is a natural progression from the previous stage that focused on their newfound sense of autonomy.

If children are given the opportunity to take initiative and assert themselves, they will feel secure about their ability to lead others and make decisions. If their boundaries are too tight (from either criticism or control from parents and/or primary caregivers), children will feel guilty about their desire to take initiative and explore new things. They will soon cease to do so and lack initiative in their exploration and experiences.

If you have ever spent time with a child in the 0–3 age range, you are probably thinking that what Erikson theorized is very true. Proper support, love

Figure 9.2 Infant and Toddler Parallel Play With Water Tables and Water Toys

and freedom help children's confidence and social skills grow. With Erikson's words in mind, now let's discuss the actual social skills and behaviors of infants and toddlers. As a parent or caregiver for these children, it is important for you to know and understand the different skills and be able to appropriately respond to them (Berk, 2012, 2015, 2018a, 2018b; Erikson, 1950; Zero to Three, 2010a; 2010b).

The Social Skills and Behaviors of Infants and Toddlers

Children come into the world ready to socialize with other human beings. Their social skills and expressions gradually increase with both age and experience. Infants and toddlers' motivation and ability to communicate, interact and play with their peers grows each day of the first three years of life. It is in these years that children learn to communicate with peers, play with peers, exhibit prosocial behaviors and manage conflicts with peers and their negative feelings. They gain the ability to use positive social skills, assert themselves and negotiate conflicts and disagreements without aggression. It is important to recognize and respond to all social behaviors so that infants and toddlers know they are being heard and learn what a response to their social communications looks like.

Infants (0–1 year)

Infants are born ready to socialize and communicate. In the first few months of life, they focus on caregivers' faces when they are spoken to and recognize familiar caregivers. Their cries are *always* communications; each cry is a request for a different need to be met, whether it be hunger, sleep or comfort. When caregivers respond to those cries (all of the time!), infants learn social and interactional skills. They learn that their social communications are heard and will be responded to, and they will continue to communicate.

In the first three months, infant socialization is focused on meeting their basic needs: eating, sleeping, elimination and body positioning. They learn to self-regulate their social interactions and reactions based on the amount of stimulus around them and how much it interests them. Young infants will also imitate caregivers in order to socially interact (try making eye contact with an infant and then stick your tongue out; the infant will do the same). Around 6 weeks, infants start to smile at people, toys or anything new and interesting. They will continue to socially smile if their smile is returned. They will also use other gestures and movement to non-verbally socially communicate with their caregivers.

Around 3 months, infants move out of the "fetal stage" and begin to socially interact even more. They will reach for familiar people, play actively with a toy or on a play mat with toys for longer periods of time, and engage in games such as peek-a-boo with caregivers. They are actively seeking interaction and reciprocation of their communications and will continually communicate if they are responded to. Their communications will not necessarily be directed at someone all of the time, but if you verbally and non-verbally respond, they will continue.

By the time infants reach 6 *months*, they are actively exchanging in interactions with their caregivers. They will respond to a smile with a smile and play back and forth games like peek-a-boo. They will take objects from your hand and somewhat hand them back (or at least offer it to you by holding it in the air) and reach for objects just out of their reach. Infants will also begin to participate with their caregivers in spoon feeding, dressing and other daily routines and activities. If you place an infant at this age in front of a mirror, she will talk and laugh at the baby looking back at her. If you place a sticker on her nose and put her in front of a mirror and she reaches to remove the sticker, she probably recognizes herself as the person in the reflection.

Infants at this age will interact differently with strangers and may experience stranger anxiety. Infants will look at their caregiver when meeting a stranger and use the caregiver's reaction to gauge whether or not the stranger is a safe person. If the caregiver smiles and greets the person warmly, the infant will feel that the stranger is safe and may feel less anxiety. If the caregiver reacts negatively or without emotion, the infant will tend to not engage the stranger in any social interaction. This is called *social referencing* and continues into the toddler years.

As infants move toward 9 *months old*, they may experience separation anxiety, where they do not want to be separated from the caregivers to whom they are attached. Infants might cry or cling to their caregiver to show their desire to be near them. While this is very normal attachment behavior, it is also social communication. The infant is communicating his desire to interact with the people he is most comfortable with. Caregivers must carefully and appropriately transition infants into a new environment and help the infants feel comfortable with any new caregivers.

Infants at this age also begin to initiate even more interactions and activities with others. They will work to get their caregivers' attention, strain to reach an object out of their reach and "talk" to their caregivers by babbling and pointing to objects. They will mouth many objects as a way to explore it and understand everything about it and watch as others manipulate objects to see what they can learn. At this point, they recognize themselves in the mirror and will initiate social interactions by reaching for and talking to themselves.

As infants approach 1 *year old* and the end of their infant years, they are interacting with whatever and whomever they can get their hands on. They babble and begin to say specific words to label objects and actively seek eye contact and social interaction with others. Their desire for independence is growing, so you may find that they push away from caregivers to do something on their own and might get frustrated when they can't. But infants at this age will still look to their primary caregivers for comfort and the meeting of their needs. If these primary caregivers have been responding to the infants' attempts at social interaction throughout the first year, the infants will continually seek interactions with them because they know their social communications will be reciprocated.

Caregivers can encourage infant social development by simply interacting verbally and physically with infants. Caregivers should *smile and talk to infants often*. Narrate what you are doing, describe an experience or just tell them about your day. *Make eye contact and touch* infants often. This shows infants acceptance and approval and that you are interested in socially interacting with them. *Pick up* infants when they reach their arms out to you. They are initiating a social interaction when they do this, and it is important to respond. When you are not interacting with them, give infants *time in front of a mirror*. They love to look at the baby in the reflection (who they eventually realize is them!) and talk to and try to touch them. And finally, *acknowledge and make a big deal about small accomplishments*. Any time an infant does something on his own or even somewhat successfully, point it out and cheer for him! This reaction helps him to become more confident in himself and his abilities and tells him that his efforts are supported.

Below is a chart of typical social gestures and interactions made by infants, and an appropriate caregiver response. Remember that caregiver response in the first year is crucial to the development of the child. Appropriate responses show the infant that their communications were heard, were understood and are important. The caregiver response also begins to teach the infant the art, or "dance," that is social interactions (Berk, 2012, 2015, 2018a, 2018b).

Table 9.1 Infant Social Gestures and Appropriate Caregiver Responses

Social Gesture/Interaction	Appropriate Caregiver Response
Cry	Assess what need the cry is requesting and fulfill it calmly and quickly
Eye contact	Return eye contact and say "hi"
Arms reaching up	Pick infant up and verbally greet him
Babble	Repeat sound or babble and then verbally respond in normal language (not baby talk)
Point to object; may say name of it, ask "dat?" or babble	Make eye contact, point to object or pick it up and say its name; hand to infant and watch their exploration of it
Looks at you when meeting a stranger whom you know and trust	Verbally greet the person and smile; encourage infant to smile and greet the person
Looks at you when meeting a stranger to both of you	Smile and say hello to stranger to model positive social interaction

Source: (Berk, 2012, 2015, 2018a, 2018b; Zero to Three, 2010a; 2010b).

Figure 9.3 Infant and Toddler Exploring Snow Together

Toddlers (1–3 years)

As infants progress into the toddler years, they take the social experiences from the first year of their life with them. If they have had caregivers who responded to their communications and attempts at initiating interaction, they will seek to interact further with others. If they have had caregivers who talked to them and initiated verbal and non-verbal interactions with them, they will consider the world a place of social interaction and seek out social experiences with others. Infants who did not have caregivers who responded to their social interactions and did not interact with them often may not initiate social interactions as easily. It is important to remember that social skills are learned behaviors, and the infant years are an important time to instill social and interactional skills in children. But it doesn't mean that a toddler cannot be taught appropriate social skills. It takes time to "retrain" their brain to recognize interactions and communications and respond to them, but it can be done.

Regardless of the social interactions that a toddler had in the infant years, his social skills and social development center on his interactions with other people, especially other children. From *ages 1 to 2*, toddlers begin to acknowledge others in their play and will initiate play interactions with people that are closest to their play. Play is still parallel most of the time, although toddlers are slowly moving to more cooperative play. Interactions between the children will occur more often and involve frequent reciprocal imitation. Toddlers will chase after each other, move their bodies or bang on a toy together. These imitations of each other and turn-taking actions help the toddlers to create joint understandings. These understandings will help the toddlers to verbally communicate with each other, which is another step in socialization. Toddlers will want to help with tasks and "share" materials they are holding by holding it out to show you and possibly let you take for a moment. Toddlers also begin to show concern for others and can be seen comforting another child who is upset.

Verbal and physical tantrums are a common social communication in the toddler years; they are still learning to express their excitement and frustrations appropriately. Caregivers must acknowledge these communications and work with the toddler to express them in a more appropriately and less energy-draining manner.

Toddlers are also in the business of testing limits. Often. They test limits to find the limit—to find the "line" that they cannot cross. It is a healthy and necessary social practice. Toddlers crave limits and actually have difficulty in the social world if they don't know what they can and cannot do. These social learning experiences allow toddlers to experience negative emotions when they violate rules or a limit. Through this, they are learning to control their desire to behave negatively and recognize limits in the social world.

As toddlers approach 2 years old, their continuous limit testing helps them to gain the ability to internalize those limits and other rules. They can anticipate disapproval when they are testing the limits and might even look you in the eye as they do it to see your reaction. This is healthy and necessary; they learn by doing and seeing others, so teach them the limit and always enforce it consistently! Toddlers are also beginning to use self-control to resist engaging in behavior that they know is inappropriate or unacceptable.

From *ages 2 to 3*, toddlers are aware of right and wrong and will begin to show signs of distress when they do something wrong. The feeling of guilt also emerges, and they will generally want to behave in socially appropriate ways because of the positive response it garners from others. They will be empathetic toward others in distress or trouble and acknowledge appropriate social behavior. They will also use more and more words to communicate with others. Older toddlers will talk with other children about each other's behaviors and influence each other's behaviors. This reciprocal play between toddlers paired with positive emotions and interactions are a frequent part of older toddlers' interactions with familiar playmates. This is the beginning of genuine peer relationships for the children.

Caregivers should actively encourage toddler's social development by giving them opportunities to play with other children. It is in these years that children learn to be with other children and negotiate their place in a play situation. Caregivers should stay close by and observe toddlers at play. Quietly observe their social interactions and intervene if you see an opportunity to help a toddler more appropriately socially communicate. When you do intervene, identify toddlers' emotions and talk them through the use of appropriate social skills. This constant recognition and modeling of social skills and communications is how toddlers learn to participate appropriately in social interactions. It is also good to have a quiet place for toddlers to be alone if they want to. There are times when emotions and feelings are overwhelming for a toddler, and they may need time to cool down and relax before returning to social situations.

Other than working with toddlers to acquire appropriate social skills, caregivers should encourage toddlers to express themselves and use their imagination. Giving toddlers the room to verbally and non-verbally communicate tells them that they are in a safe and comfortable social world that recognizes them as individuals. These feelings breed appropriate social skills. Caregivers can also play games and initiate explorations that involve turn-taking, which further gives toddlers the opportunity to learn appropriate social skills.

Having a secure attachment with toddlers helps them to learn from your modeling of appropriate social behavior. This secure attachment creates an environment where toddlers will look to these caregivers for social skills and communications. Caregivers should express positive emotions to toddlers to show toddlers their social interactions are acknowledged and discuss all behaviors openly. Recognize and describe the emotions and expressions of toddlers and establish rules and limits that cannot be broken without consequence. Define acceptable and unacceptable social behavior, and work toward continuous expression of the acceptable behavior (Berk 2012, 2015, 2018a, 2018b).

Table 9.2 Summary of the Social Behaviors of Infants and Toddlers

Summary of the Social Behaviors of Infants and Toddlers
0–3 months
Orienting behaviors: Visual fixation, visual tracking, listening, rooting and adjustment of body when held to fit holding position
Sucking and grasping to gain and maintain contact
Smiling, crying and vocalizing to signal caregiver to come close
4–8 months
Discriminates between familiar and unfamiliar people—different response (smiling, vocalizations, crying)
Seeks proximity to primary caregivers (around 7 months)—vocal and physical movements; following, approaching, clinging to promote active contact
Voluntary movements of hands and arms
Physical manipulations and movements contribute to concept of "self" and "not self"
8–12 months
Interactions with others increasing (mobility allows this)
Very egocentric about materials and people
Keeps caregivers in sight (comforting)
12–18 months
Egocentric; at end of this period they begin to differentiate their "self" from other objects and people
Interactions with others provides first experiences with self-image
Recognize differences in people and adjust their interactions with these different people
Solitary play and some parallel play
Prefers older children and adults to own age children

(*Continued*)

Table 9.2 (Continued)

Summary of the Social Behaviors of Infants and Toddlers

18–24 months
Still developing senses of self (I, mine, me and you are common words)
Recognizes other's feelings and is developing empathy

24–30 months
Beginning to interact and enjoy being around other children
Interactions with other children are usually about disagreements about possessions
Recognize emotions in others
Enjoys helping with tasks

30–36 months
Egocentric; does not fully understand that people have a consistent identity over time regardless of appearance
Still possessive of toys/materials they are using
Still seek assistance from others and will be very directive toward other people as a way to control them and get them to do what they want them to do
Self-control is increasing
Pro-social skills are increasing, especially if they have had caregivers who have done the following: Cooperating with them, put aside their needs to attend to them, showed empathy, concern, respect and nurturance toward them

Source: (Berk, 2012, 2015, 2018a, 2018b; Zero to Three, 2010a, 2010b).

Social Behaviors and Caregiver Strategies

Now that you are aware of the social development of infants and toddlers and the different social skills and communications they express, it is important for you to focus on the strategies you should use as a caregiver to respond to these skills and communications. Utilizing these strategies will allow you to help infants and toddlers learn how to appropriately behave in the social world.

Table 9.3 Social Behaviors of Infants and Toddlers and Corresponding Caregiver Strategies

Age	Social Behaviors	Caregiver Strategies
Birth–4 months	Smiles, establishes eye contact, coos Laughs and talks (babbles and makes noises)	Return smile, make eye contact, talk and sing, hold infant to body, place infant in visual proximity so they can watch you Return laugh, talk back and converse with infant
4–8 months	Shows intense pleasure *and* frustration with primary caregiver(s) Seeks caregiver's attention through verbal and non-verbal communications	Accept and share pleasure; calm and soothe during frustration Respond to child's communications immediately; stay close while infant plays

Age	Social Behaviors	Caregiver Strategies
	Recognizes self in mirror; interested in self Seeks independence in tasks and play Observes and imitates other people	Place infants in front of mirrors; place dots on hands and feet to extend interest in self and body Allow infant to practice and accomplish tasks in play how they wish Play games with infants where you imitate each other (sticking tongue out; pat-a-cake); allow infant to be close to and safely touch other infants/children
8–12 months	Initiates interactions and play experiences with others while still keeping caregiver in sight May be assertive or possessive of people and materials (egocentric) May demand attention or act shy/clingy	Respond to behavior (talking, playing) and allow infant to play with others while staying in sight) Closely observe infant for aggressive behavior; verbalize and model clear limits; provide enough toys so infant does not have to share Allow infant to follow you around; provide both verbal and physical attention
12–18 months	Egocentric Seeks caregiver presence; acts differently toward different people Plays games and occasionally shares; solitary and some parallel play Uses different behaviors to gain attention	Support toddler as an individual Allow toddler to follow you around; accept their choices of who to interact with and how Provide enough materials to encourage sharing but not force it; provide materials and spaces for toddlers to play near each other Know and respond to toddler's attention-seeking behaviors
18–24 months	Egocentric: materials belong to self; uses words like "I, mine, me and you" Seeks to increase social relationships: seeks attention, imitates; looks to others for help; becoming aware of other's feelings Wants to help Difficulty sharing; engages in parallel play May do opposite of what is requested	Help toddler identify own feelings and ideas; provide feedback about self; acknowledge and allow ownership of toys; respond to and reinforce when toddler separates self from others Identify and verbalize other's feelings; explain how their actions make others feel; encourage interactions with others and praise for completing tasks *and* asking for help when they need it

(Continued)

Table 9.3 (Continued)

Age	Social Behaviors	Caregiver Strategies
		Complete tasks with child and encourage them to help you with tasks
		Provide materials and space for children to play near each other; suggest alternating toys/taking turns
		Request specific behavior in different ways; tell child what they *should be doing*, not what they did wrong
24–30 months	Recognizes own skills and wants to practice them Independent but still wants to please and help others Recognizes other's emotions/feelings and shows theirs to others Understands "mine" versus "yours" and may begin to share	Provide materials they can use and new ones that slightly challenge Provide verbal and non-verbal attention and feedback; follow a routine Label and verbalize emotions/feelings/behaviors Begin to engage the children in group interest centers; provides materials and spaces where some sharing is necessary—acknowledge and encourage attempts to share
30–36 months	May act possessive about materials and people Will seek assistance Will direct *and* help others Will engage in more cooperative play, sharing and taking turns	Provide enough materials so child can control use of them for a period of time Be available as a resource Provide opportunities for child to exert an acceptable amount of control over others; praise spontaneous helping and ask them to help you Provide the materials, space and time for this pro-social behavior to occur; provide some opportunities to share and take turns

Source: (Berk, 2012, 2015, 2018a, 2018b; Zero to Three, 2010a; 2010b).

Social Development With Peers

Interactions and quality peer experiences among infants and toddlers are fundamentally important to development in the first three years of life. Interacting and playing with other children allows children to not only develop their social skills but also their language, self-concept, and sensorimotor abilities. Children learn skills in their peer relationships that they do not learn in their adult relationships. Vygotsky emphasized that children learn about their culture and the culture of others through peer interactions. Piaget emphasized that children construct knowledge about how to play with peers and how to cooperate and negotiate through these important social interactions.

Positive caregiver-child and teacher-child relationships do impact how a child thrives socially. Adults must not only socially interact with infants and toddlers, but they must also observe the infants and toddlers' peer social interactions to see what social skills they are exhibiting and what social skills are lacking. They can then support the continuance of the strong interactions and support the development of the weaker ones.

Infants and toddlers have the amazing ability to interact and communicate with each other even when they lack the verbal ability to do so. These non-verbal communications eventually transition to a combination of verbal and non-verbal communications and then finally to solely verbal communications. Toddlers, for example, use sounds, words and laughter to inform and direct others in their interactions with them. These gestures (gestural language) are usually understood by other toddlers, even when adults could not decode the communications.

Toward the end of the infant years (around 9–12 months), children will show numerous non-verbal communications as a way to socially interact with each other. Parents and caregivers should be aware of these non-verbal communications and know what they look like so they can correctly decipher the child's communications. Adults can decipher the non-verbal communication and then provide the verbal descriptions for the children to hear. Hearing the

Table 9.4 Non-Verbal Communications and Appropriate Caregiver Responses

Non-Verbal Communication	Appropriate Adult Verbalization
Attachment/Pacification Actions: *Touching/caressing* *Offering a toy or extending a hand* *Clapping hands* *Jumping/bouncing/rocking* *Smiling* *Leaning sideways or cocking head to side* *Making sounds* **My Own Examples:**	"You are being very gentle toward him with your hand." "You are telling me that you are happy!"
Threatening Actions that produce fear or tears in another child: *Loud vocalizations* *Opening mouth or clenching teeth* *Pointing finger* *Clenching fist or raising arm* *Leaning head or body forward* *Making boxing motion with arms*	"You are angry about ____." "You are upset that ____ happened. Let's figure it out."

(*Continued*)

212 Social Development and Interactions

Table 9.4 (Continued)

Non-Verbal Communication	Appropriate Adult Verbalization
My Own Examples:	
Aggressive Actions: Hitting Scratching Pinching Biting Pulling hair or clothes Shaking/knocking Grabbing something Throwing something **My Own Examples:**	"Your ____ hurt your friend." "You seem upset/angry that ____ happened."
Motions of fear/retreat: Widening/blinking eyes Protecting face with arms Moving head or body backward Running away Crying **My Own Examples:**	"You are unsure of ____. Let me show you it is safe." "____ is upsetting you."
Isolation: Thumb or toy sucking Tugging at hair/ear Lying down Sitting alone Crying alone **My Own Examples:**	"You need some time alone." "You seem sad/upset/tired. Let's rest quietly for a minute."

Source: (Berk, 2012, 2015, 2018a, 2018b; Zero to Three, 2010a, 2010b).

verbal descriptions can move the child closer to using words with their gestures and then eventually just words. Table 9.4 identifies different non-verbal communications and then provides examples of appropriate verbal phrases for adults to respond with. Add your own examples to your journal.

While infants and toddlers all differ in the gestures they use to communicate with their peers, they are able to read each other's behavior and decide how to respond. Children who use aggressive strategies often will be avoided by other children, and those who use many pacifying gestures and defend themselves from threatening behavior tend to be successful in peer relationships.

Infants and toddlers have been shown to have many more positive interactions with and direct more positive behaviors toward their peers versus negative ones. While it may seem that toddlers exhibit a plethora of negative social behaviors as they figure out their place in the world, they actually often interact in complimentary and reciprocal ways with their peers. They show empathy and sympathy and often respond positively and lovingly to their peers' distress. They will offer objects that they enjoy or that comfort them (such as their bottle, a special toy or food) as a way to comfort someone else. Infants exhibit these caring behaviors toward the caregivers with whom they are attached, while toddlers do so with their caregivers and their peers. Pretty amazing for such young children! It is important that parents and caregivers look for and verbally recognize these prosocial behaviors so that infants and toddlers know they are acceptable and appropriate.

There are many ways for parents and caregivers to support and facilitate prosocial development in care settings. With this adult support, children are recognized for and at the same time become aware of appropriate behaviors. Different ways to support prosocial development in a care setting for infants and toddlers are listed below. For each of the following suggestions, see if you can think of an example of what the adult's dialogue would sound like or behavior would look like. Document them in your journal.

- *Send clear messages* about how children must not hurt each other. Identify the negative act and how it made the child feel and make a clear connection between the two. Emphasize in facial expression and tone that the negative act is unacceptable
- *Give clear explanations* for why a child should or should not behave in a certain way
- *Teach alternative behaviors/communications* to negative behaviors
- *Be kind and loving* toward the children. Give hugs, use soothing words and help others in distress (or verbally recognize the distress if you can't help). The children will model the same with their peers
- *Keep children together* in care environments as they grow. They will be able to develop friendships, and their familiarity with each other will make them more likely to initiate play and interactions
- *Leave children alone* to play and interact. They will help each other, solve problems and work through conflicts if given the opportunity to do so on their own
- *Recognize and reinforce* positive social behaviors. Verbally describe what you see a child doing and let her know it is appropriate and appreciated. Emphasize how exhibiting prosocial behaviors makes others feel. When children understand the outcomes of their actions and learn that certain behaviors garner caregiver's approval, they will do them more
- *Model prosocial behaviors.* Use manners, give them food and toys in a generous and kind way and comfort them when they are in distress. This warmth and kindness allows children to feel that their physical and emotional needs are met, and they can then show the same behaviors toward others. Caregivers should also model prosocial behaviors with each other in front of the children, which creates a complete prosocial atmosphere that the children will want to participate in (Gonzalez-Mena, 2017).

The Importance of Infants and Toddlers Playing "Together"

As you read in chapter seven, play is how young children learn. This learning also extends to socialization and social skills. Notice that the word "together" is in quotes in the title of this section. As you know from chapter six, children do not really play "together" until they get close to the preschool years. Ages 2 to 3 are when that ability starts to develop, but it isn't fully developed until after the toddler years end. But this doesn't mean that putting infants and toddlers in play situations together isn't beneficial. In fact, it is vital to their social development.

Opportunities to play together gives infants and toddlers the opportunity to interact with other kids, learn how to share (or at least use materials together) and just how to get along with other children in general. Both infants and toddlers benefit socially from playtime together but in different ways. Infants are fascinated by other infants, and new play environments and materials provide new stimulation that is good for brain growth. Simply looking at another infant laying on the floor with them and touching hands is an important social interaction. Toddlers benefit from playtime with any other child of any age. They are still primarily focused on their desires and needs, so the presence of someone of any age does not alter their play plans. All play experiences with others are an opportunity for toddlers to socially interact, learn appropriate social behaviors and learn about the reactions and consequences of inappropriate social behaviors.

Both familiar and unfamiliar play locations and materials are beneficial to infants and toddlers. Familiar gives them a sense of comfort because they know what they can do with materials and in certain environments. Unfamiliar is exciting and interesting because it isn't a place or materials that they are used to. Caregivers should explore unfamiliar territory with infants and toddlers until they feel they are comfortable enough to interact and play on their own. Then caregivers can step back and let the social interactions and play unfold, while remaining close by for comfort or help when it is needed.

Infants and Their Preschool Siblings

It is important to encourage older siblings to interact with their infant siblings. This helps to create an important attachment bond between siblings, as well as provides another model for appropriate social interaction for both children. The arrival of another child means that the children must share their parents' attention and affection. This can be difficult for the older sibling, who may act out or become clingy. If the older sibling is over age 2, his or her security of attachment may decline because s/he feels threatened or displaced by the new sibling. With the right behaviors and interactions, parents can help this behavior to decline. Set aside quality one-on-one time with the older sibling, handle any misbehavior with patience and understanding, explain and discuss the infant's wants and needs and model a healthy relationship with the other parent.

Social Development and Interactions 215

Figure 9.4 Infant and Older Sibling Playing Together With the Light Table

A growing affection between siblings can grow, and soon the older sibling will be seen kissing and patting his younger sibling and alerting parents to the infant's needs. Toward the end of the first year, the siblings will spend a good amount of time together playing and interacting. The older sibling will still sometimes display anger or ambivalence toward the younger sibling (this is typical sibling behavior and usually not a cause for worry), but s/he will also be seen helping, sharing toys, imitating and being kind and friendly to the younger sibling. Infants are comforted by the presence of their older siblings, especially when their mother or other primary caregiver is absent. As they grow into toddlers, they will often imitate or join in their older sibling's play.

Children With Special Needs

Infants and toddlers who have been identified as having special needs are often delayed in their social development. It is important to recognize any delay or difficulty a child has in communicating with and developing relationships with others and support and encourage their social interactions with their peers. Children with social delays will also learn from their peers without delays, so many of the strategies discussed in this chapter will be recognized and internalized by children with special needs.

Autism

As a parent or caregiver for infants and toddlers, it is important for you to be aware of the early signs of autism as well as be familiar with the typical developmental milestones that infants and toddlers should be reaching. With the proper behavioral evaluations (there is no medical test), children as young as 1 year old can be determined as at risk for autism. Autism Speaks' website (www.autismspeaks.org) offers a plethora of information about the disability as well as provides research and advocacy information. I encourage you to review the website and be aware of the disability. You can also register for the Video Glossary, which was "designed to help parents and professionals learn more about the early red flags and diagnostic features of autism spectrum disorders (ASD)."

The following "red flags," taken directly from the Autism Speaks website, may indicate your child is at risk for an autism spectrum disorder. If your child exhibits any of the following, please don't delay in asking your pediatrician or family doctor for an evaluation:

- No big smiles or other warm, joyful expressions by 6 months or thereafter
- No back-and-forth sharing of sounds, smiles or other facial expressions by 9 months
- No babbling by 12 months
- No back-and-forth gestures such as pointing, showing, reaching or waving by 12 months
- No words by 16 months
- No meaningful, 2-word phrases (not including imitating or repeating) by 24 months
- Any loss of speech, babbling or social skills at any age (Autism Speaks, 2013)

The Role of Caregivers

Parents, caregivers and any adult whom infants and toddlers interact with play a critical role in encouraging peer interactions and relationships among children with and without disabilities. Adult behaviors and reactions are recognized and modeled by the children. When adults encourage interactions, communications and relationships between children with special needs and those without create a positive and caring environment where children learn to recognize what their peers can do—versus what they cannot do.

In a care setting, adults can try the following strategies to help children with special needs gain prosocial skills:

- Document how a child with disabilities likes to be interacted with or physically touched. Encourage these specific interactions with that child
- Place infants next to each other on the floor so they can look at each other and observe each other's actions and communications
- Provide toys and materials that children can play with together or beside each other

Social Development and Interactions 217

- Give children with disabilities a toy or material that will attract other children. Support those children in the use of the toy as they interact with others
- Verbally and physically acknowledge the behaviors of children without disabilities and encourage those with disabilities to imitate the behaviors with you
- Recognize how children with disabilities communicate (verbalizations, gestures, sign language), and interpret them out loud for the children without disabilities to hear
- Verbally acknowledge the similarities between the children with and without disabilities
- Encourage the children without disabilities to help the children with disabilities to complete a task or manipulate a material. Acknowledge the kind behavior and describe how it makes the children feel to be helped.

(www.autismspeaks.org)

For additional material, visit:
www.parentphd.org/infantandtoddlertext/ch9/

Reflection Questions

- What is the connection between attachment and social development?
- Describe *a social behavior* that you would like to encourage in children *older than age 5*.

  How would you promote the development of that behavior in infants and toddlers?

  Review the information about autism in the chapter and in the additional content for this chapter. In your own words, as if you are speaking to a parent who knows NOTHING about the disorder, briefly explain autism. Focus on the signs that a child might be on the spectrum, how it is detected, etc.

- Cite two specific examples of social skills and behaviors for infants and then for toddlers (four total).
- Based on the list of strategies in the text, cite at least two specific examples of caregivers promoting, supporting and teaching prosocial behavior. This can be in response to either verbal or non-verbal communications from the children. Describe the examples.

Bibliography

Ainsworth, M. D. S. (1982). The development of infant-mother attachment. In J. Belsky (Ed.), *In the beginning: Readings on infancy*. New York, NY: Columbia University Press.

Allen, K. E., & Marotz, I. (1989). *Developmental profiles: Birth to six*. New York, NY: Delmar.

Autism Speaks. (2013). Learn the signs of autism. Retrieved from www.autismspeaks.org/what-autism/learn-signs

Berk, L. (2012). *Child development* (9th ed.). Boston, MA: Pearson.

Berk, L. (2015). *Infants and children: Prenatal through middle childhood* (8th ed.). Boston, MA: Pearson.

Berk, L. (2018a). *Exploring child development*. Boston, MA: Pearson.

Berk, L. (2018b). *Exploring child and adolescent development*. Boston, MA: Pearson.

Douville-Watson, L., Watson, M. A., & Wilson, L. C. (2003). *Infants and toddlers: Curriculum and teaching* (5th ed.). New York, NY: Thomas Delmar Learning.

Erikson, E. H. (1950). *Childhood and society*. New York, NY: W.W. Norton and Company.

Gillies, C. (2010, December 26). Toddler social and emotional development. Retrieved from http://suite101.com/article/toddler-social-and-emotional-development-a324179

Gonzalez-Mena, J., & Eyer, D. (2017). *Infants, toddlers, and caregivers: A curriculum of respectful, responsive, relationship-based care and education* (11th ed.). New York, NY: McGraw Hill.

Hatfield, H. (2013). The abcs of toddler playdates. Retrieved from www.webmd.com/parenting/guide/toddler-playdates

Piaget, J. (1954). *The construction of reality in the child*. New York, NY: W.W. Norton and Company.

Pines, M. (1984). Children's winning ways. *Psychology Today*, 59–65.

Toddler development now: What's normal, what's not. (2013). Retrieved from www.whattoexpect.com/toddler-development/normal-child-development.aspx

Vygotsky, L. S. (1978). *Mind and society: The development of higher psychological processes*. Cambridge, MA: Harvard University Press.

Wittmer, D. S., & Peterson, S. H. (2017). *Infant and toddler development and responsive program planning: A relationship-based approach* (4th ed.). Boston, MA: Pearson.

Zero to Three. (2010a). Developing social-emotional skills. Retrieved from www.zerotothree.org/resources/series/developing-social-emotional-skills

Zero to Three. (2010b). Relationships: The heart of development and learning. Retrieved from www.zerotothree.org/resources/73-relationships-the-heart-of-development-and-learning

10 Emotional Development

The foundation of infants and toddlers' personalities is their emotional development. Emotional development is derived from both biological (nature) and environmental (nurture) factors. The "nature" that influences personality is the temperament of each child, the genetics they received from their biological parents and their gender. The "nurture" that influences personality is the quality and type of attachments each child has, the parenting styles they are exposed to and the culture that they grow up in.

Emotions come from inside a person, although they may be triggered by external events. *Feelings* are both an awareness of and an ability to respond to emotions. Expressing emotions is a way that infants and toddlers send messages and connect to other people. Temperament plays a part in how intense and frequent emotional displays are. The development of emotions and feelings in infants and toddlers moves from immediate experiences and sensations in newborns to unrefined emotional responses in infants to finally the expression and regulation of specific emotions in toddlers (Gonzalez-Mena & Eyer, 2017).

Emotional development is directly connected to infants and toddlers' attachments and socialization experiences. Infants and toddlers learn a great deal from their interactions with other people. They learn whether or not they are listened to, whether their choices are valued, if their emotional expression is appropriate and accepted, whether or not they can explore and if their needs will be met.

It is important to remember that all feelings are good; they each have a purpose and provide important information and messages about how a person is feeling. It is extremely important for parents and caregivers to acknowledge and accept all emotions and feelings of infants and toddlers as real and relevant. With this acknowledgement and acceptance, you are helping infants and toddlers recognize what emotion or feeling they are having. And with this recognition comes the ability to cope with the emotion or feeling. These coping skills contribute to infants and toddlers' self-direction and competence. Therefore, the goal of parents and caregivers should be to help infants and toddlers recognize the emotions that they are feeling and eventually regulate and express them appropriately.

Infant emotions used to be discounted as either non-existent or simply sensations. But it is now clear that you can observe infants' physical reactions to situations and clearly see their emotions in those reactions. Infants' emotional expressions are their "language" in their early relationships since they are unable to speak. In fact, researchers believe that the exchange of positive and negative emotions between infants and their caregivers help to develop their brain. For example, an infant might clench his fists or cry out in reaction to loud noises or harsh lights. On the contrary, an infant might relax his body and sigh when held by a familiar caregiver. Both of these reactions exhibit the infant's emotions. Older infants can express emotions such as pleasure, fear and anger. By around 2 years, toddlers can express emotions such as pride, embarrassment, shame and empathy.

It is important to recognize infants and toddlers' emotions when being introduced to an unfamiliar person. As we discussed in the attachment chapter, a fear or uneasiness with strangers emerges in the first year of life. A familiar caregiver can comfort these negative emotions. As we discussed in chapter 9, you might notice that an infant or toddler introduced to an unfamiliar caregiver will look to his familiar caregiver for a reaction. If the familiar caregiver smiles and acknowledges the new person warmly, the child will most likely relax. If the familiar caregiver also shows fear or uneasiness, the child will hold on to his original emotional response. These situations show that infants and toddlers can read other people's emotions and regulate their own emotions based on what they observe. This "checking in" behavior is called *social referencing*. What an amazing skill for such a young person!

Social Referencing

Social referencing is when an infant or toddler uses another person's body language, including physical posture and facial expressions, to determine her own behavior. She uses an adult caregiver's emotional expressions to regulate her own behavior. As infants approach the second half of that year, they being to evaluate objects, events and people in terms of their safety and security. This behavior carries into the toddler years.

Different research studies have been conducted where infants have been exposed to an adult's facial and verbal expressions when faced with a decision. Often, the infants' reactions were directly related to the adult's expressions. For example, a visual cliff study was done where infants crawled up to a visual cliff drop-off. Their mothers were at the other end and either encouraged or discouraged the infants to keep crawling over the visual cliff with their facial expressions. The infants who saw fear in their mothers did not cross. Those who saw happiness crossed.

Other social referencing research studies included those where infants were exposed to new toys with their adult caregivers. When the adult caregivers used facial expressions and verbal expressions of happiness, the infants picked up the toy and played. When they showed and verbalized fear, many of the infants did not.

Research studies where just facial expressions and no verbalizations were used by the caregiver, there was not as much of a distinction in the infants' behavior. This leads us to believe that vocal signals may be more influential than facial expressions. Other studies showed that infants were also influenced by the emotional signals of unknown adults. This leads us to believe that any adult can influence an infant's emotional reaction or response to an experience or person.

Social referencing research has implications for parents and caregivers of infants and toddlers. Parents and caregivers must "capitalize" on social referencing behavior and teach infants and toddlers how to react to different events (Mumme, Fernald, & Herrera, 1966).

Deciphering an Infant's Cry

Caregivers can learn a great deal about an infant's personality by listening to the way she cries. There are three basic types of cries that caregivers must learn to recognize and respond to. All three cries are common among all temperaments and personalities of infants, although the intensity of the cries will be different for each infant based on those characteristics. A *basic cry* typically derives from hunger or the desire for another basic need to be met. This cry is rhythmic that usually consists of a cry, a brief silence, a shorter and higher pitch cry and then a brief rest. This pattern then repeats. An *angry cry* is a cry that has more excess air through the vocal chords and is stronger than a basic cry. Response to this cry should be different than a response to a basic cry. A *pain cry* is different than both of the other two types of cries. This cry appears suddenly and without warning and may be followed by the infant holding her breath (Berk, 2012, 2015, 2018a, 2018b).

Temperament

Temperament is a person's individual way of reacting, behaving and responding to the world. These differences in emotions, motor response, reactivity and self-regulation remain consistent across all situations for each individual child. Though temperament is biologically based, your life experiences will influence the nature and expression of your temperament. Understanding temperament helps parents and caregivers foster positive relationships with all infants and toddlers, even those whose disposition might not be a perfect match for their own personalities.

The longest and most comprehensive study of temperament came from Alexander Thomas and Stella Chess. Thomas and Chess's research followed a varied population of children from birth into childhood. They observed the children's behaviors, talked to their teachers, interviewed parents frequently asking for factual information about how their children behaved in certain

Emotional Development 223

Figure 10.1 Infant Making Eye Contact With a Caregiver

situations and performed psychological tests on the children. They concluded that infants show a distinct temperament in the first few weeks of life, regardless of the parenting they received. They developed nine characteristics of temperament based on their research:

1. Level and degree of motor activity
2. Rhythmicity and regularity of eating, elimination and the cycle of sleeping and wakefulness

3. Response to a new object or person (accepts the new experience or withdraws from it)
4. Adaptability to changes in the environment
5. Threshold and sensitivity to stimuli
6. Intensity/energy level of responses
7. The child's general mood/disposition (cheerful/pleasant or cranky, friendly or unfriendly)
8. Degree of the child's distractibility from something he is doing
9. Attention span

Thomas and Chess also defined three different types of temperament from their work: easy, slow-to-warm-up and difficult. They concluded that 40% of children are defined as "easy," 15% are defined as "slow-to-warm-up," 10% are defined as "difficult" and 35% are defined as being a blend of the three types of temperament. While many children exhibit characteristics of more than one type of temperament, it is important for caregivers to have an understanding of each one so they can appropriately respond to every child (Thomas & Chess, 1970, 1986).

The "Easy" Child

Thomas and Chess defined "easy" children as those who are typically happy and accepting of new situations and are able to adjust calmly and easily to them. They used the term "easy" because the children presented very few problems in care and training.

As infants, "easy" children quickly established regular sleeping and feeding schedules and were generally cheerful and adaptable to new routines, food and people. As they grow up, these children were shown to adapt to new activities, situations and environments easily. Specifically, these children were shown most often to:

- Have a positive mood
- Have regular body functions
- Have a low or moderated intensity of reaction
- Be fairly adaptable and have a positive approach to new situations

(Thomas & Chess, 1970, 1986)

The "Slow-To-Warm-Up" Child

Thomas and Chess defined "slow-to-warm-up" children as typically reluctant and hesitant in new situations, although they become easier over time. These children exhibited the same behaviors as infants as they were introduced to new foods, people and routines. Specifically, these children were shown most often to:

- Have a low activity level
- Have a low intensity of reaction

- Have a tendency to withdraw/slowly adapt to a new experience or environment
- Have a slightly negative mood

(Thomas & Chess, 1970, 1986)

The "Difficult" Child

Thomas and Chess defined "difficult" children as those who are typically irritable, respond intensely to new situations and are slow to adjust to new situations. These children require a great deal of tolerance and consistency from their caregivers.

As infants, these children were often irregular in their feeding and sleeping patterns and were slow to accept new foods, routines and activities. These infants also cried often. Specifically, these children were shown most often to:

- Have irregular body functions
- Have intense reactions
- Withdraw from new stimuli
- Be slow to adapt to changes in their environment
- Have a generally negative mood
- Cry and laugh loudly
- Have tantrums as a result of frustration

(Thomas & Chess, 1970, 1986)

Table 10.1 describes the level of response to each of the nine characteristics of temperament for the easy, slow-to-warm-up and difficult child.

Suggestions for Caregiving Practices

Thomas and Chess offered suggestions for caregiving practices based on the temperament of each child. Since many children exhibit characteristics of all three types of temperament, it is important for parents and caregivers to have knowledge of the most appropriate ways to respond to children no matter how they are acting.

For children exhibiting the "easy" temperament, caregiving practices should focus on encouraging the child's declarations of individuality, while encouraging her to join constructively in activities and experiences with other children and adults.

For children exhibiting the "slow-to-warm-up" temperament, caregiving practices should focus on allowing them to adapt to new environments and experiences at their own pace. Caregivers should support these children in their transitions and not put pressure on them to move too quickly. This pressure could cause this type of child to withdraw. Simply providing new opportunities and encouraging the children to explore them is the right amount of care and attention necessary.

Table 10.1 Thomas & Chess's Nine Characteristics of Temperament

Type of Child	Activity level	Rhythmicity	Distractibility	Approach Withdrawal	Adaptability	Attention span And persistence	Intensity of reaction	Threshold of responsiveness	Quality of mood
	The proportion of active periods to inactive ones	Regularity of hunger, excretion, sleep and wakefulness	The degree to which extraneous stimuli affect behavior	The response to a new object or person	The ease with which a child adapts to changes in his environment	The amount of time devoted to an activity and the effect of distraction on the activity	The energy of response regardless of its quality or direction	The intensity of stimuli required to evoke a discernible response	The amount of friendly, pleasant, joyful behavior as contrasted with unpleasant, unfriendly behavior
"EASY"	VARIES	VERY REGULAR	VARIES	POSITIVE APPROACH	VERY ADAPTABLE	HIGH OR LOW	LOW OR MILD	HIGH OR LOW	POSITIVE
"SLOW TO WARM UP"	LOW TO MODERATE	VARIES	VARIES	INITIAL WITHDRAWAL	SLOWLY ADAPTABLE	HIGH OR LOW	MILD	HIGH OR LOW	SLIGHTLY NEGATIVE
"DIFFICULT"	VARIES	IRREGULAR	VARIES	WITHDRAWAL	SLOWLY ADAPTABLE	HIGH OR LOW	INTENSE	HIGH OR LOW	NEGATIVE

Source: (Thomas & Chess, 1970, 1986).

Emotional Development 227

Figure 10.2 Infant and Toddler Spending Time Together

For children exhibiting the "difficult" temperament, caregiving practices should focus on recognizing and coping with the children's irregularity and slow pace of adapting to new environments and experiences. Caregivers should be objective and consistent in their care and help and support the children in getting along with others and behaving appropriately. It is important for caregivers to not be inconsistent or impatient with these children because this behavior will just elicit negative behavior from the children (Thomas & Chess, 1970, 1986).

The Interaction Between the Environment and Temperament

What is important in our understanding of temperament is the fact that it is the interaction between the child's own characteristics and his environment. If these two influences are synchronized, parents and caregivers can expect healthy development of the child. If they are inharmonious, behavioral problems are almost sure to result.

Knowledge of a child's temperament can help parents and caregivers to handle the child and avoid the development of behavior problems at home and in childcare. In childcare and eventually school settings, temperament affects a child's approach to learning tasks and how he interacts with classmates and teachers. Therefore, those caregivers and teachers who care for the child in a childcare setting must be aware of temperamental traits and behaviors.

Any "demand" such as a new environment, experience or routine that conflicts with a child's temperament and/or the capacity to transition into it or accept it is likely to place a child under stress. In order to address this in the best way possible for the child, parents and caregivers should recognize what each child can and cannot do. This recognition begins with an understanding of each child's temperament, even if it changes based on a situation or experience. For example, a child who adapts well to new experiences will approach a new food differently from a child who adapts at a slower pace. Caregivers should be prepared for these different reactions and give the children the time and repeated experiences necessary to adapt. A child who has a high activity level should be given opportunities to move around often, while a child with a lower activity level can be expected to sit for longer periods of time.

This knowledge should not inhibit parents and caregivers from introducing new and exciting things for fear of a negative reaction. The key is to be prepared for possible reactions and interactions based on the temperament knowledge and approach new experiences with an *educated*, open mind.

Thomas and Chess's "Goodness of Fit" Model

Based on their research on temperament, Thomas and Chess developed their "Goodness of Fit" model. This model is the interconnection of temperament and the properties, expectations and demands of the environment. It is the degree in which a child's temperament is compatible with the expectations and/or demands of his environment. Parents and caregivers must find a balance, or "good fit," for each child that considers the child's temperament and recognizes that they must adapt to other temperaments and environmental characteristics. Parents and caregivers can also modify children's temperament with environmental influences.

Thomas and Chess's "Goodness of Fit" model encourages parents and caregivers to create a caregiving environment that acknowledges each child's different temperament while at the same time encouraging them to adapt their interactions to each of these different temperaments. For example, a caregiver would introduce a slow-to-warm up child to a new situation very differently than an easy child. This sensitive attention to each child's needs and personalities fits well with this book's emphasis on caregiving for the individual child. Each child is unique and must be acknowledged as such. Your caregiving of each child is different and respects that uniqueness. When caregivers recognize and appreciate individual differences, they are able to respond to the challenges of infants and toddlers temperaments in a caring, respectful and developmentally appropriate way (Thomas & Chess, 1970, 1986).

I do think it is important, though, to not quickly categorize children as having one of the three temperament types that Thomas and Chess have identified. While children may exhibit some or many of the characteristics of the three types, immediately assuming that child is a specific type at all times and in all situations may hurt your interactions with the child. Assuming can lead a self-fulfilling prophecy in the child, which is harmful. While Thomas and Chess believed that temperament is established by 3 months old, this is now widely disputed. Temperament develops with age and experience. Children's experiences through the infant and toddler years influence temperament, and it makes more sense to say that by the end of the toddler years (age 3), a child's temperament is more established.

Resiliency

Resilience is the ability to thrive, mature and increase ability when faced with adverse conditions. These conditions could be biological conditions such as a health issue or environmental conditions such as poverty or abuse. The conditions can be prolonged, inconsistent, severe or sporadic. In order for a person to thrive through these adverse conditions, she must use all of her biological, psychological and environmental resources. Resilience results from the work of internal (biological, psychological) and external (environmental) factors.

Resilient children rebound or recover from adversity in an adaptive manner. When discussing resiliency with infants and toddlers, we will focus on a child's inner strength and competency in "dealing with life." Fostering resiliency in infants and toddlers contributes to healthy emotional development and, consequently, leads to healthy and appropriate social skills. Our goal as parents and caregivers of young children is to teach them to act appropriately and "deal with life" in a manner that is both socially acceptable and healthy. While it is impossible to shield infants and toddlers from all types of stresses in the world, you can help them to have a positive attitude about dealing with the stresses.

The development of resilience is similar to all other areas of development: it is an interaction between nature and nurture. While resilient children are believed by some to be biologically born to be more adaptive, environment does play an important role as well. Both males and females have been shown to be equally resilient. The general characteristics of resilience seem to be *independence, internal locus of control* (the belief that life events occur based on your own actions) and *androgyny* (exhibiting both male and female characteristics).

Caregivers should promote independence, internal locus of control and androgyny in order to promote resilience in the children they care for. *Independence* can be promoted by allowing infants and toddlers to complete tasks on their own. Choosing their own activities to participate in or materials to explore are easy ways to promote independence. Caregivers can also allow infants and toddlers to wash their own hands, prepare for mealtime and eventually serve themselves. Infants and toddlers should also participate in clean up time to the best of their ability.

Internal locus of control can be promoted by creating an environment that accepts all children. Caregivers should offer children praise and encouragement and encourage social skills and socialization. Prosocial behavior should be modeled and rewarded, and children should be given numerous opportunities to play near and with each other.

Androgyny can be promoted by simply allowing it to occur. There seem to be characteristics that are considered only male or only female. This should be ignored, and all children should be able to exhibit all characteristics and behaviors. Males should be allowed to experience and express emotions. Females should be allowed to be adventurous and assertive. In a childcare setting, it should be normal for males to play in the kitchen and girls to play with trucks. To further this movement, males should also be encouraged to be infant and toddler caregivers (Gonzalez-Mena & Eyer, 2017; Gordon, 1996, 1998).

Resilient Infants

Resilience can be seen in infants who live in stressful and economically disadvantaged circumstances. Resilient infants are active and energetic and have a laid-back personality. They have an "easy" temperament and can stimulate social interactions with others. They are responsive to others' social interactions and can therefore elicit social responses and attention from other people. Resilient infants are able to display the emotions of determination, frustration and tolerance. They can control their impulses and delay gratification (Gonzalez-Mena & Eyer, 2017; Gordon, 1996, 1998).

Resilient Toddlers

Resilient toddlers are similar to resilient infants. They are independent, although in a cooperative and compliant way. They are able to engage in positive interactions with others, which garners positive responses from others. They are less timid and less hostile with others. These characteristics have them often accepted by their peers. Resilient toddlers have also been shown to be more intelligent than their non-resilient peers.

Research has also differentiated resilient toddler males from resilient toddler females. Resilient toddler males have been shown to be more socially active, expressive and dominant. Their social skills and expression are strong, as well as their affective expression and demonstration of emotions. Resilient toddler females are also quite social, active and adaptable, and they enjoy exploring their environment. They tend to be more coordinated and less timid than their non-resilient peers (Gonzalez-Mena & Eyer, 2017; Gordon, 1996, 1998).

Implications for Childcare

Parents or other primary caregivers of resilient infants and toddlers have been shown to be responsive to the children's verbal and non-verbal

Emotional Development 231

Figure 10.3 Infant and Toddler Sibling Attachment

communications. They feel confident in and enjoy parenting and their children. These caregivers provide time for the child to explore appropriate materials, pictures and toys. They cuddle their children and show affection; body contact occurs often. The care they provide is consistent, responsive, stimulated and organized. Birthdays and other special events are documented and celebrated.

Research has shown that there are environmental characteristics that allow for infant and toddler resilience when they live in impoverished or stressful environments. If caregivers provide this kind of environment, an infant or toddler is more likely to show the characteristics of resilience. Resilient children understand that everything happens for a reason, which is an understanding of cause and effect. They actively look for solutions to problems, have a positive attitude toward life and tend to socialize easily. As parents and caregivers of infants and toddlers, your goal should be to help each child in your care to exhibit these resilient characteristics. So how do you do it?

First, it is important to know each child in your care well and build a relationship with each one. When you do this, you are also working toward the healthy social-emotional environment that was discussed in chapter two. Remember that this environment is a place where every child feels as though he belongs and is an important member of the classroom or home community. The environment must also be predictable and make the children feel safe.

As caregivers build relationships with the children, they must also do so with the families of the children. As discussed in chapter three, this relationship must be of both trust and respect. Caregivers in childcare settings can be influential in providing social support for resilience-promoting behaviors. They should be emotionally supportive to parents in their daily interactions and care for their children. A supportive adult peer is very helpful for these parents. Smile, listen to the parents as they express their concerns or talk about their experiences with their children. Be sympathetic and empathetic and always be encouraging. Caregivers can also support parents by providing information about support groups and relief care agencies.

Curriculum for infants and toddlers can also promote resilience. Curriculum must be meaningful and developmentally appropriate for the age of the children. Children need to be allowed to be independent in their explorations and encouraged by their successes. This type of environment supports infants and toddlers' internal locus of control. Parents should also be shown how to emulate this appropriate environment at home. When learning relates to the children's lives and life experiences, it is relevant to them, and they are more apt to pay attention and learn from it. When you authentically assess the learning that occurs in these learning experiences through documentation of the children's explorations and communications, you are further emphasizing the relevance of their learning.

Finally, another aspect of resiliency is the ability to transition back and forth between positive and negative feelings. Caregivers who help a child reestablish previous positive feelings when a child feels negative ones will help a child to psychologically realize that when things are bad they can be made better. This leads to healthy brain development and helps to strengthen a healthy attachment relationship with a caregiver. People who are resilient are able to cope despite any obstacles put in front of them.

Strategies for Helping Infants and Toddlers Cope With Strong Emotions

Caregiving in group settings can either buffer or increase stress levels in children. This is why it is so important that childcare centers provide high-quality care. There must be supportive and nurturing environments for the children and their families, where caregivers understand emotional development and milestones. Healthy emotional development is the basis for all relationships in the childcare setting and for any learning that occurs. Caregivers must understand that there is a connection between feeling and behavior, and they must observe and work to understand each child's emotional world.

Any adult who cares for infants and toddlers must learn to embrace strong emotions, not shy away from them. When caregivers stay emotionally connected to a child expressing strong emotions, whether they are positive or negative, the child learns that his strong feelings are tolerated and can be worked through. Caregivers should attend to the safety of the emotional environment of their classroom just as must as they attend to the safety of the physical environment. They can do this by ensuring that:

- Each caregiver practices thoughtful and responsive caregiving—they understand emotional development and how to care for infants and toddlers and their emotions in a developmentally appropriate manner
- Each child has at least one caregiver who knows him well and cares for him like he needs it
- Each parent and child is greeted warmly by name and given at least a moment to connect when they enter the classroom
- There are consistent, predictable responses to staff concerns and support for all staff members
- Caregivers smile, laugh and have fun—shared laughter, joy and fun between caregivers and children helps the brain grow!

Chronic stress has been shown to decrease memory, the ability to control behavior and the ability to focus attention. It also can decrease the strength of the immune system. Strong attachment relationships can act as a "buffer" for stress. Sensitive, attentive and loving caregiving can help to decrease stress levels and then subsequently increase these different positive abilities. Fearful children in secure attachment relationships can be in an unfamiliar situation and not show signs of stress. On the other hand, children with a similar temperament in an insecure attachment relationship will show signs of stress in the same situation. Children exhibit attachment behaviors when they experience fear and uncertainty.

Respectful parents and caregivers pay attention to and reflect on the emotions that they see coming from a child. They feel that all emotion is relevant and important to recognize and that their job is to teach the child to deal with every emotion in the most healthy and appropriate way (versus trying to eliminate it). Respectful parents and caregivers do not discount or minimize any emotions and do not ask children to justify why they are feeling how they are. They acknowledge and then observe and analyze in order to determine the best way to intervene and support if it is necessary. Empathy and tolerance are key behaviors in these responsive parents and caregivers. Therefore, when working with infants and toddlers, parents and caregivers should always:

- Accept all emotions as valid and acknowledge them as real
  - Verbally acknowledge the emotion while standing as close to the child as possible
  - Place your hand on the child's arm or shoulder as a way of physically comforting the child through light contact
- Support children in finding ways to cope with the emotion and/or help them cope with the emotion
  - For infants, physical contact for comfort and verbally acknowledging the emotion will usually suffice

234 *Emotional Development*

- o For toddlers, your behaviors need to extend to asking the child to tell you why she might be feeling the emotion or what exactly is causing her to feel the emotion. You can then work with her to cope with it.
- Prepare infants and toddlers for situations that may elicit strong emotions
  - o Infants can be held by a trusted caregiver who exhibits comfort and strength
  - o Toddlers can be told what is going to happen and then "talked through" the situation
- Couple the unfamiliar (meeting a new caregiver) with the familiar (do it in an environment that the child knows well and is comfortable in)
- Always give infants and toddlers time to adjust to new situations and observe their reactions and behaviors for clues as to how they feel and how comfortable they are
- Allow the infant or toddler to have the emotion and express it and then work to understand it, cope with it or redirect it. If a child is exhibiting a negative emotion like angrily throwing toys, for example, give her a beanbag or ball to throw as a way to redirect the energy.
- Acknowledge each infant or toddler's self-calming technique (such as thumb sucking or cuddling a familiar toy or blanket), and see when he

Figure 10.4 Infant Exploring Outdoors

turn to the calming technique. This can help you to understand if and how he is coping.

(Berk, 2012, 2015, 2018a, 2018b)

Maslow: Self-Direction and Self-Regulation

People's emotions and self-calming techniques relate to their self-direction toward growth and maturity. Abraham Maslow saw this self-direction as a process he called *self-actualization*. To Maslow, healthy people are always self-actualizing. These people are aware of their potential and strive to make choices that move them toward that potential. Self-actualized people perceive reality clearly and are open, alive, spontaneous, objective and creative. They have the ability to love and have a strong sense of self.

The key to being self-actualized, though, is to have all of your physical, emotional and intellectual needs met. Below is Maslow's "Hierarchy of Needs," which exhibits the progression of needs he perceived are necessary to be met in the order he believed they must be met. As a lower level of needs are met, a person can move up to the next level and have the next set of needs met. While children's needs must be met promptly most of the time, it is important to point out that Maslow did not advocate for the immediate meeting of all needs at all times. Delay, limits and discipline are also necessary in order for children to learn limitations that the physical world puts on their gratifications. In chapter two, we discussed the idea of determining the

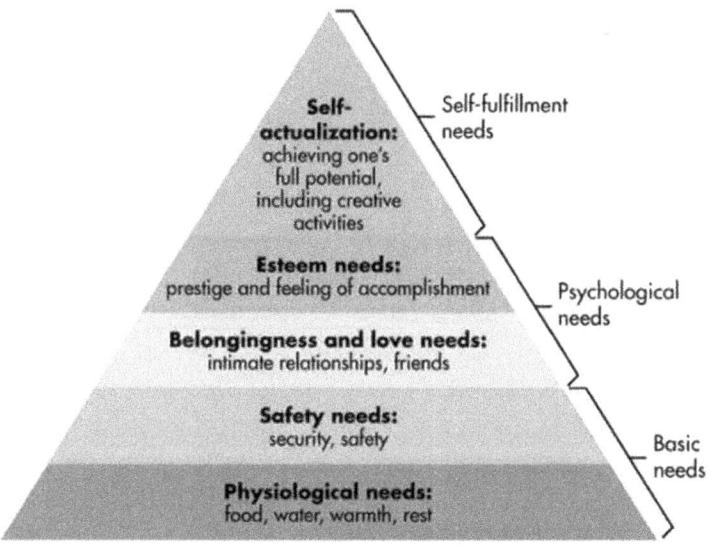

Figure 10.5 Maslow's Hierarchy of Needs
Source: McLeod (2018, May 21).

optimal stress level for a child and then responding. This idea adheres well to Maslow's acknowledgement of delaying gratification at times (Maslow, 1943; Maslow & Frager, 1987).

The Development of Self-Regulation

As infants and toddlers work to become "self-actualized," they are learning *self-regulation*, or self-control. Humans are not born with this ability, but it is one of the most important developmental tasks. Self-regulation allows people to control their emotions, respond in appropriate ways to frustration, get along with other people well and be independent.

Parents and caregivers can foster self-regulation in infants and toddlers by helping children pay attention to and define their feelings and emotions. Give them the language that they might be lacking to describe how they perceive a situation. There are also times when you can leave the child alone to focus on his experiences and react how he sees fit. When you provide an appropriate, safe and comfortable environment for infants and toddlers, you allow for the children's own self-direction toward what they need and want to do when they are ready to do it. Finally, provide choices and encourage independence. Doing this will allow infants and toddlers to truly learn from their experiences, which helps them to become a more competent person and confident decision maker.

A child's early relationships with adults greatly influences the development of self-regulation. Parents and caregivers must provide experiences that allow infants and toddlers learn to control themselves and support and encourage them in this important development. Some specific strategies parents and caregivers can use are:

- Pay attention to children's signs that they are frustrated, hungry or tired. Consistently respond to these needs and work with the child to verbally express them to you. Be empathetic toward children and show them that you understand that their needs and feelings are important
- Provide many opportunities for children to be independent and make choices. Give them a few acceptable options (three outfits you like; two snack choices) and give them the freedom to choose
- Remind children to "make good choices" often and keep frustration to a minimum by giving them warnings for change or to do something you are requesting. For example, give a five-minute, two-minute and then one-minute warning for cleaning up. When you get to the actual clean up time, they will be ready for it
- Remind children of behavioral expectations and what they can expect in different situations

Emotional Development 237

- Create a safe, quiet place where children can go in order to be alone for a break if they need to
- Talk about what children *can* do, not what they can't do
- Teach children to wait. Wait times do not need to be long, and you can give them something to do during the wait period.

(Gillespie & Seibel, 2006)

Encouraging Infants and Toddlers

Self-Confidence and Self-Control

As a caregiver for infants and toddlers, it is important for you to continuously promote and encourage self-confidence *and* self-control in the children you care for. Your interactions with and actions around the children will influence how they feel about those who care for them and the world they live in. These feelings then directly influence how they feel about themselves. Your behaviors and communications also teach infants and toddlers to develop self-control. This ability gradually grows as they get older but also requires guidance and modeling from caregivers.

Figure 10.6 Infant Calmly Bathing

Emotional Behaviors and Caregiver Strategies

Now that you are aware of the emotional development of infants and toddlers and the different emotions they express, it is important for you to focus on the strategies you should use as a caregiver to respond to them. Utilizing these strategies will allow you to help enhance infants and toddlers' emotional development. Table 10.2 describes the different emotions present during each age period and different strategies you can implement as a caregiver to respond to emotions and help promote emotional development. It also describes the level of control the child has over his emotions and emotional expression and how emotions are most often expressed.

"The Happiest Toddler on the Block"
By Dr. Harvey Karp

Just as we look to Dr. Karp to help us calm infants, we should also look to him to help us understand toddlers. Dr. Karp's book gives some excellent tips about how to help toddlers recognize, cope with and appropriately express their emotions. He reminds us that the left side of a toddler's brain (the part that controls conversation, patience and logic) is continually overpowered by the right brain (the part that focuses on impulse, emotion and understanding non-verbal communication such as facial expressions, tone of voice and sign language). When toddlers get upset (angry, frustrated), the unbalance is often severe and causes the child to cry, scream and physically show her unhappiness.

Dr. Karp offers the following suggestions for helping toddlers cope with and express their emotions appropriately:

- Use short phrases—long ones are hard to understand (one to three words for young toddlers, three to five for older toddlers)
- Repeat yourself—upset toddlers need to hear something five to ten times
- Be expressive when you talk—the way you speak is just as important if not more important than the words you say (reflect one-third of the child's tone of voice, facial expressions and body gestures so she sees that you care *and* understand exactly how she feels)

Dr. Karp offers the following suggestions for preventing tantrums with toddlers:

- Play and talk together often—intervals of two to ten minutes of play and interaction with you will satisfy them, prevent tantrums and create a cooperative and caring relationship with you
- Be clear and consistent with the limits you set, pick your battles and only set limits you can definitely enforce
- Respect toddler's words and actions, and he will become a respectful child

(Karp, 2008)

Table 10.2 Infant and Toddler Emotions and Corresponding Appropriate Caregiver Strategies

Age	Types of Emotions	Caregiver Strategies	Control of Emotions
Birth–4 months	Excitement/enjoyment Stress/anger/frustration/fear	Show the same through verbal and non-verbal communication Determine the cause and remove/reduce it; hold and comfort child	Reflected verbally through sounds Expressions seem automatic
4–8 months	Joy, happiness, pleasure in watching others and in repetitive play Fear of strangers, falling, depression, frustration, rage	Share and reflect back feelings through verbalizations, actions and games; provide opportunities to watch and play with favorite toys Affirm and acknowledge; allow expression; comfort when needed	Can be calmed when held, comforted, talked to, sung to
8–12 months	Joy, happiness, pleasure Affection Preferences for toys/people Independence Self-esteem Anxiety Fear Anger/frustration/tantrums Rejection of items/situations	Share and reflect back feelings; acknowledge and provide preferences; allow time and opportunities for independence; provide positive affirmations of infant through voice, looks, touch; praise for self-control; use "no" and commands sparingly Remove source; redirect child to something different; calm through cuddling, singing, talking; acknowledge and allow for choices	Begins to obey "No" and "Stop" Sometimes inhibits own behavior
12–18 months	Excitement/delight Humor Affection Expanded independence Fear of strangers Dependent on caregiver for security Negativism Has tantrums	Consistently accept and return emotions; allow for independence Provide choices; determine cause of stress and either remove or comfort child; can ignore some tantrums Clearly verbalize right and wrong behavior Praise for controlling behavior	Shows emotions in behavior and language Recognizes emotions of others Uses play to express emotions and resolve conflicts Learning right and wrong Repeats desirable behavior

(*Continued*)

Table 10.2 (Continued)

Age	Types of Emotions	Caregiver Strategies	Control of Emotions
18–24 months	Seeks approval Seeks security in routines Continually developing/changing feelings about self Increases fantasy Developing new fears Aggressiveness Shyness May reject parent/caregivers	Provide verbal and non-verbal approval Provide consistent routines and feedback Identify emotions and clearly respond to them Listen to and accept fantasies Listen and accept as real; reassure child of your concern Remain close and remind child or remove from situations Allow rejection and shyness and reassure of your affection for child Use words, facial expressions and gestures to show approval and disapproval of behavior Prepare child for change Allow all emotional expressions; help child work through all of them	Uses the actions of others to control behavior May resist change Can show more than one emotion at the same time Emotions change from one extreme to the other quickly
24–30 months	Comfortable with self Feels both positive and negative self-worth	Provide opportunities for child to feel success Give positive feedback Be sensitive to frustrations with tasks and socialization Accept all feelings as honest and true	Expresses emotions
30–36 months	Enthusiastic Mastering skills Reacts strongly Can act negatively	Reinforce excitement Provide challenging opportunities Provide experiences where child needs to master skills Accept initial response and work toward appropriate expression Rephrase suggestions to child and give choices Provide opportunities to work out feelings and need for control	Can be physically aggressive

Source: (Berk, 2012, 2015, 2018a, 2018b).

For additional material, visit:
www.parentphd.org/infantandtoddlertext/ch10/

Reflection Questions

For the following three events in a toddler's day, how would you act and interact with each of the three temperaments of easy, slow-to-warm-up and difficult?

- Eating:
- Free play:
- Large group story time:

Describe a resilient infant.
Describe a resilient toddler.
Read the article "What to do for a Fussy Baby" in the additional content for this chapter. What did you learn from this article about calming a fussy baby that you didn't know before?

- Identify at least two strategies that the caregivers use to help children cope with their emotions and feelings. Identify the feeling and then describe the strategy used.
- What are some temperamental differences that you observed in your classroom/field experience?
- Describe a self-calming behavior that you have observed with an infant and with a toddler.

Bibliography

Berk, L. (2012). *Child development* (9th ed.). Boston, MA: Pearson.
Berk, L. (2015). *Infants and children: Prenatal through middle childhood* (8th ed.). Boston, MA: Pearson.
Berk, L. (2018a). *Exploring child development*. Boston, MA: Pearson.

Berk, L. (2018b). *Exploring child and adolescent development.* Boston, MA: Pearson.

Chess, S., & Thomas, A. (1987). Temperamental individuality from childhood to adolescence. *Journal of Child Psychiatry, 16,* 218–226.

Douville-Watson, L., Watson, M. A., & Wilson, L. C. (2003). *Infants and toddlers: Curriculum and teaching* (5th ed.). New York, NY: Thomas Delmar Learning.

Gilkerson, L. (1998). Brain care: Supporting healthy emotional development. *Child Care Information Exchange, 5,* 66–68.

Gillespie, L., & Seibel, N. (2006, July). Self-regulation: The cornerstone of early childhood development. *Beyond the Journal,* 1–6.

Gonzalez-Mena, J., & Eyer, D. (2017). *Infants, toddlers, and caregivers: A curriculum of respectful, responsive, relationship-based care and education* (11th ed.). New York, NY: McGraw Hill.

Gordon, K. A. (1996, June). Infant and toddler resilience: Knowledge, predictions, policy and practice. Paper delivered at Head Start National Research Conference, Washington, DC.

Gordon, K. A. (1998). Infant and toddler resilience. *Early Childhood Education Journal, 26*(1), 47–52.

Izard, C. E. (1982). *Measuring emotions in infants and young children.* New York, NY: Cambridge Press.

Karp, H. (2008). *The happiest toddler on the block: How to eliminate tantrums and raise a patient, respectful, and cooperative one- to four-year-old* (2nd ed.). New York, NY: Bantam.

Klinnert, M. D., Emede, R. N., Butterfield, P., & Campos, J. J. (1986). Social referencing: The infants' use of emotional signals from a friendly adult with mother present. *Developmental Psychology, 22*(4), 427–432.

Maslow, A. H. (1943). A theory of human motivation. *Psychological Review, 50,* 370–396.

Maslow, A. H., & Frager, R. (1987). *Motivation and personality.* New Delhi: Pearson Education.

McLeod, S. A. (2018, May 21). Maslow's hierarchy of needs. Retrieved from www.simplypsychology.org/maslow.html

Mumme, D., Fernald, A., & Herrera, C. (1966). Infant's responses to facial and vocal emotional signals in a social referencing paradigm. *Child Development, 66,* 3219–3237.

Schore, A. N. (1996). The experience-dependent maturation of a regulatory system in the orbital prefrontal cortex and the origin of developmental psychopathology. *Development and Psychopathology, 8,* 59–87.

Shonkoff, J. P., & Phillips, D. A. (2000). *From neurons to neighborhoods: The science of early childhood development.* Washington, DC: National Academy of Sciences.

Siegel, D. J. (1999). *The developing mind: How relationships and the brain interact to shape who we are.* New York, NY: The Guilford Press.

Speaks-Fold, V. (2008). Accommodating different personalities and temperaments. Retrieved from www.earlychildhoodnews.com/earlychildhood/article_view.aspx?ArticleID=303

Sroufe, L. A., Egeland, B., Carlson, E. A., & Collins, W. A. (2005). *The development of the person: The Minnesota study of risk and adaptation from birth to adulthood.* New York, NY: The Guilford Press.

Thomas, A., & Chess, S. (1986). The New York longitudinal study: From infancy to early adult life. In R. Plomin & J. Dunn (Eds.), *The study of temperament: Changes, continuities and challenges* (pp. 39–52). Mahwah, NJ: Lawrence Erlbaum Associates.

Thomas, A., Chess, S., & Birch, H. G. (1970). The origin of personality. *Scientific American, 223*(2), 102–109.

Zero to Three. (2010). Relationships: The heart of development and learning. Retrieved from www.zerotothree.org/resources/73-relationships-the-heart-of-development-and-learning

11 Language and Literacy Development

Language and literacy development begins with conversations between caregivers and infants. Caregivers lay the foundation for this important area of development by talking with infants, repeating back babbling, asking questions, reading books and singing songs. Caregivers should use simple words, keep a balance between listening and talking with the child and provide an environment rich with literacy experiences and interesting things to talk about.

Language is the communication of thoughts and feelings through a system of arbitrary signals, such as voice sounds, gestures or written symbols. The sounds, symbols and interactions that people experience early in life directly relate to the way they think about and understand the world.

Language allows infants and toddlers to communicate. They facilitate conversations with others, clarify needs, gather information, label their experiences, develop reasoning skills, increase their adaptation and coping skills and express what they know. The abilities to communicate and acquire language are innate, and the course of language development is incredibly complex. It varies among children and has multiple "bursts" and "plateaus." Social experiences and interactions foster this innate ability and lead to children acquiring language. Through natural and genuine conversations with adults, children acquire language and the ability to communicate by listening to and then imitating their caregivers. As they mature, children refine their language, learn words and grammar rules and understand symbols.

As with all areas of development, nature (biology) and nurture (life experiences and interactions) work together for healthy brain growth and the development of language. There is a strong connection between brain development and language experience. Infants' brains are wired to learn any language, and they are capable of perceiving nearly all of the speech contrast used in natural language. In the first few months of life, an infant's brain is very flexible and responsive. This "neuroplasticity" is why infants tend to respond to any sound or language. As they get older, neuroplasticity lessens, and if certain sound patterns aren't heard with regularity, they will not be commonplace for the child to say and understand.

Language development is dependent on the stimulation of the synapses in infants' brains. This stimulation occurs through responsive interactions with other people. While an infant may be physically capable of producing a sound, without a response and an interaction with another person when that sound is made, the sound will likely not be made for much longer. When pleasant language experiences are repeated, the connections between neurons in the brain become stronger and shape how infants and toddlers continue to learn language. Infants need to have opportunities to listen to adults talk to them and then have opportunities to respond in order for the neurons and synapses in the brain that are related to language to develop.

As language abilities increase, so do cognitive abilities and their use in daily life. For example, infants and toddlers' memories increase as they gather labels for experiences and objects, and their memory bank eventually forms groups and categories to further understand the world. The ability to reason and to put their experiences in a logical order are also cognitive abilities that develop as language does. This leads to self-regulation, where a toddler can plan and monitor her own behavior. The ability to adapt and the development of coping skills soon follow as toddlers become more skilled at organizing the information they are taking in and learning on a daily basis. None of this would be possible without the development of language.

> Early experiences can determine how proficient a child becomes in his or her native language. Researchers found that when mothers frequently spoke to their infants, their children learned almost *300 more words by age 2* than did their peers whose mothers rarely spoke to them. Furthermore, studies have suggested that **mere exposure to language such as listening to the television or to adults talking amongst themselves provides little benefit**. Rather infants need to interact directly with other human beings, to hear people talking about what they are seeing and experiencing, in order for them to develop optimal language skills.
>
> (www.zerotothree.org)

Early social interactions allow infants to experience and imitate feedback from adults. Cooing turns into babbling, and babbling turns into first words. Conversations soon develop. It is incredibly important to talk to infants and respond to any sounds and verbal gestures that they make. Each sound and gesture is an attempt to communicate with you. If you respond, infants will continue to attempt to communicate. If you don't, they will eventually stop because they aren't getting a response to reinforce their communications.

Infants and toddlers' vocabulary is directly linked to how much interaction they experience. They need to hear words and have those words linked to objects and events. These valuable experiences create permanent neural connections in the brain because they are meaningful. When infants and toddlers interact with real people (versus watching a television for example), they learn and practice language. Talk to them and let them respond to you (Anisfield, 1984; Bates, Thal, Finlay, & Clancy, 1992).

Figure 11.1 Expressive Infant

Receptive and Expressive Language Development

Understanding both receptive and expressive language gives some insight into the progression of language development, as well as how much of an impact social interactions have on language development. Infants react to being spoken to from birth. At first, it is just the pitch or tone of your speech. Eventually, it becomes the actual sounds, words and phrases of your speech. When infants reach this point, they are responding to the actual meaning of what you are saying. When you speak to infants in meaningful ways, they understand you very early in life.

When an infant takes in and understands language, it is called *receptive language*. Essentially, they are "receiving" language from another person and are working to understand and process it. As infants continue to "receive language," they soon make connections between sounds or sound patterns and actual events or objects. When you hand an infant an object and say the name, a connection will be made. When you read a familiar storybook, he will begin to recognize the same sounds and words with the same pictures. When you perform a caregiving practice like eating or diapering, he will begin to recognize the familiar words and phrases that you say as the routine occurs.

As you have read in previous chapters, it is very important to talk to infants and to respond to their cries and vocalizations. As their cries and vocalizations are responded to, infants learn to refine them. As they refine their communications, they become more skilled at sending them. They will use the same ones at the same times—hunger, discomfort, frustration, pleasure. The first clear expression using gestures, sounds or words is called *expressive language*. The key to expressive language development is adults responding to the expressions. Again, if cries and vocalizations are not responded to, infants will give up and no longer attempt to communicate.

The majority of young children acquire first words and their meanings fairly quickly, even though they don't express them correctly right away. The words they hear most frequently by caregivers will be the words they express first and more often. By the toddler years, many children also use *fast mapping* to acquire language quickly. Fast mapping is when children use context clues to figure out the meaning of something unfamiliar. The child can gain a partial understanding of a word after only hearing it one time and then can acquire similar words from that one original meaning. The child uses familiar contexts and repetition to generalize the meaning of new words. Errors do occur, but the appropriate meanings of the words will eventually be learned through more practice and repetition. By age 2, children can make fairly efficient and appropriate use of many sources of information to determine what speakers are referring to and evaluate how the words they are hearing can be used in future situations.

As children refine and develop their language, they learn grammatical rules and the correct way to say words and phrases. There is no need to correct infants and toddlers, although you can respond with the appropriate word or phrase as a way to acknowledge the child's communications and respond. For example, if a child says "nakmin" instead of "napkin," you can say "Oh, you would like a napkin?" as a response to the child. This response will exhibit the correct pronunciation in a developmentally appropriate way. Saying "No, it's not nakmin; it's napkin" is not appropriate and will thwart the child's attempts to try and communicate for fear that he will say something wrong (Morrow, 2019).

Here are some simple tips for promoting receptive and expressive language development in infants and toddlers:

Tips for Promoting Receptive Language Development

Provide children with opportunities to:

- Hear language and new vocabulary
- Associate language with pleasure
- Discriminate and classify sounds
- Listen to each other
- Follow directions
- Hear good models of standard English

(Morrow, 2019)

Figure 11.2 Infant Exploring Letters

Tips for Promoting Expressive Language Development

Provide children with opportunities to:

- Pronounce words correctly
- Increase speaking vocabulary

- Speak in complete sentences
- Expand syntactic structures
- Communicate with each other
- Develop contextual language (subjects in school)

(Morrow, 2019)

The Development of Communication Skills: Hearing/Understanding and Talking Milestones

While every child is different, there is a typical progression of speech and language development that parents and caregivers of infants and toddlers should be aware of. Language tends to progress from responding to the spoken word by babbling to using single words to convey their needs in this general order: names objects, uses short sentences, clearer speech and then using more complex sentences (asks questions and uses nouns, verbs and conjunctions).

From birth to age 1, infants play with sounds, understand more than they can say and eventually produce one-word utterances. From ages 1 to 2, speech sounds begin to have more adult intonations, and telegraphic speech (expressing or describing thoughts, feelings or perceptions by articulating words) is often used. From ages 2 to 3, speech development is more functional, and telegraphic speech is more detailed. Children speak with more confidence and play and repeat language often.

Children will not master all of the skills listed in each category until they reach the end of the age range; if a child has not mastered every skill in the category before she moves up, it does not necessarily mean there is a problem. Remember that we look at development as something that happens *in time, not on time*.

Birth–4 months:

Hearing and Understanding

- Increases or decreases sucking in response to hearing a sound
- Startles at loud sounds
- Recognizes your voice and quiets/smiles when spoken to

Talking

- Makes pleasure sounds—"coos" are vowel-like
- Plays with tongue and makes noises with saliva in mouth
- Cries differently for different needs
- Initiates making sounds; experiments with sound; will repeat/practice sound
- Smiles when she sees you
- Responds vocally to someone

Caregiver Strategies:

- Talk with and sing often
- Answer infants with sounds and words; repeat infants' sounds
- Respond to cries immediately; hold infants often

4–8 months

Hearing and Understanding

- Responds to changes in your tone of voice
- Notices that toys make sounds
- Will move eyes in the direction of different sounds/looks for the person who is speaking
- Is attentive to music (pauses, turns eyes, head or body toward the sound)
- Looks when name is called

Talking

- Verbalizes both excitement and displeasure
- Giggles/chuckles/laughs
- Makes gurgling sounds to communicate with you
- Responds to talking with cooing/babbling/smiling
- Makes babbling sounds that sound more speech-like and have many different sounds (adding consonants; two to three syllables)
- Uses intensity/volume/pitch/rhythm in speech

Caregiver Strategies:

- Respond with talk and talk directly to infants (face them so they can see you when you are talking to them)
- Change your voice to reflect the mood
- Use normal speaking patterns and tones (no baby talk!)

8 months–1 year

Hearing and Understanding

- Turns and looks in the direction of sounds
- Listens when he is spoken to
- Recognizes the names of common items such as "cup," "book" etc. (words are learned in context; they associate words with a specific object or action)
- Responds to familiar sounds, words and own name
- Begins to respond to requests such as "want more" or "come over here"
- Enjoys playing peek-a-boo and pat-a-cake with you

Talking

- Uses gestures to communicate
- Imitates different speech sounds and uses sounds to get and keep attention
- Babbling has long and short groups of sounds; beginning of conversation-like sounds
- Speaks one or two words by age 1, although they may not be totally clear
- Repeats/practices sounds over and over
- Makes sounds that reflect emotions
- Intentionally communicates to get something accomplished/what they want

Caregiver Strategies:

- Continuously name objects while pointing to them
- Respond with talk and verbally reinforce talking with reciprocal conversation
- Respond to and verbally label emotions and actions
- Label common behaviors and verbally respond to infants' use of them

1–2 years

Hearing and Understanding

- Points to body parts when asked
- Points to pictures in books when they are named
- Listens to simple stories/songs/rhymes
- Understands simple questions ("Where is your cup?") and follows simple commands ("Throw the ball")

Talking

- Says more and more words each month (uses in context; identifies familiar pictures)
- Uses approximations for some words
- Says two words together ("No shoe") and asks one- and two-word questions ("What's that?" or "That?")
- Uses many different consonant sounds at the beginning of words
- Imitates the sounds of people and objects
- Responds with gestures and conversation (even to questions and commands they cannot say)

Caregiver Strategies:

- Become familiar with toddlers' sounds and words so you can respond appropriately

- Play with sounds and enjoy toddlers' sound explorations
- When toddlers look/point/reach for something, say the name and ask toddlers if they can name them
- Be consistent with questions and commands so toddler learns what they mean and will begin to verbally respond
- Recognize that toddler talk is about immediate needs and desires (not past or future situations)

2–3 years

Hearing and Understanding

- Listens to and attends to longer stories
- Can follow two directions at the same time ("Get your cup and put it on the table")
- Understands differences in meaning (stop and go; big and little, up and down)

Talking

- Uses language to: reflect own meaning, communicate socially (hello/please/thank you), label objects, express needs/desires, direct others, ask questions ("What's that?" is very common)
- Speech is understood the majority of the time
- Uses two- and three-word phrases
- Asks for/directs attention to things by naming them
- Sounds expanding to use k, g, f, t, d and n
- Uses nouns, verbs and pronouns
- Has a word for almost everything
- Calls self by name
- Constructs sentences versus reproducing them from memory:

    o *Demonstrative naming*—first word points out object, second word names it ("that ball")
    o *Attribution*—gives objects attributes to distinguish it from others ("blue shoe")
    o *Possession*—associates person with object ("Daddy's chair")
    o *Action sentences*—separates action from actor ("I run")
    o *Recurrence*—tells of a thing or event that happens again ("more juice")
    o *Negation*—something that is desired or expected is not there/child can't do something ("No cup" and "No hit")
    o *Increased vocabulary*—associates more words with objects
    o *Improves syntax*—clear word order, longer sentences, two- to three-word sentences
    o *Improves word forms*—uses plurals and past tense

Caregiver Strategies:

- Continue to verbally label everything—expand to full sentences
- Consistently use social words in their context (hello, please, thank you)
- Listen to child's expressions of needs and commands and respond verbally and with actions
- Answer their questions (even the ones they ask over and over again) with simple answers
- Use both short and long sentences
- Make sure child is aware you are giving directions and make them simple (American Speech-Language-Hearing Association, 2013; Morrow, 2019; Nilsen, 2016; Zero to Three, 2019a, 2019b, 2019c)

Literacy Development

> *Language provides the foundation for the development of literacy skills. Learning to communicate through gestures, sounds, and words increases a child's interest in—and later understanding of—books and reading. Talking, reading aloud, and singing all stimulate children's understanding and use of language, and help them learn to become good communicators and eager readers.*
>
> (www.zerotothree.org)

Literacy is the ability to listen and speak, and then eventually read and write. Oral language development is the cornerstone of literacy development. Children's literacy development begins very early on when they use "symbols" such as words, gestures, marks on paper and objects modeled out of materials in different activities such as talking, play, scribbling and drawing and pretend reading and writing. The following are some early literacy behaviors that you will see in infants and toddlers:

- Handling of books (page turning, chewing)
- Looking at and recognizing pictures in books (pointing, gazing at, laughing at)
- Understanding and comprehension of pictures and stories (imitating an action, talking about events)
- Story-reading (babbling in imitation of reading, running fingers along printed words)
- Holding writing utensils (markers, crayons) and making marks on paper

Early literacy is directly connected to children's relationships and activities. To understand the beginnings of literacy, we must study the environments that children grow up in and how these environments provide opportunities for the children to be exposed to literacy materials such as books, paper and writing materials. The people that children are surrounded by in their daily lives are who make reading and writing interesting and meaningful to young children. If you consider how many hours per day an infant or toddler spends in your care, you realize that you are one of these important people. You have an impact on the children in your care's literacy development.

Parents and caregivers serve as models and demonstrate literacy skills; provide literacy materials; and instruct, communicate and encourage children to practice literacy in their lives. Their attitudes and expectations about literacy are directly communicated to the children every day. Literacy development can be fostered in infants and toddlers with the appropriate environment and materials—and plenty of time to play.

For many children, play is where reading and writing begin. As you read in chapter seven, play is where children make connections to their world and the people in it. They emulate activities and experiences from their lives as a way of understanding them. Just as children play with materials, they play with reading and writing.

Play is linked to literacy development in two ways: as a symbolic activity and as a representation of an experience. As a symbolic activity, pretend play gives children the opportunity to use symbols to represent experiences and create imaginary worlds. They will then use these skills when they begin to read and write. As a representation of experience, play makes the actions of reading and writing that different characters perform more meaningful and accessible to children.

When children play with reading and writing, they become familiar with the tools of literacy and begin to learn how to use and control them. Play allows children to come to understand what reading and writing consist of and what they can do with them. Books, paper and writing materials should be available as often as toys and manipulatives so that children can incorporate reading and writing into their play. Children will experiment with written language and learn important information and skills about reading and writing through this type of play.

There are also connections between play and storytelling and the reading of and listening to books. Creating imaginary situations in play is a similar experience to what children create in their heads as they listen to storybooks and when they read or write stories on their own. Many children make up their first stories during their pretend play; they create and act out dramatic narratives and reenact stories they have heard. This later transfers to the writing and reading of their own pictures and stories. As children grow older, their play and imaginations become more extravagant, complex and abstract. There is often abundant and rich language used between children during play. Children discuss the characters they are portraying, the settings of their play and the plots of the experiences they are creating or recreating. Pretend play is almost dependent on language to create the worlds and characters and communicate meanings between the children.

Children also "play" with written language materials such as paper, pencils, markers, crayons and paper. They participate in the acts of writing and reading and take on the roles of writer and reader. If a character they are portraying reads or writes, the children will practice those skills with whatever

Figure 11.3 Toddler Drawing

understanding or experience they have with them. Play can make children feel like writers and readers long before they actually have the skills and knowledge to write and read (Morrow, 2019).

Infants and Toddlers With Books

Infants and toddlers should be exposed to a variety of books and stories from the beginning of life. Book experiences provide them with both interaction and literacy learning time. Infants and toddlers will listen to and visually attend to books, as well as explore them using their sense of touch, smell and taste. The more infants and toddlers are involved in book-reading experiences, the stronger their cognitive and literacy skills are. Book experiences lengthen their memory and attention span and teach them to attend to words on a page. They learn that the pictures tell the story and that they can read the story by looking at the pictures.

There are different types of books that you can provide for infants and toddlers, as well as specific features that cater to children in the first three years. Different types of books include:

- Story books
- Nonfiction books
- Wordless books
- Interaction books
- Concept books
- Predictable books

Figure 11.4 Infant Reaching for a Book

- Reference books
- Alphabet and word books
- Novelty books
- Paperbacks and magazines
- Teacher- and child-made books
- Therapeutic books
- Seasonal and holiday books
- Books with audio tapes
- Infant-toddler books
- Multicultural books

Infants and toddlers are also drawn to different features of books based on their age and developmental level. Use the following lists to help you choose the right books for the age of children you either live with or care for:

0–6 months:

- Simple, large pictures
- Bright colors
- Stiff/cardboard chunky board books
- Cloth/soft vinyl books

6–12 months:

- Board books with:
    - Photos of other babies
    - Bright colors
    - Photos of familiar objects (balls, bottles)
    - Sturdy pages that can be propped up or spread out on the floor
- Plastic/vinyl/washable cloth books
- Small plastic photo albums with pictures of family and friends

12–24 months:

- Sturdy board books they can carry around
- Books with:
    - Photos of children doing familiar activities such as sleeping, eating or playing
    - A few words on each page
    - Simple rhymes
    - Predictable text
- Goodnight books for bedtime
- Animal books
- Books about saying hello and goodbye

24–36 months:

- Books that have:
    - Simple stories
    - Rhymes they can memorize
- Books about:
    - Bedtime
    - Counting
    - Alphabet
    - Shapes
    - Sizes
    - Animals
    - Vehicles
    - Playtime
    - Saying hello and goodbye

(Morrow, 2019)

It is clearly important for parents and caregivers to participate in reading experiences with infants and toddlers. Now that you are aware of what types of books to provide and what features infants and toddlers attend to as they grow, it is important for you to know just *how* to engage in book experiences with the children. Here are some simple guidelines for sharing books with infants and toddlers:

- Make it part of everyday
    - Mealtimes
    - In the car/bus
    - Childcare drop off
    - Doctor's office
    - Grocery store
    - Naptime
    - End of the day
    - Bath time
    - Bedtime
- Show that it is fun
- Do it for as long as the child will sit (a few minutes is fine)
- Talk or sing about the pictures
- Let the children turn the pages
- Show the cover page and point out the title, author, illustrator and cover photos/art that tells what the story is about
- Point to the words as you read
- Read with animation and inflection
- Talk about how your lives relate to the story plot and characters
- Ask questions about the story/let children ask questions
- Let the children "read" or tell the story to you

(Morrow, 2019)

Caregiver Strategies to Promote

Language and Literacy Development

Now that you are knowledgeable about the language and literacy development of infants and toddlers, it is important for you to learn different strategies that you can use when caring for this age group of children. This next section will provide you with overall strategies for helping infants and toddlers develop their language and literacy skills and then break those strategies down into specific age groups. If you use these strategies as a guideline for your work with infants and toddlers, you can be sure that the children's literacy and language will grow.

Caregiver Strategies to Help

Infants and Toddlers Develop Their Language

- READ, READ, READ!—Point out pictures, rhyming words/sounds and characters

Figure 11.5 Infant Reaching for Letters

- Talk to children long before they can talk
  - Use real talk
  - Speak in short sentences
  - Clearly articulate when speaking
  - Talk about the situation the child is involved in—describe what is happening as it occurs and use labels that children need to learn
  - Expand on what child says (fills in missing words)
  - Extend what child says
  - Imitate what child says
  - Ask questions and encourage them to ask you questions when they need more information
- Encourage children to talk to each other
- Play with children using sound and word games
- Give toddlers plenty of experiences to talk about
- Engage children in conversation during caregiving and play times
- Provide children with interesting experiences that can provide conversation material

(Gonzalez-Mena & Eyer, 2017)

260 Language and Literacy Development

Caregiver Strategies to Foster

Infants and Toddlers' Literacy Development

- Talk to them often
- Create a print-rich environment full of reading opportunities
- Demonstrate your own interests in books and the world
- Provide a social environment that gives infants and toddlers opportunities and watch and interact with each other
- Go on walks outside—talk about what you see, provide information, ask questions and ask the children what they see
- Explore the environment with young children—look out the window or around the room and explore materials

Figure 11.6 Toddler Writing Example

- Provide materials that allow talking, listening, drawing, and reading
- Provide a sensory-rich environment that includes verbal interactions, singing, shared book experiences and pictures and artwork on the wall
- Be attentive to child-initiated literacy and language interactions
- Provide numerous types of books for children to read and explore and encourage free exploration
- Initiate storybook/picture book sharing often
- Understand that the family setting, where parents express pleasure in reading and writing, plays an important role in emergent literacy
- Incorporate reading into the daily routine and into transitions
- Read books that have:
  - Bright colors
  - Realistic pictures
  - Rhythmic writing
  - Simple but engaging plots
  - A small amount of words (gradually increase as children get older)
- Point out words everywhere—not just in books
- Provide writing utensils for exploration (crayons and paper)
- Provide play experiences that promote hand-eye coordination (pouring water or sand)—this will help with writing in the future
- Make books about children's lives (families, their neighborhoods or home) using realistic pictures

(Gonzalez-Mena & Eyer, 2017)

Caregiver Strategies by Age
Infants: Birth–1 year old

- Read to infants everyday:
  - Start with short board books with pictures only or one word and a picture
  - Take the time to describe what is happening on the page
  - Incorporate books throughout the day (bedtime, when waiting somewhere)
  - Use animation and inflection when you read
  - Allow infants to mouth the books
  - Repeat books and stories often
- Sing songs (even those that you make up)—infants like hearing your voice
- Play peek-a-boo and back-and-forth games—they are practice for conversation later
- Reinforce infants' communication by looking at them, speaking to them and imitating their vocalizations

- Repeat/imitate laughter and facial expressions
- Describe their feelings and experiences and put words to their sounds
- Teach turn-taking in conversations by teaching infants to imitate actions such as clapping, blowing kisses and waving goodbye
- Narrate what you and others are doing out loud so infants can hear you
- Verbally identify characteristics of different things (color, size, sounds) while pointing to them
- Count out loud (fingers and toes, going up steps)

Younger Toddlers: 1–2 years old

- Read to toddlers everyday:
    - Expand to books with pictures and longer phrases or sentences
    - Take the time to describe what is happening on the page
    - Name pictures in books, talk about the pictures in a book, ask toddlers to point to pictures as you name them or to name the pictures as you point to them
    - Ask questions while you read
    - Follow toddlers' lead when they do not seem interested in a book after a few reads and move on to a different one *or* take a play break in the middle of a book and come back to it
    - Let toddlers move around while you read if they want—they are still listening
    - Tell stories as much as read stories
    - Let toddlers "read" the book to you if they wish
- Narrate what you are doing and what you see when you go places (stroller walks should be full of "I see a bird" and "The tree is green," etc.)
- Talk with toddlers often—the more they are talked to and with, the larger their vocabularies are
    - Use simple and grammatically correct speech that toddlers can understand and imitate
- Introduce phonics by pointing out the sounds of objects and the noises they make
- Use many new words with toddlers—describing words to talk about what you are doing/how you are doing it
- "Read" the environmental print around you—signs, menus, etc.
- Expand on the words toddlers use (They say, "bird," and you say, "That's right. That is a bird in a nest.")
- Do not correct speech mistakes; simply say it correctly when you respond
- Translate for your child if others do not understand what she is saying

Older Toddlers: 2–3 years old

- Read to toddlers everyday:
  - Expand to books with longer stories/more words
  - Ask toddlers to describe what is happening on the page/"read" the story to you by looking at the pictures
  - Ask comprehension questions after reading (who/when/where/sequence of events)
  - Let toddlers choose the books they want to read and capitalize on a specific character/book they are interested in by finding more that are similar, have the same character or are by the same author
- Tell stories and ask toddlers questions about the who/what/where/why/how of the story and the sequence of events
- Talk with toddlers often— expands vocabulary and exposes them to complex sentence structures
- Use simple and grammatically correct speech that toddlers can understand and imitate
- Talk about the characteristics of things (size, shape, color)
- Make up rhymes, recite poems and fingerplays and sings songs with toddlers
- Repeat what toddlers say and expand on it (They say, "blue car," and you say, "Yes, that is a blue car. It is driving down the road.")
- Ask toddlers to repeat what you don't understand so they know their speech is valued
- Ask toddlers open-ended questions and questions that require them to make a choice—wait for an answer and reinforce successful communication
- Strengthen comprehension skills by asking many questions, ask for descriptions and ask for recall of memories
- Give toddlers toys and props that they can use to "act out" literacy
- Build on toddlers' interests by finding literacy materials to read about/look at on the topic (the public library is a great resource)
- Expand toddlers' vocabulary by continually introducing new words and descriptions:

  - Name everything you see
  - Describe everything that you see and its use
  - Ask toddlers to name objects and what they see in pictures (books, magazine, environmental print)
  - Write simple sentences under pictures to show that oral language can be read from print

(Gonzalez-Mena, 2017; Morrow, 2019; Rosenkoetter & Barton, 2002; Roskos, Christie, & Richgels, 2003; Zero to Three, 2019a, 2019b, 2019c)

Bilingual Children

As infant and toddler caregivers, you are sure to encounter children in your care whose home language is not English. As a parent of an infant or toddler, you and your children are sure to encounter families in your daily lives whose home language is not English. You may also want your children to learn a second language. Regardless of your situation, you must all support children in whatever language or languages they are speaking and learning.

All of the literacy strategies that you would use when caring for monolingual children are the same as those for bilingual children. Therefore, this section will give you some information about how to *support* bilingual children and their families in infant/toddler settings. First, though, I ask that you refer to children who are learning English or children whose home language is not English as "bilingual" or "emergent lingual." They are, after all, a speaker of two languages and are in the process of learning both at this stage of their lives. The language that they speak at home that is not English should be referred to as their "home language." That most correctly defines the language that they speak at home with their families, not the one that they speak while in care.

Since infants and toddlers are in the beginning stages of learning any language, they can acquire their home language at the same time as they are acquiring English in childcare. In fact, as children become more proficient in their home language, they can more easily learn a second language. Caregivers can learn simple phrases in the child's home language to help the transition and speak to child in English using the same literacy strategies they use for the English-speaking children. Infants and toddlers may simply listen and respond at first and then gradually start to communicate in English as they both become more comfortable using it and become more and more proficient in their home language. Caregiver support during this "silent period" is important.

From 6–12 months, infants' brains begin to focus on the languages they hear frequently. If an infant is exposed to only one language in the first 6 months, she will begin to lose the ability to hear the differences in sounds of other languages. But if an infant is exposed to more than one language during this period, she will remain open to hearing the sounds in other languages. Her brain will actually stay more "flexible" to learning more languages.

Children are introduced to their cultural community as infants and toddlers. They learn their culture's way of interacting, of learning and many important stories and traditions. Caregivers should ensure the continuity and connection between home and school in order to support this important early learning. Supporting infants and toddlers' families is just as important as supporting the children. It is important that the child's home language is acknowledge and supported. Families should be encouraged to speak their home language with their children as they normally would. Because reading to children is so important as well, families should also be encouraged to read to their children in their home language. They key is to continually remind families that exposure to *any* oral and written language is beneficial for children.

Language and Literacy Development 265

Along with supporting the families and the infants or toddlers' acquisition of both their home language and English, there are specific strategies you can use to support the children while they are in your care:

- Ensure that the children hear both languages often and in many circumstances
- Provide opportunities for the children to use both languages
- Read books in both languages
- Be consistent in your talk to the children—what language you use when, how often, when you switch languages, etc.
- Encourage children to use both languages often—if you want them to speak a specific language in specific situations, positively encourage it and provide words/assistance when they need it
- If children are having difficulty learning either language well, check for a hearing problem

(Lowry, 2016; Marcos, 1998; Morrow, 2019)

Warning Signs for Communication Disorders

The earlier a child's speech and language delay is identified and treated, the less likely it is that the delays will persist or get worse. These types of delays are combatable if they are identified and addressed. This section will provide you with specific "warning signs" in children ages 0–3 that might mean they have a communication disorder. It is important to document your observations and then consult with a professional to accurately diagnose a child.

Birth–8 months

- Lack of interest in social contact
- Lack of response to human voice or other sounds

8–9 months

- They stop babbling (deaf infants babble at first and then stop)
- No interest in interacting with objects and caregivers in familiar environments

9–10 months

- Doesn't follow direction of a point

11–12 months

- Child does not give, show or point at objects; doesn't play games like pat-a-cake and peek-a-boo

12 months

- Does not use gestures such as shaking head or waving
- Is not speaking at least two consonants (p, b)
- Isn't communicating with you when he needs something

15 months

- Doesn't understand or respond to "no" or "bye-bye"
- Does not say at least one to three words
- Does not say "mama" or "dada"

16 months

- Does not point to body parts when asked

18 months

- Does not say at least 15 words

19/20 months

- Does not point out things of interest

20 months

- Does not speak at least six consonant sounds

21 months

- Does not respond to simple directions
- Does not pretend with dolls or self

24 months

- Uses 25 or fewer words
- Does not imitate actions or words of others
- Cannot point to named pictures in a book
- Cannot put two words together
- Does not know the function of common household objects

26 months

- Does not use simple two-word sentences

30 months

- Cannot name at least three body parts
- Cannot be understood by any family members

32 months

- Has difficulty singing parts of nursery rhymes

36 months

- Does not ask questions
- Cannot be understood by strangers at least 50% of the time
- Cannot articulate initial consonants
- Cannot name most common household objects
- Has limited vocabulary
- Uses short/simple sentences
- Has difficulty talking about the future
- Makes grammar errors others aren't making
- Misunderstands questions
- Misunderstood by others
- There is a lack of social play
- Has difficulty carrying on a conversation

(www.babycenter.com)

Creating a Literacy Environment for Infants and Toddlers

As you have read in this chapter, the infant/toddler years are incredibly important in the development of language and children's attitudes about literacy. Whether you are in the home or in a childcare center, creating a literacy environment for infants and toddlers is easy to do. Caregivers must plan oral language experiences (firsthand experiences, conversations and engagement in songs, rhymes, and other playful language games) and create an environment that promotes oral language use. Books and other literacy materials should be placed throughout the classroom so that children have frequent opportunities to read and write. Here are a few tips for putting together a place where children ages 0–3 can explore literacy materials and grow their language and love of literacy.

Book Area:

- Baskets filled with soft and board books
- Bookshelves filled with hard and soft cover books
- Bookshelves should be at the height of toddlers and should be sturdy enough for them to pull themselves up while holding on
- Pillows/soft cushions to lay or sit on while exploring books

Infants and toddlers will mouth books, open and close them, turn the pages, throw them, and carry them around. Any exploration with books is good! They will also rip pages unintentionally, so introduce soft cover books together and help them to carefully explore them. Read to infants and toddlers in the book area but be prepared for them to move around. Don't worry—they are still listening! Keep reading, and they may return for another moment to sit and listen/look at the book.

Literacy Materials:

- Containers of magnetic and plastic letters
- Magnetic board to use to manipulate magnetic letters
- Letter and number puzzles (with and without handles on the pieces)

Introduce magnetic letters as soon as infants can sit up—place them in front of the magnetic board with the letters attached and watch them explore. Infants and toddlers will mouth the letters, hold them in their hands, carry them around and work to manipulate them on the board. Allow all safe exploration and talk to them about what letters they are working with. Identify letters, make words and watch their knowledge of the alphabet grow!

Writing Materials:

- Paper
- Large and small crayons
- Markers

Allow infants and toddlers to hold and carry around writing utensils. Infants will mouth the crayons and markers, so you might wait to introduce at least the crayons until they are past this stage. If the markers are tightly sealed, a quick mouthing before carrying or throwing the markers is fine; it is the first explorations. Model writing/drawing on the paper and allow the children to try it. Infants and toddlers will also hold or rip the paper as a way of exploring it; allow this and talk about what they are experiencing.

Some reminders about the *Play-Literacy Connection*:

- Play provides opportunities to promote literacy skills
- Play provides opportunities to use literacy in real-life ways
- Play themes with literacy are opportunities for social and emotional expression
- Language experiences in play build oral and written communication

(Rosenkoetter & Barton, 2002; Roskos et al., 2003)

Developmental Theory and Language Development

There are many different theories about language development and just how humans acquire and use language. Below is a brief summary of these different developmental theories so that you are aware of them:

Language and Literacy Development 269

Figure 11.7 Toddler Writing

Behaviorist Theory:

- Language is observed and produces speech that occurs in an interaction between speaker and listener
- Adults provide language model that children learn through imitation
- Reinforcement from adults is key

Nativist Theory:

- Language develops innately
- Motivation to learn language is inside children
- As children mature, their language grows

Piaget

- First words are egocentric
- Early language relates to experiences

Vygotsky

- Zone of proximal development important in language acquisition

Language and Literacy Development

- Adults interact with, encourage, motivate and support children in language development
- Expansion and extension of language through social interactions

Constructivist Theory:

- Process of acquiring language is continuous and interactive and takes place in the social context of the child's interacting with others
- Children try out new words and make errors
- Language is an active, social process

Halliday:

- Language is learned when it is relevant and functional

    o Instrumental— satisfy need/get something done
    o Regulatory—control behavior of others
    o Interactional—get along with others
    o Personal—tell about themselves
    o Heuristic—find out about things/learn things
    o Imaginative—pretend/make believe
    o Informative—communicate information to someone

(Nilsen, 2016)

For additional material, visit:
www.parentphd.org/infantandtoddlertext/ch11/

Reflection Questions

As an infant/toddler caregiver or a student in a fieldwork setting, respond to the following:

- How are the caregivers in your classroom/field experience building the children's vocabulary?
- You are working with a toddler who speaks a language no one else speaks in the program. How would you communicate with the child? What would you do to facilitate his/her interactions with other children?
- You are working with a child with a communication disorder/delay. What would you need to consider? What kinds of language learning activities would you try?
- How do the adults in your classroom/field experience use books with the children? What approaches do they use to keep children's attention on the books?
- Describe two examples of the "Caregiver Strategies to Help Infants and Toddlers Develop Their Language" that you see in your classroom/field experience setting.
- Describe two examples of the "Caregiver Strategies to Foster Infants and Toddlers' Literacy Development" that you see in your classroom/field experience setting.

Bibliography

Anisfield, M. (1984). *Language development from birth to three*. Hillsdale, NJ: Lawrence Erlbaum Associates.

American Speech-Language-Hearing Association. (2013). How does your child hear and talk? Retrieved from www.asha.org/public/speech/development/chart/

Bates, E., Thal, D., Finlay, B., & Clancy, B. (1992). Early language development and its neural correlates. In I. Rapin & S. Segalowitz (Eds.), *Handbook of neuropsychology: Child neurology* (2nd ed., Vol. 6, pp. 1–62). Amsterdam: Elsevier.

Douville-Watson, L., Watson, M. A., & Wilson, L. C. (2003). *Infants and toddlers: Curriculum and teaching* (5th ed.). New York, NY: Thomas Delmar Learning.

Gonzalez-Mena, J., & Eyer, D. (2017). *Infants, toddlers, and caregivers: A curriculum of respectful, responsive, relationship-based care and education* (11th ed.). New York, NY: McGraw Hill.

Lowry, L (2016). Bilingualism in young children: Separating fact from fiction. Retrieved from www.hanen.org/Helpful-Info/Articles/Bilingualism-in-Young-Children – Separating-Fact-fr.aspx

Marcos, K. M. (1998, Fall). Second language learning: Everyone can benefit. *The ERIC Review*, 6(1), 2–5.

McLane, J., & McNamee, G. (1991, September). Beginnings of literacy. Retrieved from www.zerotothree.org/early-care-education/early-language-literacy/beginnings-of-literacy.html

Morrow, L. M. (2019). *Literacy development in the early years: Helping children read and write* (9th ed.). New York, NY: Pearson.

Nilsen, B. (2016). *Week by week: Plans for documenting children's development* (7th ed.). Florence, KY: Cengage.

Parlakian, R., Lerner, C., & Im, J. (2008). Getting ready to read: Helping your child become a confident reader and writer starting from birth. *Zero to Three*, 1–13.

Purcell, J., Lee, M., & Biffin, J. (2006). Supporting bilingual children in early childhood. Retrieved from www.learninglinks.org.au/supporting-bilingual-children-in-early-childhood/

Rosenkoetter, S., & Barton, L. (2002, February-March). Bridges to literacy: Early routines that promote later school success. *Zero to Three*, 33–38. Retrieved from www.zerotothree.org/child-development/early-language-literacy/vol_22-4f.pdf

Roskos, K., Christie, J., & Richgels, D. (2003, March). The essentials of early literacy instruction. *Young Children*, 52–60.

Schickedanz, J. (1999). *Much more than the ABCs: The early stages of reading and writing.* Washington, DC: NAEYC.

Swingley, D. (2010). Fast mapping and slow mapping in children's word learning. *Language Learning and Development*, 6, 179–183.

Warning signs of a toddler's language delay. (2011, December). Retrieved from www.babycenter.com/0_warning-signs-of-a-toddlers-language-delay_12293.bc

Wittmer, D. S., & Peterson, S. H. (2017). *Infant and toddler development and responsive program planning: A relationship-based approach* (4th ed.). Boston, MA: Pearson.

Zero to Three. (2003). BrainWonders and sharing books with babies. Retrieved from www.zerotothree.org/BrainWonders

Zero to Three. (2019a). Developing school readiness: Skills from 0-12 months. Retrieved from www.zerotothree.org/resources/series/developing-school-readiness-skills-from-0-12-months

Zero to Three. (2019b). Developing school readiness: Skills from 12-24 months. Retrieved from www.zerotothree.org/resources/series/developing-school-readiness-skills-from-12-24-months

Zero to Three. (2019c). Developing school readiness: Skills from 24-36 months. Retrieved from www.zerotothree.org/resources/series/developing-school-readiness-skills-from-24-to-36-months

12 Cognitive Development

As you already know from previous chapters, experience helps the brain grow. This chapter will continue to emphasize that point and explain how specific cognitive skills and understandings result from the experience/brain growth connection. At birth, the brain is unfinished but ready to grow and develop. All of the hardware is present but dormant, and it is waiting for connection to activate it. As infants have experiences and then repeated experiences, the connections activate the hardware, and the brain grows. This lays the foundation for lifelong learning.

Every experience in infants and toddlers' lives contribute to their learning and their building of cognitive knowledge and skills. Understanding how infants and toddlers learn is necessary in order to create a developmentally appropriate environment that will foster cognitive development. Infant and toddler caregivers must continually promote cognitive development through the materials and experiences that they provide for the children to explore.

Infants are innately curious and use this curiosity in their early experiences to gain knowledge and develop problem-solving skills. They begin their learning by exploring the world with their bodies. Mouthing, grasping and reaching are typical exploratory actions that you will see in infants. They use their senses to explore and then display what they are learning from those explorations in their physical movements. Infants repeat actions over and over again until they master them. This "mastery learning" transfers these repeated actions into more sophisticated cognitive skills. These sophisticated cognitive skills continue to develop as children move through infancy and into the toddler years.

The brain processes new information by finding meaning in it and making sense of it. As infants and toddlers have experiences, they find patterns in the information from those experiences and connect it to what they already know. And as infants and toddlers are exposed to experiences, people and objects, their brain cells create more and more connections (synapses). When the same things happen over and over again, the brain cell connections become permanent (this includes experiences and language) (Rovee-Collier, 1999).

From birth to age 3, these connections grow at a faster rate than any other time in a person's life. New connections are formed daily, and the more each one is used, the stronger that part of the brain becomes. Connections (synapses) that are rarely used are weak and are eventually discarded by the brain. Emotions also affect brain function and memory. Cognitive development can only occur with emotional security and social stability. When infants and toddlers feel content, their brain will release endorphins that enhance memory skills.

Language also plays a significant role in cognitive development and in this gradual acquiring of skills. As infants and toddlers explore with their senses, repeat actions and develop skills, they need labels to categorize what they are doing and to help remember them. Language creates these labels. As infants and toddlers continually create labels, their language grows, and they increase their ability to communicate and regulate their own behavior. This allows them to understand the world in continually more sophisticated ways. (AAP, 2013).

The two main theorists that infant and toddler caregivers must be aware of when studying cognitive development are Jean Piaget and Lev Vygotsky. Piaget stressed the biological changes that contribute to cognitive development, while Vygotsky stressed how social interaction can transform a child's thinking and problem-solving skills. Together these two theories help us understand cognitive development. Neither theory alone can thoroughly explain cognition nor how young children learn. In understanding their theories as well as where they agree and conflict, infant and toddler caregivers can begin to form their own theories about how young children learn.

Jean Piaget

Jean Piaget was a significant contributor to early childhood practitioners' understanding of young children's cognitive development. Piaget was interested in how children come to know the world, especially the quality of children's understanding and how they can explain it. He believed that the knowledge and information gained from experiences is functional and helps a child adapt to the world. Interaction with people and the environment is essential in order to construct new knowledge. Piaget believed that children discover learning through their play experiences and then take that learning into their social interactions with others.

Piaget was a stage theorist, which means that he explained children's cognitive development by progressive age groups. He believed that development precedes learning. Children begin in the first stage at the appropriate age (birth) and move through the stages as they age. Each stage is tied to a specific age range. To Piaget, children's growth is gradual and continuous. A skill or ability later in life depends on the maturing and improving of earlier skills and achievements. Therefore, you cannot push development; children will develop skills at the appropriate age and with the appropriate background knowledge.

Cognitive Development 275

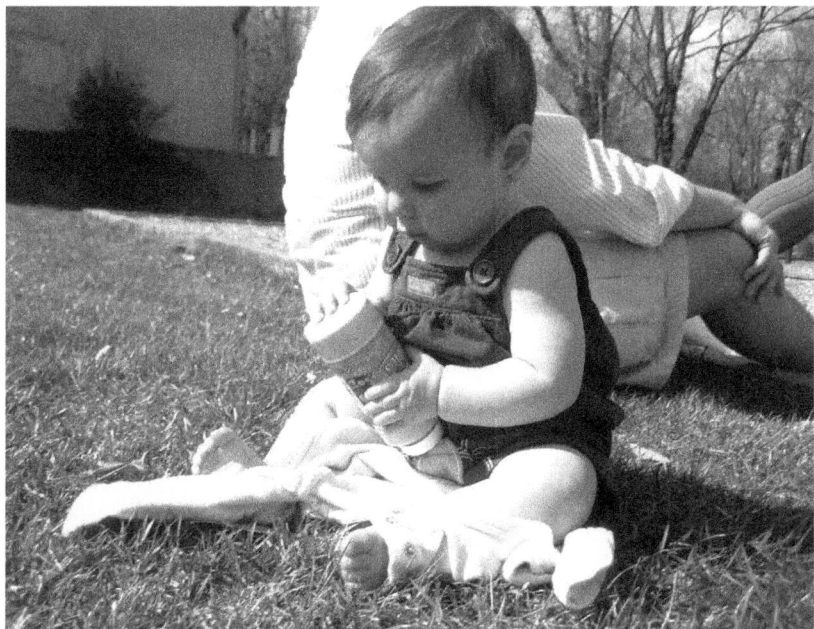

Figure 12.1 Infant Exploring a Bubble Container

This text will discuss all of stage one (the sensorimotor stage) and a part of stage two (the preoperational stage) in Piaget's theory of cognitive development. In the *sensorimotor stage*, which begins at birth, infants obtain information in this stage through their senses and motor activity. They move themselves, move other people and manipulate objects using their senses. When they continually interact with the environment, they are refining their senses and gradually moving from reflexive actions to coordination of senses and their actions.

Piaget believed that when children begin to use language and have the ability to pretend, they move on to the preoperational stage. In the *preoperational stage*, which begins at age 2 (but ends at age 7—quite a long age range!), a great deal of cognitive development occurs. Children are developing better reasoning skills, language and the ability to pretend. They have an increased memory and the ability to recall past events. They can remember what happened yesterday and the day before, and their ability to predict is increasing. They use symbols, such as words, to label things and can use mental images in their thinking processes (Gonzalez-Mena & Eyer, 2017; Nilsen, 2016).

Table 12.1 provides specifics from each stage to help in your understanding of Piaget's theory:

Table 12.1 Piaget's Theory of Cognitive Development – The First Two Stages

Stage and Age	Description
Sensorimotor Stage 0–2 years	0–1 month: inborn/simple reactions to the world
	1–4 months: refines simple behaviors and repeats/combines them
	4–8 months: interacts with objects around them; repeats pleasurable actions
	8–12 months: goal-directed behavior and intentionality; understanding of cause and effect
	12–18 months: changes behaviors to produce desired outcome; experiments with objects to create new events
	18–24 months: imagines events and solves problems; symbolic thinking; begins to use words
Preoperational Stage 2–7 years	12–18 months: experiments to find new ways to problem solve
	18–24 months: can solve problems mentally (versus just by doing), showing evidence of having insight
	24–36 months: classification is developing, though it isn't consistent
	Within 12–36 months:
	– mentally sorts objects and actions
	– beginning to classify objects (limited understanding of quantity, number, space and time)

Source: (Gonzalez-Mena & Eyer, 2017; Nilsen, 2016).

Within the stages of his cognitive theory, Piaget emphasized three key terms that help to explain how the children are learning: assimilation, accommodation and object permanence. *Assimilation* is when children take in new information, process it and then fit it into what they already know. *Accommodation* is when children take in new information, process it and then change what they previously thought. The new information refines or expands their prior knowledge. It is through the ongoing process of assimilation (taking in new experiences) and accommodation (adjusting to it) that children learn about and adapt to the world.

If you think about assimilation and accommodation in terms of infants and toddlers, it connects well to how they explore and learn about the world. Infants are fascinated with their own bodies. The early actions that they practice and combine involve their own movements and how their own bodies feel. That fascination soon starts to move away from their own bodies to the effects their actions have on others and their environment. This shift from self to environment shows that they are beginning to realize that they are separate from the objects in their environment (Gonzalez-Mena & Eyer, 2017; Nilsen, 2016).

As infants grow into toddlers, they explore new objects and approach new experiences using assimilation and accommodation. Toddlers will first explore an object's characteristics and attempt to figure out "what it does." The same goes for experiences—toddlers approach experiences with a curiosity of what it entails and what they can do in or with it. Toddlers then progress to more intentional actions and explorations, focusing on the product of their manipulations and explorations. With all of this exploring and experimenting, toddlers develop abilities to anticipate what will happen and remember what happened the last time they performed a specific act or skill.

Another key term from Piaget is *object permanence*, which is the ability to remember an object or a person even though they cannot be seen, touched or heard. Young infants lack object permanence. When you think about infants' understanding of the world and how it completely revolves around what they can explore with their own senses, this lack of understanding makes sense. When you hide a toy from a young infant lacking object permanence, they think it is gone and will not be able to look for it. Make it reappear, and the object has been re-created for them. This is why peek-a-boo is so exciting for infants; your face actually "disappears" for a moment to the infant and then reappears when you do. This is also why young infants become distressed with their caregivers leave their sight. They truly think that they are gone. When caregivers reappear into their sight, infants are calmed. Gradually infants come to realize that objects continue to exist even if they are out of their sight, and object permanence is achieved (Gonzalez-Mena & Eyer, 2017; Nilsen, 2016).

Figure 12.2 Older Infant Playing With Puzzle Pieces

278 Cognitive Development

Figure 12.3 Older Infant Placing Puzzle Pieces

Finally, Piaget emphasized that *schemes*, or organized ways to making sense of experiences, change with age. *Adaptation* is when infants and toddlers build schemes through their direct interaction with the environment. This is when assimilation and accommodation occur. Schemes then shift from adaptation to *organization*. Organization occurs internally, apart from direct contact with the environment. When children form new schemes, they then rearrange them and link them with their other schemes to form a strong and interconnected cognitive system. Piaget also believed that children develop *intentionality* in the first few years of life, which is their ability to construct a plan. As infants and toddlers explore things in the world and interact with people and the environment, they construct plans about what they are doing and experiencing. This continual construction of plans is how they learn (Berk, 2012, 2015, 2018a, 2018b; Piaget, 1952).

Lev Vygotsky

Lev Vygotsky had a more open-ended view of how young children learn. His ideas were not in stages but rather discussed as an overall idea of what influences children's learning. A key to Vygotsky's beliefs about cognition is that he strongly believed that cognitive activities have their origins in *social interactions*. He continually emphasized the importance of social interactions in order to know and understand the world. This is very different from Piaget's view of cognitive development, which focuses on cognitive development occurring in stages and through biological growth.

Similar to Piaget, Vygotsky believed that children construct their understanding of the world. Vygotsky, though, believed that this is a *co-constructed experience*. Vygotsky emphasized that young children acquire knowledge and skills with the help of other, more experienced learners. For example, if a child was given a toy to explore on her own and then with a peer, Vygotsky believed that more learning would occur when the toy was explored with a peer. This idea of *assisted learning* emphasizes that children are constantly learning from others and they make that learning their own through play and exploration. Vygotsky also emphasized that the cultural context in which a child lives affects how and what he learns. Social interactions and the social processes/speech within this cultural context shape how children learn (Nilsen, 2016).

These ideas bring up another key term of Vygotsky's: the *zone of proximal development*. The ZPD is the difference between what children can do on their own (independent performance) and what they can do with help and guidance from someone else (assisted performance). Vygotsky believed that if caregivers appropriately assist children in problem solving, children will stay in the situation longer and learn more. This assistance can also come from a more experienced peer or simply a peer who is exploring and learning along with the child. This co-partner might discover something that the original child did not and share it, and then they both learn something new. Think of this idea in your own lives—if you explore something on your own, you learn about it based on only your explorations and discoveries. Now imagine if you explore something with another person. Now a whole new group of ideas and explorations is thrown into the equation. You will most assuredly learn more with that other person involved than if you were all alone. (Nilsen, 2016)

Along with these mental and physical explorations comes the importance of language. Vygotsky believed that language plays a central role in the cognitive development of young children. Language is the first type of communication between infants and adults, and the numerous caregiving experiences that you read about in earlier chapters provide many opportunities for language and communication. As children move through infancy and toddlerhood, the gestures, words and symbols they have experienced and learned in their social interactions become internalized. This internalized language allows the child to communicate with himself, which Vygotsky believed is important in cognitive development. Vygotsky acknowledged that language and cognition develop separately but that they merge in social interactions. The language of others has a profound effect on how a child organizes and regulates her own behavior (Berk, 2012, 2015, 2018a, 2018b; Vygotsky, 1978).

Tables 12.2 and 12.3 summarize the similarities and differences between Piaget and Vygotsky. These tables will help you to further understand their theories and ideas, as well as help you to develop your own theory of how young children learn:

280 Cognitive Development

Figure 12.4 An Infant and a Toddler Exploring Music Together

Comparing Piaget and Vygotsky: Similarities

Table 12.2

Piaget and Vygotsky Both Believed That:
Young children construct their knowledge and build information based on experience
Young children build their own understanding of their world
Young children acquire abilities when they are ready and previous skills are the basis for new learning
Play is an important opportunity to learn and practice life skills
Language is important in order for cognitive development to advance
Cognition is fostered by both nature and nurture
Young children use creativity to make sense of their experiences

Source: (Gonzalez-Mena & Eyer, 2017).

Comparing Piaget and Vygotsky: Differences

Table 12.3

Piaget	Vygotsky
Knowledge is self-constructed	Knowledge is co-constructed (assisted performance/discovery)
Biological maturation (moving through the stages) allows cognition to advance	Learning can be advanced with the assistance of an "expert" or "more capable peer"
Development leads learning	Learning leads development
Hands-on, sensory-rich play is important to learn knowledge and skills	Pretend play is also important in learning about objects, cause and effect and the world
Language provides labels for previous experiences; emphasized egocentric speech	Language is absolutely essential for mental growth; emphasized self-talk
Stages of his theory are universal and apply to all children around the world; thinking is independent of culture	Stressed the important of culture, society and life experience; culture influences the course of cognitive development and knowledge and skills develop at different ages in different cultures

Source: (Gonzalez-Mena & Eyer, 2017).

Pretend Play and Cognition

Chapter seven described play and its importance in young children's learning and development. All play promotes learning, but here is a brief reminder about the importance of *pretend play*.

Participation in *pretend play* usually begins around 18–24 months and is an important part of cognitive development. Children represent their world through this type of play and utilize language and actions to show what they have learned and what they have experienced. Participating in this play with other children enhances the experience even more because the other child can offer different perspectives and ideas that add to the original child's knowledge and skills. Language and vocabulary also increase as children listen to and communicate with each other.

When pretend play begins in the toddler years, the child is the center of his play. This gradually changes over the next year, and the child is able to remove himself as the object of attention. For example, a 1-year-old will pretend to feed himself, an 18-month-old will feed a doll, and by 2 years old the doll will be an active participant in the play experience. As the child continues to grow, pretend play becomes more complex, and she can substitute one object for another (such as using a block for a phone) (Bergen, 2002).

Figure 12.5 Two Toddlers Working on a Puzzle Together

Cognitive Development of Infants and Toddlers

The cognitive development of children in the first three years of life is detailed and complex. Infant and toddler brains are constantly changing, adding new knowledge and refining what is already known. While we can assume they learn from any hands-on and exploratory experience, it is important to understand just how their brains work at different periods in the first three years.

Infants and toddlers have specific approaches to learning that are built into their brain circuitry through the influence of both genetic (nature) and environmental (nurture) information. They use *attention*, which is the ability to focus on one experience or interaction without being distracted. They use *curiosity*, which is the desire to explore. They use *information gathering*, where they collect information about the sounds of their home language, how people behave around each other and the rules are of their families/culture. They use *memory*, which is the ability to take in new information while still holding onto the information they already know. They continuously *problem solve* in their daily interactions with the world. They *persist through frustration* when they persist through a challenge to find a solution (Gonzalez-Mena & Eyer, 2017).

Infants and toddlers encounter things every day that require them to think. Parents and caregivers need to observe this thinking process and allow the children to figure out as much as they can on their own. They can ask questions and provide assistance and encouragement. The next section provides specific information about the cognitive understanding of children ages 0–3.

Cognitive Development 283

All Infants (0–12 Months)

- Can see and hear what is happening around them
- Can communicate their interests and needs to others
- Have the ability to see faces and objects of different colors, shapes and sizes

Infants (0–4 Months)

Young infants in these first few months of life enjoy interacting with you, like repetitive activities and will demand your attention to their needs. Talking to infants, describing what you see or what they are doing, and changing your voice and facial expression are all learning experiences for them. These young infants also enjoy looking at a mirror at that very interesting baby looking back at them. Their actions are focused on repeating interesting motor activity and actions that produce interesting effects in their world. Specifically, 0–4-month-old infants:

- Perform reflexive actions
- Will imitate familiar behaviors
- Have an awareness of object properties
- Shift gradually from passive to active search
- Follow objects with eyes when they move

Infants (4–8 Months)

Infants at this age are moving into the mobility stage of the infant years. Interacting with you, repetitive activities and demanding your attention are still common and preferred behaviors. They will enjoy looking at other babies, watching your face appear and disappear behind something and waving bye-bye. Toys that provide a "surprise" such as popping up or noises at the touch, are interesting and exciting. Specifically, 4–8-month-old infants:

- Have basic numerical knowledge
- Have improved physical knowledge—they look for an object, reach for it and touch it
- Intentionally repeat an interesting action
- Are continually developing hand-eye coordination

Infants (8–12 Months)

As infants move toward the final months of their infant years, their brains are moving as quickly as their bodies! They give and reciprocate affection and love and will play simple games with you. These infants are very aware of strangers and prefer their parents/primary caregivers. Anxiety at separation and fear at new situations are all signs that their brains are processing information and attempting to understand it. Specifically, 8–12-month-old infants:

- Can attend to simple commands and imitate your actions
- Have object permanence
- Have the ability to solve problems by referring to a previous similar problem
- Can feed themselves and help with simple household tasks
- Understand that others cause actions
- Imitate others actions and uses actions as play

All Toddlers (12–36 Months)

Infants have now moved into the very active and exciting toddler years. They recognize themselves in mirrors, show a wide range of emotions and want to be independent. Toddlers can play for longer periods of time, enjoy any exploration that is messy and very physically involved and will imitate other people's actions. Imitation has actually become a large part of their behavior.

Emotions change often and are strong as toddlers try to understand them and when they feel them. Frustration, pride, jealousy and the desire to be the center of attention are all present. Toddlers will also notice distress in others and work to comfort them.

Toddlers will approach everything as a learning experience. They concentrate, gather as much information as they can, and can draw on prior knowledge to make decisions and find solutions. Toddlers will tend to select activities that are challenging yet not beyond their abilities. They can also evaluate their own performance as either a success or failure and will look for approval from others when successful and disapproval when they fail.

Matching and sorting everyday materials is interesting, as well as collecting natural and man-made materials for these tasks. They can learn the names of their body parts if you point them out often and will begin to use art materials in an exploratory manner. Specifically, all toddlers by the age of 36 months:

- Have object permanence
- Will move one object aside to get to another/use one toy to reach another/recognize that an object is upside and down and turn it right-side up
- Will take things apart to see what is inside
- Imitate others
- Match words with concepts (identify pictures in a book)
- Understand cause and effect
- Learns by:
    - Using the senses
    - Experimenting
    - Manipulating objects

Toddlers (12–24 Months)

- Can infer other's intentions
- Employs trial-and-error
- Copies behaviors of others and this imitation becomes ritualistic
- Imitates past events and can test out ideas based on past concrete past events

Toddlers (24–36 Months)

The second half of the toddler years is just as active and exciting. Now, though, toddlers can play with other children and be even more independent in their daily activities. They want to help you and do everything they can on their own. They have clearly defined internal standards for their own performance and the performance of others and experience pride or shame based on how they met these standards.

Older toddlers are also becoming able to control their bladder and bowel functions, which means that they could be mentally ready to potty train. They can follow simple rules and enjoy the daily routines they have come to expect. This also means that a change in routine or experience might be difficult and will take some time to process and fully understand. A wide range of emotions are still visible and can still change rather quickly.

Sorting, categorizing and identifying the characteristics of everything they see and touch is interesting and are big learning experiences. The learning process is becoming more thoughtful now, and older toddlers will use mental images and mental trial and error as much as physical problem solving. Memory and intellectual abilities are developing rapidly, and they are starting to understand time and the relationships between objects.

Play has also become more complex. Older toddlers will string together activities and explorations into a logical sequence, rather than just randomly moving from one toy or play experience to another. They feel that everything that happens in the world is because of something they have done. Logical reasoning is still not developed, though, and they still see the world in very simple terms.

- The following cognitive skills begin to develop by 24 months and are developed by 4 years old:

    o Intense increase in representational activity as language, make-believe play, understanding of symbol/real world relationships and categorization develop
    o Can take the perspective of others in familiar situations and face-to-face communications
    o Can distinguish animate from inanimate objects
    o Can reverse thinking

- o Understands cause and effect in many familiar contexts
- o Categorizes and sorts objects based on commonality and hierarchy

Here are some specific cognitive skills that increase understanding from 24–30 months:

Toddlers (24–30 Months)

- Quantity—understand some, more, gone and big
- Number—understand more
- Space—understand up, down, behind, under and over
- Time—understand now and soon

Toddlers (30–36 Months)

- Quantity—use words to label quantity
- Number—use words to label the number of something to compare it the number of something else
- Space—understand up, down, behind, under and over
- Time—understand now, soon, before and after

(Berk, 2012, 2015, 2018a, 2018b)

Supporting Cognitive Development

As with most areas of development, cognitive development can only be promoted appropriately if the child feels security and attachment with both their caregivers and their environment. Infants with secure attachments cling to their caregivers, showing intentionality, which is a mark of early cognitive behavior. Their need for comfort and security is both purposeful and intelligent.

As you read about the chapter on attachment, meeting the needs of infants and toddlers is extremely important in their overall development. As you might have guessed, it is especially important in their cognitive development. Children whose needs are consistently met are comfortable with and trust their environment. This trust and comfort allows them to explore the environment. This exploration is how they learn. If a child is not comfortable exploring her environment or playing freely, she is losing out on learning opportunities.

The key to helping and guiding infants and toddlers is to do it appropriately. This does not mean showing them how to do something or how something works if they cannot figure it out. What it does mean is being respectful and responsive to the child's actions, explorations and language. It means providing assistance in problem solving but not controlling the experience. Interactions should be collaborative. This guided and socially shared cognition is at the cornerstone of Vygotsky's theory about the cognitive development of young children.

Caregivers of infants and toddlers should promote cognitive development by providing a sensory-rich environment that invites exploration, imagination and play. Infants and toddlers should be allowed to play with objects in any way that they wish. This open-ended play gives them an opportunity to problem solve in ways that are meaningful and interesting to them. Planned activities with specific outcomes are inappropriate for infants and toddlers and do not promote their cognitive development. The process will not matter to the children, and you will often find in these experiences that the children will just let their caregivers complete the process and make the product for them versus becoming actively involved in the experience. Real-life, everyday explorations and play experiences are how young children learn, and allowing them to be creative in every experience is all that you need to do to help them learn and grown appropriately. You should also encourage the children to interact with each other during these explorations and play experiences. Children from infancy to toddlerhood can communicate with each other in their own ways, and if you promote it and foster it, they can learn from each other. Interactions with both objects *and* people promote cognitive development.

Strategies for Encouraging Cognitive Thinking and Development

Now that you understand infants and toddlers' cognitive development, it is important to learn specific strategies to support it. This next section will first provide you with a list of strategies that you should know and perform as a caregiver for infants and toddlers. This all-encompassing list will help you to set up an appropriate infant/toddler environment and act as a responsive caregiver. I then provide you with information and strategies by age group (infants, young toddlers and older toddlers) in the following categories: materials and manipulatives, communications, explorations and problem solving and play. This section is more specific and will guide you in what to provide for the children to explore, how to provide it and what to do and say while they are exploring. While there is different information for each age group, you can extend any of it beyond the age it specifies if you feel it is appropriate.

Overall Strategies for Infants and Toddlers

- Keep infants in comfortable positions, talk quietly to them and look at/manipulate things together so they can keep an alert state of attention
- Keep toddlers focused and attentive by limiting distractions and interruptions
- Express interest, curiosity and encouragement in infant and toddlers' activities; observe and reflect on what you believe they are trying to accomplish
- Offer materials in new ways and in new areas of classroom to spark curiosity

- Provide materials that are challenging but not impossible
- Offer choices when it is possible
- Provide a variety of sensory exploration experiences
- Keep the routine and room arrangement predictable and talk about what children do and did during the day in order to help them develop memories; talk about passage of/concepts of time
- Provide many materials and opportunities to categorize, match, sort, compare, contrast as well as promote awareness of shape, size, amounts, numbers and one-to-one correspondence
- Encourage problem solving by letting the children figure things out on their own as much as possible
- Help develop object permanence by playing peek-a-boo and read books with hidden pictures/pictures under flaps and about parents coming and going
- Provide toys that respond and encourage understanding of the use of space: balls, push lights/switches, stacking cups, stacking rings and tunnels to crawl through
- Provide manipulatives that help the children understand the use of tools: markers, paint, water, play telephones, keys and replicas of household tools
- Scaffold the children's play by providing language, ideas and materials
- For toddlers:

    o Stress and reinforce independence and self-reliance
    o Encourage them to compete task on their own and to complete it well
    o Provide a cognitively stimulating environment
    o Encourage and support them in a positive manner so they enjoy new challenges and feel confident about mastering tasks

Strategies by Age

Infants (0–12 Months)

- Materials and Manipulatives

    o Books
    o Interesting objects that attract the five senses
    o Typical household items are interesting and can be explored
    o Different textures and fabrics
    o Balls of sticky masking tape
    o Wooden and metal spoons
    o Ball of different textures (smooth, bumpy) and sizes

- Communications

    o Respond to all communications

Cognitive Development 289

- o Narrate actions to describe what you see/what they are doing
- o Express excitement and happiness at infants' actions and explorations (verbally and non-verbally)
- o Be clear about what infants can and cannot touch in the house; provide "yes touch" materials throughout the house and redirect to them when necessary

- Explorations and Problem Solving
  - o Give her a chance to figure something out and then provide help when needed (remember optimum stress level?)
  - o Support and encourage them to reach goals/accomplish things
  - o Encourage all kinds of exploration and narrate what you see
  - o Model problem solving (they will learn through imitating you)

Figure 12.6 Infant Exploring a Play Mat

- o Take walks inside and outside often; talk about what you are seeing and doing and allow them to touch as much as possible while you describe the experience
- o Involve them in daily routines; they will learn how things work and how to imitate the actions of others
- Play
  - o Play peek-a-boo and other disappearing/reappearing games with your bodies and objects (develops memory and object permanence)
  - o Plenty of opportunities to play and explore materials on her own

Young Toddlers (12–24 Months)

- Materials and Manipulatives
  - o Books
  - o Toys and materials that they can shake, bang, open/close, take apart, fill/dump
  - o Water
  - o Sand
  - o Materials collected from nature (leaves, rocks)
  - o Grocery store items (talk about colors, size, weight)
  - o Props to encourage imagination (pretend food, dress-up clothes)
- Communications
  - o Continue to be clear about what they can and cannot touch in the house; provide "yes touch" materials throughout the house and redirect to them when necessary
  - o Provide opportunities for them to make choices
- Explorations and Problem Solving
  - o Follow their lead in gross and fine motor explorations; give them the words for their actions (up/down, in/out), let them do something over and over again, provide alternatives when necessary
  - o Support problem solving by helping but don't complete a task for them—builds thinking skills and self-confidence
  - o Encourage them to participate in self-care tasks; they will learn how familiar objects work and how to problem solve through a daily care task
  - o Allow them to help around the house—builds self-esteem and self-confidence
  - o Expand thinking skills by expanding a favorite action to other materials or environments
  - o Sort/categorize everything you can (nature materials, clothes in the laundry basket, cups in the kitchen)

- Play

    - Pretend play to help build imagination
    - Plenty of opportunities to play and explore materials on their own

Older Toddlers (24–36 Months)

- Materials and Manipulatives

    - Books
    - Props for pretend play
    - Familiar/unfamiliar objects
    - Natural/man-made objects

- Communications

    - Don't always answer questions immediately; take time to think or ask them what they think the answer is
    - Ask why questions throughout the day—shows interest in their ideas and keeps their minds working
    - Observe them and see what they are interested in then ask questions and engage with them to build on their curiosity and love of learning
    - Connect the past to the present—logical connections make life clearer
    - Help their understanding of time by using timers and pointing out the time changes on clocks
    - Talk about feelings (theirs, yours and others) and provide the appropriate vocabulary

- Explorations and Problem Solving

    - Provide opportunities to explore familiar/unfamiliar objects, natural/man-made materials
    - Point out and discuss patterns in everyday routines
    - Sort and categorize everything you can
    - Suggest different ways to solve a problem when they are having a hard time

- Play

    - Pretend play where one child is the leader and you ask questions to extend the play—strengthens thinking skills and development of original ideas
    - Make up and change the words to songs—promotes logical thinking and the understanding of the connection between ideas

(Berk, 2012, 2015, 2018a, 2018b; Zero to Three, 2017)

292 *Cognitive Development*

Specific Toys and Activities That Promote Cognitive Development

Many of the previous chapters have provided you with developmentally appropriate toy and manipulative examples for infants and toddlers. Table 12.4 provides you with the specific cognitive connections of one example for each age group. Think about other toy/activity examples and hypothesize about the cognitive connections.

Some of these ideas were taken from Guyton (2011), and others are from my experience as an infant/toddler caregiver and parent. Many of the toy/activity suggestions can be used with any child ages 0–3. They will all explore and learn from the toy/activity differently based on their age and cognitive abilities.

Cognitive Delays

This next section provides some specific warning signs that there might be a cognitive delay in an infant or toddler. It is important to thoroughly observe and assess the child with the help of a professional. If a child exhibits one of the warning signs listed, it does not automatically mean he has a cognitive delay. Again, always consult a professional (the child's pediatrician, for example) before drawing any conclusions.

Figure 12.7 Toddler Exploring Sand and Sand Toys

Table 12.4 Toys and Their Cognitive Connections

Age	Toy/Activity	Cognitive Connections
0–9 months	Play/Activity mats with mobiles overhead—*lay infant on his back (and then eventually sitting up) and dangle safe materials over him to grab and bat at*	– Cause and effect – Sound and texture discoveries – Hand-eye coordination
9–12 months	Open and reveal books and toys—*any book, game or covered pictures where infants have to move something to "reveal" what is under it will be exciting and interesting*	– Object permanence – Cause and effect – Identification of objects in pictures
12–18 months	Books—*board, paper, big and small*	Early Literacy Skills – Language – Vocabulary – Prediction – Who/what/when/where/why questions
18–24 months	Telescopes—*paper towel/toilet paper rolls or paper rolled and taped into a tube can be used to look at items up close and focused—ask them to look for specific things or ask them what they see through*	– Classification – Recognition – Language – Vocabulary – Perspective taking – Focused attention
24–36 months	Puppets—*use them to tell stories or act out situations and ideas; use socks, paper bags or pictures glued to popsicle sticks*	– Imagination – Abstract thinking – Language – Sequence of events
All Infants and Toddlers (0–36 months)	Sensory Bottles—*fill empty water or soda bottles with colored water and glitter, beads, rocks, sand, etc. Infants will shake the bottle and listen to the different sounds it makes and turn it over in their hands to watch the materials inside move*	– Cause and effect – Intentionality – Sound and sight discoveries

Source: (Guyton, 2011; Zero to Three, 2017).

0–6 Months

- Assessing infants in the first six months is difficult; they are so new to the world and are adapting to it. Cognitive skills are gradually developing during these first few months of life. Be aware, though, if a young infant does not exhibit the following behaviors by 6 months old:
    o Makes eye contact (this should occur soon after birth)
    o Looks at objects in hand

294 *Cognitive Development*

Figure 12.8 Toddler Exploratory Play

- o   Looks after a toy which is dropped
- o   Uses a two-hand approach to grasp toys
- o   Turns head to voice, follows with eye

6–8 Months
- Avoids close contact or cuddling
- No attempts to get the attention of others
- Does not respond to sounds
- No visual tracking
- Not starting to repeat actions of others and produce pleasurable results
- Has difficulty self-soothing or regulating reactions
- Cannot be consoled at night in order to rest
- Is not interested in games and interactions such as peek-a-boo

By 12 Months
- Limited or inconsistent eye contact
- No interest in children his age
- Inflexible/rigid with routine, food, clothing, etc.
- Does not search for hidden or removed objects
- Has extreme difficulty waiting for something
- Does not participate in functional play

- Does not anticipate an effect of an action (blocks falling over)
- Still uses repeated actions versus trial and error when problem solving

18–24 Months

- Not interested in children his age
- Does not imitate verbalizations, actions or behaviors
- Does not understand the functions of common objects
- Has extreme difficulty waiting for something
- Has difficulty remaining engaged/attending to something on his own and without constant attention from an adult
- Is still using predominantly the mouth and other sensory exploratory behaviors in play
- Is extremely passive

By 36 Months

- Abnormally aggressive
- Has extreme difficulty separating from parent/primary caregiver
- Not initiating or reciprocating interactions with other children his age
- Unable to show simple categorization of objects
- No interest in pretend play

(Berk, 2012, 2015, 2018a, 2018b; Gonzalez-Mena & Eyer, 2017)

The Project Approach With Toddlers

The Project Approach is an approach to developing curriculum in early childhood education. The premise behind the approach is that curriculum is developed based on the children's interests. Teachers listen to the children's play, conversations and explorations, and take the main themes and interests from those experiences and create curriculum. This approach is typically used in preschool but has been adapted for toddlers. For more information on The Project Approach, read the following book that outlines it completely:

> Helm, J. H., & Katz, L. G. (2016). *Young investigators: The project approach in the early years* (3rd ed.). New York, NY: Teachers College Press.

The following article explains how to use The Project Approach with toddlers. It is a wonderful way to create curriculum and truly relevant learning for young children:

> LeeKeenan, D., & Edwards, C. (1992). Using the project approach with toddlers. *DigitalCommons@University of Nebraska – Lincoln.*

Some features of project work are of value for toddlers, while others are best left until children are older. This article shares the process through which teachers and administrators at a private school in Mexico City gained awareness of the importance of listening, observing, and documenting children's activities to determine how to adapt features of the Project Approach to meet the needs and interests of toddlers. This adaptation of project work, called "project practice," engaged toddlers in developmentally appropriate activities that involved exploration, representation, and the search for understanding.

(Article Abstract)

Kogan, Y., & Pin, J. (2009). Beginning the journey: The project approach with toddlers. *Early Childhood Research & Practice, 11*(1).

For additional material, visit:
www.parentphd.org/infantandtoddlertext/ch12/

Reflection Questions

- Explain brain development, specifically memory development, in infants and toddlers. How can this brain development be nurtured? Reference at least TWO articles or videos from this chapter's additional materials.

In your own words, define the following "Approaches to Learning" for infants and toddlers. Then, describe one or more examples of an infant or toddler using each of the approaches that you have seen in your classroom/field experience.

- Attention
- Curiosity
- Information gathering
- Memory

- Problem solving
- Persistence through frustration

Choose one of the Approaches to Learning examples you provided above and compare Piaget versus Vygotsky's thoughts on the observation. What would Piaget say about it? What would Vygotsky say about it?

Read the information about science and math with infants and toddlers in the additional materials for this chapter. Based on what you read, describe a science experience and a math experience that you have seen *naturally occur* in your infant and/or toddler field site. Then, describe the caregiver's role in each experience.

Bibliography

American Academy of Pediatrics. (2013). Ages and stages. Retrieved from www.healthychildren.org/english/ages-stages/Pages/default.aspx

Bergen, D. (2002). The role of pretend play in children's cognitive development. *Early Childhood Research and Practice, 4*(1).

Berk, L. (2012). *Child development* (9th ed.). Boston, MA: Pearson.

Berk, L. (2015). *Infants and children: Prenatal through middle childhood* (8th ed.). Boston, MA: Pearson.

Berk, L. (2018a). *Exploring child development.* Boston, MA: Pearson.

Berk, L. (2018b). *Exploring child and adolescent development.* Boston, MA: Pearson.

Douville-Watson, L., Watson, M. A., & Wilson, L. C. (2003). *Infants and toddlers: Curriculum and teaching* (5th ed.). New York, NY: Thomas Delmar Learning.

Early Intervention Support.com. (2012). Cognitive development in infants, toddlers and children. Retrieved from www.earlyinterventionsupport.com/development/cognitive/default.aspx

Gonzalez-Mena, J., & Eyer, D. (2017). *Infants, toddlers, and caregivers: A curriculum of respectful, responsive, relationship-based care and education* (11th ed.). New York, NY: McGraw Hill.

Guyton, G. (2011). Using toys to support infant-toddler learning and development. *Young Children,* 50–56.

Nilsen, B. (2016). *Week by week: Plans for documenting children's development* (7th ed.). Florence, KY: Cengage.

Piaget, J. (1952). *The origins of intelligence in children.* New York, NY: International University Press.

Rovee-Collier, C. (1999). The development of infant memory. *Current Directions in Psychological Science, 8,* 80–85.

Schiller, P., & Willis, C. (2008, July). Using brain-based teaching strategies to create supportive early childhood environments that address learning standards. *Beyond the Journal,* 1–6.

Shonkoff, J. P., & Phillips, D. A. (2000). *From neurons to neighborhoods: The science of early childhood development*. Washington, DC: National Academy of Sciences.

Vygotsky, L. S. (1978). *Mind and society: The development of higher psychological processes*. Cambridge, MA: Harvard University Press.

Wittmer, D. S., & Peterson, S. H. (2017). *Infant and toddler development and responsive program planning: A relationship-based approach* (4th ed.). Boston, MA: Pearson.

Zero to Three. (2017). Rocking and rolling: Empowering infants' and toddlers' learning through scaffolding. Retrieved from www.naeyc.org/resources/pubs/yc/may2017/rocking-and-rolling-empowering-infants-and-toddlers

13 Early Intervention

What Is Early Intervention?

Early Intervention (EI) is comprised of services for infants and toddlers who have disabilities or developmental delays. In the first three years of life, if an infant or toddler is not developing skills at the "typical" rate of their age group, EI can help that child to do so. With parental consent, a child is evaluated to determine whether or not he is eligible for the services. A parent can request an evaluation based on concerns they have for their child's development, or a pediatrician can recommend the child based on concerns they have at the child's routine check-up.

A child can also be diagnosed at birth with specific conditions that require EI services. These conditions can be biological or developmental conditions or can be because of conditions present at birth for the child (prematurity, low birth weight, illness, etc.). In these cases, parents are given a referral for EI services before the infant leaves the hospital. Children can receive EI services up to and sometimes beyond their third birthday.

If a child is referred to EI and/or a parent requests an evaluation for developmental delays and/or disabilities, an evaluation team will work together on both the initial screening and full evaluation. The members of this team will have different expertise and experience and together will have a full understanding of infant and toddler learning and development. They will have expertise in working with young children and will work both individually and together to:

- Observe the child
- Ask the child to complete specific tasks
- Talk to the child to help determine if there is, in fact, a delay present

The goal of the team is to determine how the child functions in the following developmental areas:

- Adaptive
- Cognitive

300 *Early Intervention*

- Physical (includes vision and hearing delays)
- Communication
- Social/emotional development

When determining whether a child is eligible for EI Services, both the child *and* the family are involved in the evaluation process. The family evaluation is voluntary but is important to complete because it determines the family's concerns, resources and priorities in connection with the goal of enhancing the development of the child.

An evaluation of a child will not need to occur if he or she is automatically eligible for EI services because they have been diagnosed with a mental or physical condition that has been determined to have a high probability of resulting in a developmental delay. Some examples of these conditions are:

- Down syndrome
- Fragile X syndrome
- Chromosomal abnormalities
- Genetic or congenital disorders and/or infections
- Sensory impairments
- Inborn errors of metabolism
- Disorders reflecting disturbance of the development of the nervous system

Figure 13.1 Toddler Reading With an Infant

- Severe attachment disorders
- Disorders because of exposure to toxic substances (ex: fetal alcohol syndrome)

(Division for Early Childhood, 2014)

The Importance of the Family and the Building of Relationships

Early Intervention places the family at the center, with the services revolving around them. Parents and professionals work together to determine the needs of the child and then create an Individual Family Service Plan (IFSP) that addresses the needs of the child *and* the family.

The integration of the family systems approach into special education emphasized that the family is an active system in which the interactions and behaviors of one member of the family affects all other members of the family. The time frame for intervention is not only determined by the child's need but also how much time is necessary to help the family members develop social-emotional and relationship skills (Christian, 2006).

Most families are seeking both information and emotional sensitivity when going through EI with their children. A key aim of EI is to balance goals and methods so that the family can learn and grow along with the child during their intervention. EI professionals must share their knowledge and skills in a way that fosters a respectful and collaborative relationship with the families. In doing this, both family and child capability is strengthened.

Part C of The Individuals With Disabilities Education Act (IDEA)

> The Individuals with Disabilities Education Act (IDEA) is a law ensuring services to children with disabilities throughout the nation. IDEA governs how states and public agencies provide early intervention, special education and related services to more than 6.5 million eligible infants, toddlers, children and youth with disabilities.
>
> (https://sites.ed.gov/idea/)

Under Part C of IDEA, the following services must be provided to families at no cost:

- The development and review of the IFSP
- Evaluations and assessments
- Service coordination
- Child Find services

(https://ectacenter.org/partc/partc.asp)

Figure 13.2 Infant Bonding With Her Father

Other services are available but may have fees that the families must pay, either through health insurance or out of pocket. Services cannot be denied for a child because his family cannot pay for them.

Early Intervention Services

Everyone involved in a young child's life affects how he learns and grows, and reciprocal and responsive early relationships influence this growth and development. Learning is a social experience, which means that "how" we are with children is just as important as "what" we are doing with them. A child's sense of self develops from what he thinks of himself, as well as how other see him and relate to him. A child's sense of achievement is driven by both his accomplishments and the expectations and approval of the people he spends his time with. These ideas are important to remember when discussing and planning for Early Intervention services for a child.

The goal for children with delays should be to enable him to form a sense of self and see himself as purposeful and interactive individuals. EI strategies must have a social-emotional goal as much as a physical/language/cognitive goal. Professionals must participate in the intervention *with* the child instead of "doing" the intervention *to* the child. The child is an active participant in the functional and meaningful activities developed for him, and his interests, actions and enthusiasms are all considered when the tasks are developed and implemented. Interventions are most successful when they become a natural part of the child's day and focus on practical activities and pleasant interactions.

EI services for eligible infants and toddlers and their family members include but are not limited to:

- Family education, training and counseling, home visits and parent support groups
- Special instruction
- Speech and language services
- Medical services
- Occupational therapy
- Physical therapy
- Psychological services
- Service coordination
- Nursing services
- Nutrition services
- Social work services
- Vision services
- Assistive technology devices and services

(Division for Early Childhood, 2014)

Services may also be provided to address the *needs and priorities of the child's family*. Family-directed services are meant to help family members understand the special needs of their child and how to enhance his or her development.

The Council for Exceptional Children

The Council for Exceptional Children (CEC) is the largest international professional organization dedicated to improving the educational success of individuals with disabilities and/or gifts and talents. The CEC advocates for appropriate governmental policies, sets professional standards, provides professional development, advocates for individuals with exceptionalities and helps professionals obtain conditions and resources necessary for effective professional practice. The CEC is considered "the voice and vision of special education."

CEC's Division of Early Childhood

Within the CEC is the Division for Early Childhood Education.

> The Division for Early Childhood (DEC) promotes policies and advances evidence-based practices that support families and enhance the optimal

development of young children (0–8) who have or are at risk for developmental delays and disabilities. DEC is an international membership organization for those who work with or on behalf of young children (0–8) with disabilities and other special needs and their families.

DEC Recommended Practices in Early Intervention/ Early Childhood Special Education: www.dec-sped.org/ dec-recommended-practices

Individual Family Service Plan

When an infant or toddler has a documented disability or special need that requires outside intervention, the center and families create an "Individual Family Service Plan (IFSP)." This plan documents and guides the implementation of the early intervention process for children with disabilities and their families in accordance with the Individuals with Disabilities Education Act (IDEA). An IFSP describes the services necessary to facilitate a child's development and includes information about the family's participation in the intervention services. Family members and caregivers work as a team to plan, implement and evaluate the intervention services. An IFSP is written with the idea that the family is the child's greatest resource and that the best way to meet a child's needs is to support the family and build on their strengths. The goals are written within the context of the family and have outcomes targeted at both the child and the family members and family as a whole.

The IFSP process begins by assessing the child and family. An effective assessment process addresses each family members' questions and concerns about the child and determines if a child is eligible for services. This determination comes from observations and assessments of the child in a setting that is familiar to the child. The child's strengths; needs; and preferences for activities, materials and environments are documented. The family and the interventionists then create goals for the child. From these goals, strategies and outcomes are developed, and intervention responsibilities are assigned. The intervention strategies should occur within everyday natural environments and should enable the child to become more independent in his world.

An IFSP must contain the following information:

- The child's present levels of functioning and need in the areas of physical, cognitive, communication, social/emotional and adaptive development
- The family's resources, priorities and concerns relating to enhancing the development of the child with a disability
- The major outcomes/results that are expected to be achieved for the child and the family
- Specific Early Intervention Services that the child will be receiving, including specific procedures and a timeline
- The natural environments (home, community, childcare center) in which services will be provided (if the services are not provided in a natural environment, a statement must be included justifying this decision)

Figure 13.3 Infant and Toddler Bonding With Their Mother

- Number of days/sessions for the services, the projected dates for the services and the anticipated duration
- Whether the services will be one on one or part of a group
- Who will pay for the services
- The name of the service provider who will be responsible for implementing the plan and coordinating with other agencies and persons
- Steps to support the child's transition out of early intervention to preschool or other appropriate services

An IFSP is reviewed every six months and is updated at least once a year. The families and the intervention team will look at the child's progress and decide how (or if) the IFSP needs to be changed to reflect both the child's growth toward the goals that were set and other family changes or needs. Questions such as the following are asked and discussed in these review meetings:

- To what extent and at what rate is the child making progress toward attaining outcomes?
- Are the selected intervention strategies and activities promoting gains in development?
- Do changes need to be made in the intervention plan?

(Bruder, 2000)

306   *Early Intervention*

The additional materials for this chapter provide a plethora of resources and information that expand on the ideas presented in this chapter. Please visit the website for additional content about Early Intervention services.

For additional material, visit:
www.parentphd.org/infantandtoddlertext/ch13/

Reflection Questions

- What does IFSP stand for (the actual letters are what words)?
- Define in your own words what an IFSP is.

Now, obtain an IFSP from your school/classroom or field experience and complete the following analysis:

Read the child's information and think about the following:

- What the child's delay is in that area
- What the child SHOULD be able to do at his age in that area

Read the Family and Transportation information and think about the following:

- What family members are in the child's life?
- How can each of those family members help the child's progress through the intervention process?
- How will the transportation information influence the implementation of intervention services?

Now, complete the required information in the IFSP template below. Refer to your specific knowledge of what the child should be able to do in each area at the child's ACTUAL AGE and then refer to information about the child's delay in that area. You must also take into consideration the family and transportation information when you are suggesting strategies.

Physical (small muscles, big muscles including hearing, vision, and health status):

- Identify what the child's physical skills should be:
    - Small muscles/Fine motor:
    - Big muscles/Gross motor:
    - Hearing/Vision/Health:
- Identify a SPECIFIC STRATEGY you would implement to address the child's delays AND to get him where he needs to be for the following areas:
    - Small muscles/Fine motor:
    - Big muscles/Gross motor:

Cognitive (thinking and reasoning skills):

- Identify what the child's cognitive skills should be:
    - Thinking:
    - Reasoning:
- Identify a SPECIFIC STRATEGY you would implement to address his delays AND to get him where he needs to be for the following areas:
    - Thinking:
    - Reasoning:

Communication (talking and understanding language):

- Identify what the child's language skills should be:
    - Talking (Expressive):
    - Understanding (Receptive):
- Identify a SPECIFIC STRATEGY you would implement to address his delays AND to get him where he needs to be for the following areas:
    - Talking (Expressive):
    - Understanding (Receptive):

Social and Emotional (play skills and interacting with others):

- Identify what the child's social and emotional skills should be:
  - Play skills:
  - Interactions with others:
- Identify a SPECIFIC STRATEGY you would implement to address his delays AND to get him where he needs to be for the following areas:
  - Play skills:
  - Interactions with others:

Adaptive (self-help, feeding, dressing, etc.):

- Identify what the child's adaptive skills should be:

Self-Help/Self-Care skills:

- Identify a SPECIFIC STRATEGY you would implement to address his delays AND to get him where he needs to be for the following areas:

Self-Help/Self-Care skills

Bibliography

Bruder, M. B. (2000). The individual family service plan (IFSP). *ERIC Clearinghouse on Disabilities and Gifted Education*, E605, 1–8.

Christian, L. (2006). Understanding families: Applying family systems theory to early childhood practice. *Beyond the journal*, (January 2006), 1–8.

Division for Early Childhood. (2014). DEC recommended practices in early intervention/early childhood special education 2014. Retrieved July 24, 2016, from www.dec-sped.org/recommendedpractices

Jennings, D., Hanline, M. F., & Woods, J. (2012). Understanding Routines-Based Interventions in Early Childhood Special Education. *Dimensions of Early Childhood*, 40(2), 23–13. Retrieved July 22, 2016, from www.southernearlychildhood.org/upload/pdf/Using_Routines_Based_Interventions_in_Early_Childhood_Special_Education_Danielle_Jennings_Mary_Frances_Hanline_Juliann_Woods.pdf

Shonkoff, J. P., & Meisels, S. J. (2000). *Handbook of early childhood intervention*. Cambridge: Cambridge University Press.

Thorp, E. K., & McCollum, J. A. (1994). Defining the infancy specialization in early childhood special education. In L. J. Johnson, R. J. Gallagher, M. J. Montagne, et al. (Eds.), *Meeting early intervention challenges: Issues from birth to three* (pp. 167–83). Baltimore, MD; Paul H. Brookes.

Index

Note: Page numbers in italics indicate figures and page numbers in bold indicate tables.

accommodation 276–277
active listening 88–90
activities 153
adaptation 278
Ainsworth, M. 177, 179–182
allergies 30
American Academy of Pediatrics (AAP) 26–28, 30, 33, 119
androgyny 229–230
Anecdotal/Running Records 18–19
angry cry 222
anxious-ambivalent attachment 179–180, **180–181**
anxious-avoidant attachment 179–180, **180–181**
assimilation 276–277
assisted learning 279
attachment: anxious-ambivalent 179–180, **180–181**; anxious-avoidant 179–180, **180–181**; Bowlby's theory of 177–179; brain development and 182–184; caregivers and 184–186; comfort/transitional objects and 184, *184*; critical period of 178; defined 173; disorders of 187–188; Early Intervention services and 186; formation of 173–174; infants and 174–180; insecure and unhealthy 177, 181, 195; issues in 185–186, 195; phases of 178–180; principal 174; relationships in 174–177; reunion behavior **181**; secure and healthy 176–177, 179–180, **180**, 181–182; sense of self 174; separation anxiety **180**; separation distress 178–179, 185; social development and 198–200; stranger anxiety **181**; Strange Situation (Ainsworth) 179–182; as stress buffers 233; toddlers and 184–185
Attachment Parenting: attachment theory and 188; Baby B's 190–192; babywearing 191, *193*; balance in 189, 191–192; bedding close to baby 191; belief in language of baby's cry 191; benefits of 192–194; beware of baby trainers 191; birth bonding 190–191; breastfeeding 191; criticism of 194–195; emotional bonding and 194; independence and 189, 192–193; parent expertise in 188–189; physical/emotional closeness and 189
attachment theory 188, 194–195
attention 282
attention span 105, 120
auditory perception *see* hearing (auditory perception)
autism 215–216
Autism Speaks 216
autonomy 200–201
axons 183

Baby B's 190–192
baby sign language 49–50
baby trainers 191
babywearing 191, *193*
Back to Sleep campaign 48
balance 189, 191–192
bargains 72
basic cry 222

bathing 39, 40
bedding close to baby 191
bed-sharing 194
behaviorist theory 269
belief in language of baby's cry 191
Berke, K. 57
bilingual children 83–84, 264–265
birth bonding 190–191
body awareness 66
body growth 129–131
books/stories 254–258, 261, 267–268
bottle-feeding 27–28
Bowlby, J. 177–179, 182
Bowlby's theory of attachment: infant need for 177–178; internal working model and 178–179; maternal deprivation hypothesis 178; proximity maintenance 178; safe haven 178; secure base 178–179; separation distress 178–179
brain development: attachment and 182–184; axons 183; bilingual children and 264; dendrites 183; infant/toddler 6–7, 131; language development and 244–245; mirror neurons 183; myelinization and 131; nature (genes) and nurture (environment) 183; neural pathways 183; neuroplasticity and 244; neurotransmitters 183; synapses 183; television and 119–120
breastfeeding 27, 191
breast milk 27–28
Bredekamp, S. 12–13
bribes 72

calming 46–47
calming reflex 46
caregiver/family relationship: benefits of 80–81; bilingual children and 264–265; cultural identity and 83; documenting a child's day 87–88; family caregiving practices and 84; family pictures and 83; family-to-school communication forms 96–99; incident reports 87–88, 94; making families comfortable 81–83; multicultural/multilingual curriculum 83–84; ongoing/open communication 88–89; parent conference form 94–95; parent conferences 89–91; portfolios and 89–90, 95; reporting child abuse 91; resiliency and 232; special needs children 91–93; working through conflicts 84–87
caregivers: active listening and 88–90; adult relationships and 4; attachment and 184–188; cognitive development and 287–288; developmentally appropriate practice (DAP) and 13–14; diapering 35–36; documentation 18; emotional behaviors and 238, **239–240**; gender roles and 67–68; intentionality and 12–13; interactions with 4–5, 8; knowledge/skills of 26; language and literacy development 258–261; learning environment and 8–9; modeling socially acceptable behavior 71; motor development facilitation 135; observation 18; play and 152–158; positive relationships and 211; potty training 36; problem solving feedback and 12; promotion of independence 229; reading to children 257–258, 261–263; resiliency and 230–232; response and 4, 9; self-confidence and 237; self-control and 237; self-regulation and 236–237; sense of engagement with 53; socialization and 204, 207, 216–217; socialization strategies **208–209**, 208, **210**; strong emotions and 232–234; temperament responses and 225, 227–229
caregiving curriculum 25–26, 232; see also caregiving routines; early childhood education
caregiving routines: bathing 38–39, 40; calming strategies 46–47; communication and 49–50; consistency in 25; diapering 35–36; dressing 38, 41; eating/feeding 27–34; group 24, 73; individualized 24, 72; infants and 26–33, 35–36, 39, 41–50, 72–73; involving infants/toddlers in 26–27; naps 44; potty training 36–38; sleeping 41–49; toddlers and 26–27, 33–39, 41, 43–44, 73
cephalocaudal principle 131
Chess, S. 222, 224–225, **226**, 228–229
child abuse 91
child behavior 55
child development: age groupings 2; brain development 6–7; infant/toddler 5–7, 26; major areas of 18;

newborn vs. four-month-old babies **47**; play and 148–150; social/emotional 7–8; *see also* cognitive development; emotional development; perceptual development; social development
children with disabilities: early childhood education and 303–304; Early Intervention (EI) and 186, 300–301; IFSP and 304–305; social development and 217; *see also* special needs children
chronic stress 233
cognitive development: assisted learning and 279; attention and 282; biological changes and 274; brain cell connections and 273–274; caregiver strategies for 287–288; co-constructed experience and 279; delays in 292, 293–295; emotions and 274; infants and 282–284, 288–290; information gathering and 282; language development and 245, 274; mastery learning and 273; persisting through frustration in 282; Piaget on 274–276, **276**, 277–278, **280–281**; play and **168**, 287; preoperational stage 275, **276**; pretend play and 281; problem solving and 282; Project Approach 295–296; sensorimotor stage 275, **276**; social interactions and 274, 278–279; supporting 286–287; toddlers and 282, 284–286, 290–291, 295–296; toys/activities promoting 292, **293**; Vygotsky on 274, 278–279, **280–281**, 286
communication: active listening 88–90; baby sign language and 49–50; caregiver/family 88–89; families with special needs children and 91–92; family questionnaire 98–99; family-to-school forms 96–99; infants and 49–50; infant/toddler peers and 211; milestones in 249–252; non-verbal 211, **211**, 212, **212**; open-ended questions 90; parent conferences 89–91; *see also* language development; literacy development
communication disorders 265–267
constructivist theory 270
cooperation 169
Copple, C. 12–13
co-sleeping 194
Council for Exceptional Children (CEC) 303–304

cries 222
cultural identity 66, 83
curriculum *see* caregiving curriculum

dendrites 183
depth perception 113
developmentally appropriate practice (DAP): defined 12–13; in the home 57–59; infants and 56; intentionality in 12; key aspects of 13–14; play and 154–167; toddlers and 57
diapering 35–36
"difficult" children 225, **226**, 227
discipline 68–70; *see also* guidance; redirection
Division for Early Childhood (DEC) 303–304
documentation 18, 87–88
Dodge, D. 57
dressing 38, 41
dual language learners 83–84

early childhood education: attachment and 177; beliefs about 3; child development and 26; children with disabilities and 303–304; curriculum development in 295; developmentally appropriate practice (DAP) in 12–13; modeling in 69; NAEYC criteria for 15–17; nature versus nurture in 5; play and 148; Project Approach 295–296; Psychosocial theory and 199; *see also* infant/toddler care
Early Intervention (EI): attachment disorders and 186; children with disabilities and 186, 300–301; evaluation for 299–300; family needs and priorities 301, 303; IDEA and 301–302; services included in 303; social-emotional goals of 302–303
"easy" children 224–225, **226**
eating/feeding: bottle-feeding formula 27–28; breast milk 27–28; cups and 33–34; dairy products 31; finger foods 32–33; infants and 27–28, 30–33; seats for 32, **32**; silverware and 33; sippy cups 31; sleeping and 45–46; solid food introduction 28–31; toddlers and 33–34
emotional development: caregivers and 225, 238; caregiver strategies for **239–240**; emotions in 220; feelings in 220, 232; infant cries 222; infants and

Index 311

221–222, 229; nature (genes) and nurture (environment) 220; play and **167**; preventing tantrums 238; resiliency 229–232; self-actualization and 235–236; self-confidence and 237; self-control and 237; self-regulation and 236–237; social referencing 221–222; strong emotions and 232–234; temperament 222–225, **226**, 227–229; toddlers and 221, 229, 238
emotions 220, 232–234, 274
environments: designing spaces in 59, 61; physical/learning 52–61, 64–65; quick evaluation of 75, 77–78; routines and transitions in 52, 72–75; sense of security in 53; social/emotional 52, 65–72; temperament and 227–228; *see also* spaces
Erikson, E. 199–201
exploration 135, 149–152, 232
expressive language 246, *246*, 247–249
Eyer, D. 26, 57, 67

family questionnaire 98–99
family systems approach 301
family-to-school communication forms 96–99
fast mapping 247
feelings 220, 232
fine motor skills 18, 57, **60**, 129, 131, 133, 142
finger foods 32–33
formula 27–28
free play 149

Gak 144
gender identity 66–67
gender roles 67–68
Gerber, M. 17, 154–155
Gonzalez-Mena, J. 12–13, 26, 57, 67
"Goodness of Fit" model 228–229
Greenman, J. 57, 75
gross motor skills 11, 18, 57, **60**, 61, 129, 131–132, 142
guidance: bargains versus bribes approach 71–72; limits in physical environment 68–69; modeling socially acceptable behavior 71; positive reinforcement and 71; preventing harmful situations 71; redirection and 69–71; social/emotional environments and 68–69
Guyton, G. 292

Halliday, M. 270
happenings 153
Happiest Baby on the Block, The (Karp) 46, 238
hearing (auditory perception): infants and 109–112, 117–118; milestones in 110–112; music and 118; parentese 110, 117; promoting development of 117–118; reading and 118; toddlers and 112, 117–118; understanding and 249–252
hearing loss 112
Hierarchy of Needs 235, *235*
home language 264–265, 282
homes: developmentally appropriate environments in 57–59; limits in physical environment 68–69; multisensory experiences in 120–121, 124; play experiences in 165–167; restricting toddlers in 152; safety gates in 59, 68–69

IDEA *see* Individuals with Disabilities Education Act (IDEA)
IFSP *see* Individual Family Service Plan (IFSP)
incident report 94
independence 189, 192–193, 200, 229, 236
Individual Family Service Plan (IFSP) 92–93, 301, 304–305
Individuals with Disabilities Education Act (IDEA) 301–302, 304
infant classrooms: limits in 68; mouthable 116; NAEYC criteria for 15–16; routines and transitions in 52, 72–73; touchable 116
infant daily sheet 97
infants: abilities and characteristics **47**; attachment and 174–180; bathing 38–39, 40; bilingual 264; books for 256–257; calming strategies 46–47; cognitive development and 282–284; cognitive development strategies 288–290; communication and 49–50; deciphering cries 222; designing spaces for 59–60, **60**; developmentally appropriate environments for 57; diapering 35–36; dressing 38, 41; eating/feeding 27–31, *31*, 32–33; emotional development 221–222, 229; exploration and 135; expressive language and *246*, 247;

family caregiving practices and 84; individualized routines for 24; language development and 245; learning environment and 9; modeling and 69; movement and 11; newborns 110, 113; non-verbal communication 211, **211**, 212, **212**; peer interactions and communication 211–213; play and 150–152, 156–161; play materials for **62–63**, 64, 158–160, 167; practice play and 150; preschool siblings and 214–215, *215*, *231*; primary caregiving system and 25; problem solving and 11–12; reading to 160, 261–262; receptive language and 246–247; resiliency and 230; self-confidence in 237; self-control in 237; sense of self 66, 174; sippy cups 31, 34; sleeping and 42–46, *46*; social gestures/interactions **204**; socialization and 202–204, **207–210**; solid food introduction 28–29, *29*, 30–31; strong emotions and 232–234; swaddling and 44, *45*; temperament 222–224

infant/toddler care: attachment issues and 185–186, 194; "Goodness of Fit" model 228; playtime together 214, *227*, *280*; prosocial development in 213, 216–217; *see also* caregiving routines; early childhood education

infant/toddler education *see* caregiving curriculum; early childhood education

Infant/Toddler Environment Rating Scale (ITERS) 64–65

information gathering 282

intentionality 12, 278

internal locus of control 229–230

internal working model (attachment) 178–179

ITERS *see* Infant/Toddler Environment Rating Scale (ITERS)

Kaplan Early Learning Company 65
Kaplan FloorPlanner Tool 65
Karp, H. 46, 238
Katz, K. 38

language delay 120
language development: bilingual children and 264–265; brain development and 244–245; caregiver strategies for 244, 249–253, 258–259; cognitive development and 245, 274; communication disorders and 265–267; communication milestones 249–252; defined 244; developmental theories for 268–270; expressive language 246–247; fast mapping 247; hearing/understanding and 249–252; infants and 245–247; nature (genes) and nurture (environment) 244; play and **167**, 268; promoting expressive 248–249; promoting receptive 247; receptive language 246–247; talking and 249–252; toddlers and 247; vocabulary and 245; *see also* literacy development

learning environments *see* physical/learning environments

literacy development: bilingual children and 264–265; books/stories in 254–258, 261, 267–268; caregiver strategies for 260–261; creating an environment for 267–268; defined 253; literacy materials 268; oral language development and 253; play as representation of experience in 254–255; play as symbolic activity in 254; reading and 257–258, 261; relationships in 253–254; writing materials 268; *see also* language development

manipulation 133
Maslow, A. 235
mastery learning 273
maternal deprivation hypothesis 178
mirror neurons 183
modeling 69
moro reflex 44
mother/infant attachment 178–179, **180**, 181, **181**, 182
multicultural/multilingual curriculum 83–84
multisensory experiences 120–121
music and movement: environment for 142; fine motor skills 142; gross motor skills 143; hearing (auditory perception) and 118; infants and 11; materials for 143; physical development and 142–143
myelinization 131

NAEYC *see* National Association for the Education of Young Children (NAEYC)

naps 44
National Association for the Education of Young Children (NAEYC): accreditation standards 65; on caregiving routines 26; criteria for infant classrooms 15–16; criteria for toddler classrooms 16–17; on developmentally appropriate spaces 57; teacher-child ratio guidelines **53**
nativist theory 269
nature (genes) and nurture (environment) 183, 220, 244
neural pathways 183
neuroplasticity 244
neurotransmitters 183
newborns **47**, 110, 113; *see also* infants
non-verbal communication 211, **211**, 212, **212**

object permanence 276–277
observation 18
open-ended questions 90
organization 278

pain cry 222
parallel play 168, *201*
parent conference form 94–95
parent conferences: active listening and 90; conducting 90–91; form for 94–95; including children in 90; open-ended questions and 90; portfolios and 89–90, 95; preparation for 90
parentese 110, 117
parents: Attachment Parenting and 188–194; limit enforcement and 70; modeling socially acceptable behavior 71; reading to children 257–258; resiliency and 230–231; self-regulation and 236–237; sneaking out by 68, 185
peers 210–213
perceptual development: attention span 105; daily activities/explorations 121; defined 103; developmentally appropriate practice (DAP) 119–120; hearing (auditory perception) 109–112, 117–118; infants and 104–119; multisensory experiences for 120–121; promoting 114–121; sensory awareness and 104; sensory bottles/bags 125–126, *126*; sensory interactions and 104; sensory processing disorder (SPD) 122–125; sight (visual perception) 112–114, 118–119; smell 106, 114; taste 107, 114–116; television viewing and 120; toddlers and 104–107, 109, 114–118; touch 107–109, 116–117
persisting through frustration 282
physical development: body/brain growth 129–131; caregiver strategies for 135; cephalocaudal principle and 131; delays in 135, 142; exploration and 135; fine motor skills 133; Gak 144; gross motor skills 131–132; manipulation and 133; milestones in **136–141**; music and movement 142–143; play and **168**; proximodistal principle and 131; reflexes 133–135; yoga for children 144–145
physical/learning environments: caregiver/family relationship and 81–83; caregivers and 8–9; child behavior and 55; components of 52; designing spaces in 59–60, **60**, 61, **61**; developmentally appropriate 57; example of 65; healthy/sanitary 55, **55**; infants and 9, **60**; limits in 68–69; for mobile infants 60; physical layout of 55, **55**, 56, **56**; play and 148–150, 167, **167–168**; play materials 61, **62–63**, 64; rating quality of 64, **64**, 65; safety in 53, **54**, 55, 68–69; teacher-child ratios in 53, **53**, 54; toddlers and 9, *10*, 11, 61, **61**
Piaget, Jean: on accommodation 276–277; on adaptation 278; on assimilation 276–277; on cognitive development 274–276, **276**, 277–278, **280–281**; on intentionality 278; on language development 269; on object permanence 276–277; on organization 278; on schemes 278; on social interactions 211; as stage theorist 274; on symbolic play 150
"Places for Babies" (Greenman) 75
play: activities 153; books/stories in 254–255; caregivers and 152–158; child development and 148–150; choosing the right toys 164–166; cognitive development and **168**; cooperation in 169; developmentally appropriate materials/experiences 154–167; dramatic/fantasy 164; emotional development and **167**; empowerment and 150; environment for 151; free play and exploration 149–153; happenings 153; infants

and 150–152, 156–161; infant/toddler playtime together 214; language development and **167**, 268; learning and 148–150, 167, **167–168**; literacy development and 254–255; musical games/songs 163; with others 206; parallel 168, *201*; physical development and **168**; practice/functional 150; pretend 281; quiet 163; reading and 254; role for adults in 154; routines and transitions in 73; sharing and 168; social development and **167**; storytelling and 254; symbolic 150; toddlers and 150–152, *155*, 161–168, 285; unstructured 119; verbal/nonverbal communication 156–157
play materials 61, **62–63**, 64
portfolios 89–90, 95
positive reinforcement 71
Potty for Me!, A (Katz) 38
potty training 36–38, 285
preoperational stage 275, **276**
preservice teachers 25–26
pretend play 281
primary caregiving system 25–26
principal attachment 174
problem solving 11–12, 282
Project Approach 295–296
proximity maintenance 178
proximodistal principle 131
Psychosocial theory 199–202
pull-ups 37–38

Reactive Attachment Disorder 188
reading: caregiver strategies for 261–263; hearing (auditory perception) and 118; infants and 160; literacy development and 257–258, 261; play and 254
receptive language 246–247
reciprocal 4
redirection 69–71
reflexes 133–135
resiliency: androgyny and 229–230; caregivers and 230–232; defined 229; development of 229; independence and 229; infants and 230; internal/external factors for 229; internal locus of control and 229–230; stressful environments and 231; toddlers and 230; transitions in feelings 232
respectfulness 4
responsiveness 4
reunion behavior 181, **181**

RIE Educaring Approach 17, 154–155
routines *see* caregiving routines
Rudick, S. 57

safe haven 178
Safe to Sleep campaign 48
safety: emotional environment and 232–233; in the home 59, 68–69; physical/learning environments and 54, **55**, 68; routines and 72; social referencing and 221
safety gates 59, 68–69, 152
schemes 278
Sears, M. 188
Sears, W. 188–190
secure attachment 179–180, **180**, 181, **181**
secure base 178–179
self-actualization 235–236
self-concept 66–67
self-confidence 237
self-control 237
self-direction 235
self-esteem 66, 181, 198
self-image 66
self-regulation 236–237, 245
sense of self: body awareness and 66; caregivers and 67–68; cultural identity and 66; gender identity and 66–67; gender roles and 67–68; self-concept and 66–67; self-esteem and 66; self-image and 66; sneaking out and 68
sensitivity 108–109
sensorimotor stage 275, **276**
sensory awareness 103–104
sensory bags 125–126, *126*
sensory bottles 125, *126*
sensory integration 104–105
sensory light table *126*, *130*
sensory processing disorder (SPD): causes of 122; families and 124; identifying and diagnosing 122–123; over response and 121; under response and 121; treating 123–125
separation anxiety 179, **180**
separation distress 178–179, 185
sharing 168–169
siblings 214–215, *215*
SIDS *see* Sudden Infant Death Syndrome (SIDS)
sight (visual perception): depth perception and 113; infants and 112–113, 118; milestones in 113;

promoting development of 118–119; toddlers and 114, 119; walks and 119
sign language 49–50
sippy cups 31, *34*
sleeping: eating/feeding and 45–46; infants and 42–46, *46*; moro reflex and 44; naps and 44; risk of SIDS 42, 47–48; routines for 41–44; sleep sacks 44; swaddling and 44, *45*; toddlers and 43–44
sleep sacks 44
"slow-to-warm-up" children 224–225, **226**
smell 106, 114
social development: attachment and 198–199; peers and 210–213; play and 167; Psychosocial theory 199–202; special needs children and 215–217; *see also* socialization
social/emotional development 7–8
social/emotional environments 52, 65–72
socialization: attachment and 198–200; caregiver-child relationships 211; caregivers and 204, **204**, 207, 216–217; caregiver strategies for **208–209**, 208, **210**; infants and 202–204, **204**, 207–210; learning 198; limit testing and 206; playtime together 214, *227*; self-esteem and 198; siblings and 214–215, *215*; toddlers and 205–207, **207**, **208–210**
socially acceptable behavior 71
social referencing 221–222
social skills *see* socialization
solid food 28–31
spaces 59–60, **60**, 61, **61**; *see also* environments
SPD *see* sensory processing disorder (SPD)
special needs children: autism 215–216; caregiver/family relationship 91–93; family systems approach to 301; IFSP and 92–93, 304–305; social development and 215–217; *see also* children with disabilities
stage theory 274
STAR Institute for Sensory Processing Disorder 124
storytelling 254
stranger anxiety **181**
Strange Situation (Ainsworth): anxious-ambivalent attachment 179–180, **180**, 181, **181**; anxious-avoidant attachment 179–180, **180**, 181, **181**; criticism of 182; secure attachment 179–180, **180**, 181, **181**
strong emotions 232–234
Sudden Infant Death Syndrome (SIDS) 42, 47–49, 194
swaddling 44, *45*
synapses 183

talking 249–252
tantrums 206, 225, 238
taste 107, 114–116
teacher-child ratios 53, **53**, 54
teacher-child relationships 211
Teachers College Press 64
television 67, 119–120
temperament: caregiving responses to 225, 227–228; characteristics of 223–224, **226**; development of 229; "difficult" children 225, **226**, 227; "easy" children 224–225, **226**; environment and 227–228; "Goodness of Fit" model 228–229; individual differences in 222; infants and 223; "slow-to-warm-up" children 224–225, **226**; types of 224–225, **226**, 227–229
theory of attachment 177–178
Thomas, A. 222, 224–225, **226**, 228–229
toddler classrooms: center-based organization in 119; gender roles and 67–68; limits in 68; NAEYC criteria for 16–17; routines and transitions in 52, 73–75; smells in 114; touchable 116
toddler daily sheet 97–98
toddlers: attachment and 184–185; autonomy and 200–201; bathing 38–39; bilingual 264; books for 257; cognitive development and 282, 284–286, 295–296; cognitive development strategies 290–291; cooperation and 169; designing spaces for 61, **61**; developmentally appropriate environments for 57; diapering 35–36; dressing 38, 41; eating/feeding 33–34; emotional development 221, 229, 238; exploration and 135; family caregiving practices and 84; group routines for 24; language development and 247; learning environment and 9, *10*, 11; limit testing by 69–70, 206; manipulative exploration *14*; modeling and 69; peer interactions

and communication 211–213; play and 150–152, *155*, 161–168, 285; playing with others 206; play materials for **62–63**, 64, 162, 164–167; potty training 36–38, 285; preventing tantrums 206, 238; primary caregiving system and 25–26; problem solving and 11–12; Project Approach 295–296; pull-ups and 37–38; reading to 262–263; redirection and 69–70; resiliency and 230; self-confidence in 237; self-control in 237; self-regulation and 245; sense of self 66; separation feelings 185; sharing and 168–169; showing feelings 70; sleeping and 43–44; socialization and 205–207, **207**, **208–210**; strong emotions and 232–234; symbolic play and 150; vocabulary and 245
touch 107–109, 116–117

understanding 249–252

visual perception *see* sight (visual perception)
vocabulary 245
Vygotsky, Lev: on assisted learning 279; co-constructed experience and 279; on cognitive development 274, 278–279, **280–281**, 286; on language development 269–270, 279; on social interactions 150, 211, 278–279; zone of proximal development and 269, 279

water play 6

yoga for children 144–145

Zero to Three 154
zone of proximal development 269, 279